Contents

Study Guide

Development: Infancy Through Adolescence

Laurence Steinberg
Temple University

Deborah Lowe Vandell
University of Wisconsin-Madison

Marc H. Bornstein
National Institute of Child Health and Human Development

Prepared by

Kelly Bouas Henry
Missouri Western State University

WADSWORTH
CENGAGE Learning

Australia • Brazil • Japan • Korea • Mexico • Singapore • Spain • United Kingdom • United States

WADSWORTH
CENGAGE Learning

For product information and technology assistance, contact us at **Cengage Learning Customer & Sales Support, 1-800-354-9706**

For permission to use material from this text or product, submit all requests online at www.cengage.com/permissions Further permissions questions can be emailed to permissionrequest@cengage.com

ISBN-13: 978-0-618-60990-1
ISBN-10: 0-618-60990-3

Wadsworth
10 Davis Drive
Belmont, CA 94002-3098
USA

Cengage Learning is a leading provider of customized learning solutions with office locations around the globe, including Singapore, the United Kingdom, Australia, Mexico, Brazil, and Japan. Locate your local office at: www.cengage.com/global

Cengage Learning products are represented in Canada by Nelson Education, Ltd.

To learn more about Brooks/Cole, visit www.cengage.com/wadsworth

Purchase any of our products at your local college store or at our preferred online store www.ichapters.com

Printed in the United States of America
1 2 3 4 5 6 7 13 12 11 10 09

CHAPTER 1

The Study of Child Development

LEARNING OBJECTIVES

1. Name and explain the four goals of developmental psychologists.

2. Discuss how development differs from simple growth and change.

3. List and discuss the four basic questions that define the study of development.

4. List and explain the guiding principles of development.

5. Explain Freud's theory of psychosexual development.

6. Explain Erikson's theory of psychosocial development. How did it differ from Freud's theory?

7. Discuss the difference between classical and operant conditioning.

8. Explain how Bandura's social learning theory is applied to child development.

9. Discuss how Piaget's cognitive-developmental theory explains child development. List and explain the four stages of development discussed by Piaget.

10. Discuss Piaget's concepts of assimilation and accommodation with regard to how children's thinking changes over time.

11. Describe the ecological and sociocultural perspectives on development.

12. Discuss how developmental psychologists use the evolutionary perspective to explain development.

13. Explain how psychologists who subscribe to the dynamic systems perspective look at human development.

14. Describe the steps of the scientific method used by developmental psychologists.

15. Explain the differences between Naturalistic Observation, Participant Observation, and Structured Observation. Discuss the advantages and disadvantages of these methods.

16. Discuss the advantages and disadvantages of interviews, questionnaires, and tests as research methods.

17. Define reliability and validity, and explain why they are important in psychological testing.

18. Explain the advantages and disadvantages of case studies, correlational studies, and experiments.

19. Describe how experiments work. Discuss the roles of independent and dependent variables, and treatment and control groups. Explain why random assignment is important in an experiment.

20. Explain how longitudinal, cross-sectional, and accelerated longitudinal studies work. Discuss why a researcher might choose to use each of these methods.

21. Explain the role of ethics in psychological research.

OUTLINE

Developmental scientists study development from a wide variety of academic disciplines. The science of child development is based on *empirical evidence*. A central question for these scientists is to what degree traits remain stable over time.

I.   What Lies Ahead?

Five age periods characterize major transitions in child development: the **prenatal period** (conception to birth), **infancy** (birth to 2), **early childhood** (ages 2–6), **middle childhood** (ages 6–11), and **adolescence** (ages 11–20). These periods mark major developments, and the age markers are only approximate. Within each period, **physical development**, **cognitive development**, and **socioemotional development** are the major *domains* of study. The borders between these domains of study are fuzzy rather than firm.

II.   Why Study Development?

Child development experts have four major goal: (1) to *describe* developmental change, (2) to *explain* what causes it, (3) to *predict* what an individual will be like based on their present and past developmental achievements, and (4) to *intervene* with this knowledge to enhance children's lives.

    A.   Defining Development

Development is more than growth and change. **Development** is relatively *enduring* growth and change that makes an individual better *adapted* to the environment, by enhancing the individual's ability to engage in, understand, and experience more *complex* behavior, thinking, and emotions.

    B.   Basic Questions

Developmental scientists share an interest in four basic questions about the nature of human development:

      ♦   Which aspects of development are universal, and which aspects vary from one individual or group to the next?

      ♦   Which aspects of development are continuous and which are not?

      ♦   Which aspects of development are more or less fixed and which are relatively easy to change?

      ♦   What makes development happen?

    C.   Guiding Principles

Virtually all developmentalists agree that development involves constant interplay between biology and the environment; occurs in a multi-layered context; is cumulative, and continues throughout life. The pathway that connects a person's past to his or her future is known as the **developmental trajectory**.

III. Theories of Development

A scientific **theory** is a set of ideas or principles based on empirical evidence that explains related natural phenomena. Theories help scientists organize their thinking, discern what phenomena are significant, and generate new ideas. Theories are flexible, in that they may change and be replaced over time in light of new evidence.

    A.   Classical Theories
      1.   Psychoanalytic Theory

Psychoanalytic theory focuses on the inner self and how emotions determine the way we interpret our experiences and therefore how we act. Sigmund Freud, the founder of psychoanalytic theory, began his career as a physician but came to believe his patients' problems were psychological, not neurological. Freud believed that infants are born with powerful sexual and aggressive urges and seek immediate gratification for them. To the extent that these urges collide with reality, the infant is expected to learn self-control. How the conflict between personal desires and societal rules is resolved determines the child's emotional outlook, according to Freud, which is set by around age 5 or 6.

a) Freud's theory of psychosexual development
Freud divided psychosexual development into stages, named for the zone of the body a child finds most arousing at a given age: the *oral, anal, phallic*, and (after a period of latency) *genital* stages. Freud argued that healthy development involves the emergence of the *ego*, which mediates between the *id* and the *superego*. Conflicts between these structures of personality remain active in a person's *unconscious*.

b) Erikson's theory of **psychosocial development**
Erikson's theory differs from Freud's in two important ways. First, he argued that personality was not fixed but continued to develop over the lifespan. Additionally, Erikson felt that the crisis, or conflict, to be resolved at each stage of development was psychosocial in nature (based on conflicts in interaction), not psychosexual. The transition from one stage to another, according to Erikson, depends heavily on cultural norms.

2. Learning Theory
Learning theory emphasizes the role of external influences on behavior.

a) Behaviorism.
Watson studied learning based on associations, or **classical conditioning**. Skinner studied **operant conditioning**, or learning based on past consequences. Operant conditioning can be intentional or unintentional. If a behavior is not rewarded, after a time it becomes *extinguished*.

b) Social learning theory.
Social learning theory, developed by Bandura, describes how learning can be acquired by imitation of a model performing a behavior. **Observational learning** occurs most likely when the model is someone powerful or admired. **Behavior therapy** involves attempts to change an individual's behavior through the use of rewards and punishments.

3. Cognitive-Developmental Theory
Cognitive-developmental theorists see development as resulting from qualitative changes in thought. Piaget, a pioneer in this field, identified four stages of cognitive growth: the **sensorimotor stage**, the **preoperational stage**, the **concrete operational stage**, and the **formal operational stage**. Piaget argued that children achieve cognitive development via **assimilation** and **accommodation** processes. Assimilation involves fitting new information into existing ways of thinking, while accommodation involves adapting one's way of thinking to a new understanding.

B. Contemporary Theories
1. The Ecological Perspective
The **ecological perspective** emphasizes the context in which development occurs. It involves studying the child's immediate environment, as well as the network of relationships and settings the child encounters over time.

2. The Sociocultural Perspective
   The **sociocultural perspective** emphasizes the role of the *cultural* context in which development occurs, not the context in general.

3. Behavioral Genetics
   Behavioral genetics is the study of inherited behavior, focusing on the reciprocal relationship between genetics and experience.

4. The Evolutionary Perspective
   The **evolutionary perspective** focuses on how child development is adaptive in light of human evolutionary history.

5. The Dynamic Systems Perspective
   Dynamic systems theory highlights how development is part of a single, coherent yet ever-changing system. That system is viewed as having multiple layers of development and context. Changing any one part of the system can have consequences throughout the system. Consequently, the parts of the system should be studied together, not separately.

IV. The Scientific Study of Development
   A. The Scientific Method
      The **scientific method** is a systematic procedure for testing ideas. It involves formulating a question, developing a **hypothesis**, conducting a study to test that hypothesis, analyzing the study data, and publishing or presenting the findings. This final step of disseminating findings helps support **replication** of results by other peers in the scientific community. Because scientists cannot study all children, they attempt to procure a **representative sample** which might generalize to the population at large.

   B. Research Methods
      1. Observational Research
         Naturalistic observation involves observing participants in their everyday settings, usually with a checklist of predetermined guidelines and without interacting with the participants. In **participant observation**, the researcher does interact with the people he or she is observing, often interviewing them. Finally, **structured observation** involves researchers creating a setting and tasks that are likely to evoke the behavior they want to observe.

      2. Self-reports
         When individuals provide information about themselves via questionnaires or interviews, we say the method involves **self-reports**. Self-reports can be open-ended or structured. Self-reports allow researchers to collect a large amount of data at a lower cost than observations usually incur. However, people may not be fully honest on self-reports, or may misinterpret the questions, so careful wording of the questions is important.

      3. Standardized Tests
         Standardized tests are administered to all participants in precisely the same manner. They have norms that allow researchers to compare a child to others. They have usually been developed in such a way that they provide extremely consistent, or **reliable**, data. Additionally, the careful development behind them promotes **validity**, meaning the test measures what it is supposed to measure.

   C. Research Design
      1. Case Studies

A **case study** is an intensive study of one or a small number of individuals or families. They typically are open-ended, allowing the researcher to improvise. Case studies are inspiring and can help generate hypotheses, but they are not generalizable.

2. Correlational Studies
In a **correlational study**, researchers examine two or more variables to see if they are linked in any way. A correlation is a measure of a linear relationship between two things that can vary and that can be counted or measured. A **positive correlation** indicates that the two variables change in the same direction. A **negative correlation** indicates that the two variables change in different directions. Correlations can take on any value between -1.00 (a very negative correlation) and +1.00 (a very positive correlation), inclusive of those endpoints. Although correlations indicate a relationship between two variables, they do not indicate that one variable causes the other.

3. Experiments
Experiments do provide a way for researchers to determine cause and effect relationships. In an experiment, a researcher manipulates the **independent variable** and measures the **dependent variable** while holding all other conditions constant. In testing the effects of an independent variable, scientists need to be sure that their results are not merely the consequence of participating in a study, but actually due to the specifics of the variable in question. To establish this, researchers call the group that received the treatment being tested the **treatment**, or **experimental group**, and the group of participants that did not receive the specialized treatment the **control group**. Participants are assigned to these groups using a **random assignment** procedure.

Some research questions would be unethical to examine using a true experiment because it would be wrong to randomly assign participants to a harmful condition. In such instances, researchers rely on **natural experiments**, comparing individuals in the real world who have naturally grouped into such conditions based on their own life experiences.

D. Studying Change over Time
1. Longitudinal Studies
Longitudinal studies involve studying the same individual or group of individuals over a period of time with assessments at regular intervals. While they allow change to be studied directly, they are time-consuming and costly.

2. Cross-sectional Studies
Cross-sectional studies involve studying individuals of different ages at the same time. They are less expensive than longitudinal studies and give immediate results, but they do not allow for the direct study of change. Additionally, their results may be skewed by the **cohort effect**.

3. Accelerated Longitudinal Design
An **accelerated longitudinal design** is both cross-sectional and longitudinal. Different age groups are followed over time.

E. Research Ethics
Developmental scientists use the ethics code published by the Society for Research on Child Development. This code contains six main rules: (1) researchers should not use procedures that cause harm; (2) they should procure the child's informed consent and

in most cases the parents', too; (3) they must maintain confidentiality in their records; (4) they must debrief their participants following the study; (5) they must consider the implications of their findings when disseminating their work; and (6) they must comply with review board requirements or face consequences of misconduct charges.

V.   Developmental Science in the Real World
     Developmental science provides advice to parents, teachers, health-care practitioners, program developers, policy makers, and members of business and industry. Understanding child development can help individuals in these roles make better decisions about how to work with and design products and services for children.

KEY TERMS

1. **Developmental scientists** are experts who study development—regardless of their disciplinary training. (see Introductory section)

2. **Empirical evidence** is information obtained through systematic observations and experiments. (see Introductory section)

3. The **prenatal period** is the period of development from conception to birth. (see What Lies Ahead?)

4. **Infancy** is the period of development from birth to about age two. (see What Lies Ahead?)

5. **Early childhood** is the period of development from about ages two to six. (see What Lies Ahead?)

6. **Middle childhood** is the period of development from about ages six to eleven. (see What Lies Ahead?)

7. **Adolescence** is the period of development from about age eleven to age twenty. (see What Lies Ahead?)

8. **Physical development** is the domain of development that includes changes in size, shape, outward appearance, and inner physical functioning; changes in physical capabilities; and changes in the structure and function of the brain. (see What Lies Ahead?)

9. **Cognitive development** is the domain of development that involves changes in intellectual abilities, including memory, thinking, reasoning, language, problem solving, and decision making. (see What Lies Ahead?)

10. **Socioemotional development** is the domain of development that includes changes in feelings and motivation, temperament and personality, and relationships with others. Sometimes it is referred to as *psychosocial development.* (see What Lies Ahead?)

11. **Development** is the relatively enduring growth and change that makes an individual better adapted to the environment, by enhancing the individual's ability to engage in, understand, and experience more complex behavior, thinking, and emotions. (see Why Study Development?)

12. A **developmental trajectory** is the pathway of developmental change that connects the past, present, and future. (see Why Study Development?)

13. A **theory** is a set of ideas and principles based on empirical findings that explain related natural phenomena. (see Theories of Development)

14. **Psychoanalytic theory** focuses on human behavior and development. It was first articulated by Sigmund Freud, and focuses on the inner self and how emotions determine the way we interpret our experiences, and thus how we act. (see Theories of Development)

15. **Psychosocial development** is a synonym for socioemotional development. This particular terminology is associated with Erik Erikson's theory of development. (see Theories of Development)

16. **Learning theory** is a theory of human behavior based on classical and/or operant conditioning, as well as observational learning, that stresses the role of external influences on behavior. (see Theories of Development)

17. **Classical conditioning** is a process of associative learning by which a subject comes to respond in a desired manner to a previously neutral stimulus (e.g., the sound of a steel bar being hit with a hammer) that has been repeatedly presented along with an unconditioned stimulus (e.g., a white furry object) that elicits the desired response (e.g., fear). (see Theories of Development)

18. **Operant conditioning** is a process of learning in which the likelihood of a specific behavior is increased or decreased as a result of reward or punishment that follows. (see Theories of Development)

19. **Social learning theory** is a theory of human behavior that emphasizes the ways in which individuals learn by observing others and through the application of social rewards (e.g., praise) and punishment (e.g., disapproval). (see Theories of Development)

20. **Observational learning** is a process of learning based on the observation of others. (see Theories of Development)

21. **Behavior therapy** is an attempt to change behavior through the deliberate use of rewards and punishments. (see Theories of Development)

22. The **cognitive developmental perspective** is a perspective on human development that emphasizes qualitative changes in the ways that individuals think as they mature, mainly associated with the work of Jean Piaget. (see Theories of Development)

23. The **sensorimotor stage** is a period of cognitive development in Piaget's theory from birth to about age two, during which infants learn by relating sensations to motor action. (see Theories of Development)

24. The **preoperational stage** in Piaget's theory is the stage of cognitive development from approximately ages two to seven, during which children acquire a mental storehouse of images and symbols, especially spoken and written words. (see Theories of Development)

25. The **concrete operational stage** in Piaget's theory is the stage of cognitive development from approximately ages seven to eleven, during which children make giant strides in their ability to organize ideas and think logically, but where their logical reasoning is limited to real object and actual experiences and events. (see Theories of Development)

26. The **formal operational stage** in Piaget's theory is the stage of cognitive development that emerges approximately at age eleven, during which individuals develop the ability to apply logical reasoning to abstract phenomena. (see Theories of Development)

27. **Assimilation** in Piaget's theory is the child's attempt to fit new information into his or her existing way of thinking. (see Theories of Development)

28. **Accommodation** in Piaget's theory is the child's adaptation of an existing way of thinking in response to new information. (see Theories of Development)

29. The **ecological perspective** is a perspective on human development that emphasizes the contexts, both proximal and distant, in which development occurs, often associated with the work of Urie Bronfenbrenner. (see Theories of Development)

30. The **sociocultural perspective** is a perspective on human development that stresses the ways in which development involves adaptation to specific cultural demands. (see Theories of Development)

31. **Behavioral genetics** is the study of the inherited bases of behavior. (see Theories of Development)

32. The **evolutionary perspective** is a perspective on human development that emphasizes the evolved basis of human behavior. (see Theories of Development)

33. **Dynamic systems theory** is a perspective on human development that views the many facets of development as part of a single, dynamic, constantly changing system. (see Theories of Development)

34. The **scientific method** is a systematic, step-by-step procedure for testing ideas. (see The Scientific Study of Development)

35. A **hypothesis** is a prediction that can be tested empirically and supported or rejected on the basis of scientific evidence. (see The Scientific Study of Development)

36. **Replication** is the repetition of a study using the same methods. (see The Scientific Study of Development)

37. A **representative sample** is a group of participants in a research study who represent the larger population the scientist wants to draw conclusions about. (see The Scientific Study of Development)

38. **Naturalistic observation** is a method of data collection in which the researcher observes individuals in their everyday settings. (see The Scientific Study of Development)

39. **Participant observation** is a method of data collection in which the researcher observes and interacts with the individuals in their everyday settings. (see The Scientific Study of Development)

40. **Structured observation** is a method of data collection in which the researcher creates a setting and tasks that are likely to evoke a behavior of interest. (see The Scientific Study of Development)

41. A **self-report** is a method of data collection in which the researcher asks individuals about themselves, either through questionnaires or interviews. (see The Scientific Study of Development)

42. **Standardized tests** are measures that are generally accepted by the other scientists as reliable and valid, often with norms derived from their prior administration to large and representative samples. (see The Scientific Study of Development)

43. **Reliability** is the extent to which a measure yields assessments that are consistent, or the degree to which an instrument measures something the same way each time it is used under the same condition with the same subjects. (see The Scientific Study of Development)

44. **Validity** is the extent to which a measure assesses what it is supposed to measure rather than something else; also can be used to refer to the truth or accuracy of a conclusion drawn from a scientific study. (see The Scientific Study of Development)

45. A **case study** is an intensive study of one or a small number of individuals or families.

46. A **correlational study** is a study in which the researcher examines two or more variables to see if they are linked in any way. (see The Scientific Study of Development)

47. A **positive correlation** occurs when two variables are correlated such that high levels of one variable are associated with high levels of the other, and low levels of one are associated with low levels of the other. (see The Scientific Study of Development)

48. A **negative correlation** occurs when two variables are correlated such that high levels of one variable are associated with low levels of the other, and low levels of one are associated with high levels of the other. (see The Scientific Study of Development)

49. An **experiment** is a research design in which the researcher controls conditions in the hopes of drawing conclusions about cause and effect. (see The Scientific Study of Development)

50. An **independent variable** in an experiment is the element the researcher introduces, or manipulates, to examine its effects on one or more outcomes of interest; in nonexperimental research this can refer to variables that are used to predict outcomes of interest. (see The Scientific Study of Development)

51. A **dependent variable** in an experiment is the outcome of interest; in nonexperimental research, this can refer to variables that are predicted by other factors. (see The Scientific Study of Development)

52. The **treatment (or experimental) group** in an experiment is the group of participants who receive a predetermined program, intervention, or treatment and who then are compared with a control and/or other treatment groups. (see The Scientific Study of Development)

53. The **control group** in an experiment is a comparison group of participants who do not receive the predetermined program, intervention, or treatment received by the treatment group. (see The Scientific Study of Development)

54. **Random assignment** in an experiment is the practice of assigning participants to treatment or control groups on a random basis, to attempt to limit any observed differences between them to the presence or absence of the treatment. (see The Scientific Study of Development)

55. A **natural experiment** is a research design that takes advantage of naturally occurring events that affect some individuals but not others, or that makes use of an opportunity to measure development before and after a naturally occurring event has happened. (see The Scientific Study of Development)

56. A **longitudinal study** is a study in which researchers follow the same individuals over time and assess them more than once. (see The Scientific Study of Development)

57. A **cross-sectional study** is a study in which researchers compare individuals of different ages at the same time. (see The Scientific Study of Development)

58. The **cohort effect** is the influence of the fact that people of different ages grew up in different eras and had different experiences, which complicates drawing conclusions about age differences found in cross-sectional studies. (see The Scientific Study of Development)

59. An **accelerated longitudinal study** (sometimes referred to as a *cross-sequential study*) is a study that is both cross sectional and longitudinal, in which the researcher follows different age groups over time and assesses them more than once. (see The Scientific Study of Development)

FILL-IN-THE-BLANKS KEY TERMS

This section will help you check your knowledge of the key terms introduced in this chapter. Fill in each blank with the appropriate term from the list of key terms in the previous section.

1. A _____ occurs when two variables are correlated such that high levels of one variable are associated with high levels of the other, and low levels of one are associated with low levels of the other.

2. _____ are experts who study development—regardless of their disciplinary training.

3. The method of data collection in which the researcher creates a setting and tasks that are likely to evoke a behavior of interest is_____.

4. A _____ is the pathway of developmental change that connects the past, present, and future.

5. _____ is the period of development from about ages six to eleven.

6. The _____ is the influence of the fact that people of different ages grew up in different eras and had different experiences, which complicates drawing conclusions about age differences found in cross-sectional studies.

7. The practice of assigning participants to treatment or control groups on a random basis, to attempt to limit any observed differences between them to the presence or absence of the treatment is known as _____.

8. _____ is a perspective on human development that views the many facets of development as part of a single, dynamic, constantly changing system

9. A child's adaptation of an existing way of thinking in response to new information is known as_____.

10. A(n) _____ is a research design in which the researcher controls conditions in the hopes of drawing conclusions about cause and effect.

APPLIED LEARNING AND CRITICAL THINKING

The study of child development offers you a variety of opportunities to extend your learning beyond the walls of your classroom—applying what you know to real-life contexts. You can do this through service activities, internships, research experiences, and so forth. The Applied Learning portion of the Study Guide will suggest some activities that will allow you to apply the knowledge you've gained in studying each chapter to enrich your learning, and ground it in the real-world. As you think critically in these contexts, you will broaden and deepen your understanding of the material.

As this chapter provides you with a broad overview of content relevant to the study of child development, as well as information on the process by which child development is studied (i.e., research), consider the following possibilities:

1. Find an article from one of the academic journals that focuses on child development. *Merrill-Palmer Quarterly* and *Child Development* are two good examples that most college and university libraries carry. Page through and see what topics are covered in a recent issue and choose one article to read. After reading it, write a short summary of the research, being sure to identify the author(s)' research question, hypothesis, and results. Then, see if you can think of other ways that those results might be interpreted. For example, suppose a researcher compared children of different ethnicities on intelligence, and found that the intelligence test scores were higher for African American children than Hispanic American children. Suppose further that the researcher concluded that the average African American child was "smarter" than the average Hispanic child. What other explanations could you consider for the pattern of results the researcher observed? Could it be that the Hispanic children had poorer English skills and the test was given in English? Could the difference be due to difference in socioeconomic status of the children? What alternate explanations

for the pattern of results can you generate? In going through this sort of exercise, you are gaining practice in identifying threats to a study's "validity."

2. Try to identify what sorts of internships might give you experience in applying the science of child development. Of course, most education departments have student teaching experience, which would be one obvious route, but try to identify industries in your area that might benefit from expertise in child development. Is there a children's hospital nearby? Does it have a developmental scientist on staff? Are there internships there? How about a corporation that makes products specifically for children? Would someone at one of these organizations be willing to grant you an informational interview? The following website has some good pointers on how to gain an informational interview, and what sorts of questions to ask once you are visiting with the developmental scientist in that venue: http://jobsearch.about.com/cs/infointerviews/a/infointerview.htm.

3. Employment opportunities that offer you a chance to apply your knowledge about child development abound. Most day cares will hire employees who do not possess a Bachelor's degree, but do possess a certificate in child development. Consider working at one of these venues. To prepare for an interview for that purpose, write a day's "lesson plan" for what you would do with children of different ages. You might revisit this lesson plan at the end of the semester to see if you would plan it differently based on what you learned after reading the book as a whole.

4. If you don't want to pursue a job, consider volunteer work that exposes you to children and requires you to apply your knowledge. Many school districts need tutors to work with children, and many families would love to have a babysitter who knows how to play with kids instead of just "watching" them. The next time you are in such a setting, try to take note of where the child or children you are watching are in terms of their different domains of development: physical, cognitive, and socioemotional. In doing so, you can learn about how these different domains influence each other while you provide an important service.

MULTIPLE-CHOICE QUESTIONS

Quiz 1

1. Experts who study development—regardless of their training—are called

    a. psychologists.
    b. developmental scientists.
    c. sociologists.
    d. anthropologists.

2. Which of the following age periods is in the correct sequential order?

    a. adolescence, early childhood, middle childhood, prenatal period, and infancy
    b. adolescence, middle childhood, early childhood, infancy, and prenatal period
    c. infancy, prenatal period, early childhood, middle childhood, and adolescence
    d. prenatal period, infancy, early childhood, middle childhood, and adolescence

3. Cara studies how children's ability to form memories changes over time. Cara is most likely primarily interested in which domain of development?

    a. Physical
    b. Cognitive
    c. Socioemotional
    d. Spiritual

4. Development is
    a. enduring growth and change.
    b. change that makes an individual better adapted to the environment.
    c. change that makes an individual better able to engage in, understand, and experience complex behavior.
    d. All of these

5. The notion that development is cumulative, and that to understand a person in the present requires examination of their past, is essential to the notion of
    a. infancy.
    b. structured observations.
    c. developmental trajectory.
    d. the cohort effect.

6. The ideas behind psychoanalysis, or learning, or dynamic systems are all examples of
    a. classical theories.
    b. contemporary theories.
    c. hypotheses.
    d. theories.

7. According to psychoanalytic thought, the rational, adaptive part of the self is the
    a. ego.
    b. superego.
    c. id.
    d. unconscious.

8. Little Julie has learned that when her mom opens the pantry, she will get a packet of fruit chews. One day, her mom opens the pantry for another purpose, and Julie starts running for her high chair saying "fruit chews" because she anticipates the treat that usually follows. This is an example of
    a. classical conditioning.
    b. operant conditioning.
    c. social learning.
    d. observational learning.

9. Joe is 13 years old. For the first time in his life, he is really enjoying his social studies classes. The ideas his teacher talks about, like democracy, justice, and equality, seem to make sense to him. Joe is probably in Piaget's _____ period of development.
    a. sensorimotor
    b. preoperational
    c. concrete operational
    d. formal operational

10. The study of the inherited bases of behavior is
    a. the ecological perspective.
    b. the sociocultural perspective.
    c. behavioral genetics.
    d. the evolutionary perspective.

11. The way a person thinks influences the kind of social environment he or she ends up in, and that social environment influences the kinds of emotional experiences available to a person. If you change someone's social environment, you can expect to see changes in emotion as well as thought patterns. This notion of the interrelatedness of these different domains of development is consistent with

    a.   psychosocial development.

    b.   cognitive-developmental theory.

    c.   dynamic systems theory.

    d.   psychoanalytic theory.

12. Judy did a study and found that peers had greater influence on adolescents than did parents. John did the same study using the same methods and found the same result. John has

    a.   replicated Judy's study, which strengthens her results.

    b.   copied Judy's study, which undermines her results.

    c.   challenged Judy's study.

    d.   conducted a correlational study.

13. The method of data collection that involves creating a setting and task that are likely to evoke behaviors of interest is known as

    a.   naturalistic observation.

    b.   participant observation.

    c.   structured observation.

    d.   experimentation.

14. As one variable increases, a second variable decreases. This sort of relationship characterizes a

    a.   positive correlation.

    b.   negative correlation.

    c.   cohort effect.

    d.   validity study.

15. People who grew up during the Great Depression are often more frugal, relative to people who did not. This is an example of

    a.   the cohort effect.

    b.   assimilation.

    c.   reliability.

    d.   validity.

Quiz 2

Use this quiz to reassess your learning after taking Quiz 1 and reviewing the chapter.

1. The period of development that starts at approximately age 6 and goes to approximately age 11 is called

    a.   the prenatal period.

    b.   infancy.

    c.   early childhood.

    d.   middle childhood.

2. Socioemotional development is to _____ as cognitive development is to _____.

    a.   feelings; thought

    b.   thought; memory

    c.   brain function; thought

    d.   memory; brain structure

3. Sam is affected by a lot of different areas in his life. His friendships influence what he likes to do, and his family influences the opportunities that are afforded to him. The fact that he lives a middle-class life in the United States means that he has been relatively well nourished, and because he became a teenager during 2008, he is likely to enjoy technologies that weren't available in other historic periods. These different aspects of life have influenced how Sam has grown and changed over time. This best illustrates which guiding principle of the study of child development?

    a. Development results from the constant interplay of biology and the environment.
    b. Development occurs in multilayered contexts.
    c. Development is a dynamic, reciprocal process.
    d. Development is cumulative.

4. Social learning theory was developed by

    a. Watson.
    b. Freud.
    c. Bandura.
    d. Piaget.

5. Molly calls all birds "robins." This illustrates

    a. assimilation.
    b. accommodation.
    c. behavior therapy.
    d. operant conditioning.

6. The contemporary perspective on development that argues that you cannot understand development without taking into account the context in which it occurs is called the

    a. ecological perspective.
    b. evolutionary perspective.
    c. dynamic systems theory.
    d. behavioral genetics.

7. Which ordering of the steps of the scientific method is correct?

    a. analyze data, publish, make a hypothesis, conduct a study, and formulate a question
    b. make a hypothesis, formulate a question, conduct a study, publish, and analyze data
    c. formulate a question, make a hypothesis, conduct a study, analyze data, and publish
    d. analyze data, formulate a question, develop a hypothesis, publish, conduct a study

8. If a tests measures what it is supposed to measure, we say the test has

    a. reliability.
    b. validity.
    c. standardization.
    d. a positive correlation.

9. Which of the following is NOT a drawback to using self-report measures?

    a. People may answer questions inaccurately.
    b. People may not be able to remember the answer to questions.
    c. They are expensive and difficult to use.
    d. All of these

10. Leia wants to observe how friendships develop at school. She unobtrusively watches on the playground and charts who talks to whom, how often, and the duration of the conversation. Leia is conducting a(n)

    a. participant observation study.
    b. self-report study.
    c. structured observation.
    d. naturalistic observation.

11. The more deposits I make to my bank account, the more money I have in the account. The relationship between number of deposits and the account balance is

   a.   a negative correlation.
   b.   a positive correlation.
   c.   an independent variable.
   d.   a dependent variable.

12. Researchers _____ dependent variables, but they _____ independent variables.

   a.   measure; measure
   b.   manipulate; manipulate
   c.   measure; manipulate
   d.   manipulate; measure

13. Because you cannot randomly assign participants to certain, potentially harmful conditions (e.g., half the participants are assigned to smoke heavily while the other half is not), you have to rely on what sort of experimental design from time to time?

   a.   Natural experiments
   b.   Longitudinal designs
   c.   Cross-sectional designs
   d.   Experiments

14. Joe studies a group of 200 kids every year from the day they start kindergarten until the day they graduate. Joe has conducted a(n)

   a.   cohort design.
   b.   cross-sectional study.
   c.   accelerated cross-sectional study.
   d.   longitudinal study.

15. The study of child development provides advice to

   a.   parents.
   b.   teachers.
   c.   program developers.
   d.   All of these

ANSWERS TO FILL-IN-THE-BLANKS KEY TERMS

1. positive correlation (see The Scientific Study of Development)

2. Developmental scientists (see Introductory section)

3. structured observation (see The Scientific Study of Development)

4. developmental trajectory (see Why Study Development?)

5. Middle childhood (see What Lies Ahead?)

6. cohort effect (see The Scientific Study of Development)

7. random assignment (see The Scientific Study of Development)

8. Dynamic systems theory (see Theories of Development)

9. accommodation (see Theories of Development)

10. experiment (see The Scientific Study of Development)

ANSWERS TO MULTIPLE-CHOICE QUESTIONS

Circle the question numbers you answered incorrectly.

Quiz 1

1.   b is the answer.   Although psychologists, sociologists, and anthropologists may study development, not all of them do. The collective term for individuals who specifically study child development (regardless of their field) is developmental scientist. (see introductory section)

2.   d is the answer.   The correct sequential order of these ages is prenatal period (conception up to birth), infancy (birth to about age 2), early childhood (age 2 to about age 6), middle childhood (age 6 to approximately age 11), and adolescence (age 11–20). (see What Lies Ahead?)

3.   b is the answer.   Cara is probably interested in the cognitive domain, primarily, as memory is a cognitive function. The physical domain deals more directly with changes in outward appearance and brain structure and function, while the socioemotional domain focuses on changes in feelings, motivation, temperament, personality, and relationships with others. The text does not address a spiritual domain. (see What Lies Ahead?)

4.   d is the answer.   Development is all of these things. It involves enduring growth and change that makes one better adapted to the environment, and that enhances one's ability to engage in, understand, and experience more complex behavior. (see Why Study Development?)

5.   c is the answer.   Developmental trajectory is the pathway that connects one's past to one's present and future. The idea of a trajectory suggests that each step forward in one's life, developmentally speaking, builds on the steps and experiences that preceded it. This implies that development builds cumulatively over one's span of experience. (see Why Study Development?)

6.   d is the answer.   Psychoanalytic, learning, and dynamic systems theories all contain sets of ideas that explain related natural phenomena. Only psychoanalytic theory and learning theory are classical theories; and only dynamic systems theory is considered a contemporary theory. Each of these theories can be used to generate hypotheses (or predictions), but they are not in and of themselves predictions. (see Theories of Development)

7.   a is the answer.   The ego is the rational, adaptive part of the self. It mediates the sexual and aggressive urges that originate in the id, and the demands of the superego (or conscience) in light of the constraints of reality. The ego functions at the conscious level, while the id and its urges function more at the unconscious level. (see Theories of Development)

8.   a is the answer.   Classical conditioning is learning to make predictive associations. Julie has learned to predict what will happen when the pantry door opens. Operant conditioning focuses on learning based on prior consequences rather than associations with specific stimuli. And social and observational learning both have to do with learning by watching models perform behaviors and then imitating them. (see Theories of Development)

9.   d is the answer.   The formal operational period of development, according to Piaget, involves the emergence of the ability to think in abstract, hypothetical, symbolic terms that transcend space in time. Joe's interest in abstract principles, such as democracy, justice, and equality, suggests he is probably in the formal operational period of development. The other three stages (sensorimotor, preoperational, and concrete operational) do not involve the ability to understand these sorts of abstract concepts. (see Theories of Development)

10.   c is the answer.   Behavioral genetics is the study of the inherited bases of behavior. The ecological and sociocultural perspectives focus on how different aspects of context influence development, and the evolutionary perspective focuses on adaptation as an explanation for developmental change. (see Theories of Development)

11.   c is the answer.   Dynamic systems theory focuses on the connections between levels of human functioning, domains of development, and levels of context. The central idea is that these form a web, and that altering any part of the web will reverberate throughout the web, causing changes in a variety of areas. (see Theories of Development)

12.   a is the answer.   Replication is repetition of a study using the same methods, but by a different researcher using different participants. When the same results are obtained in a replication, it strengthens, or verifies, the first study's findings. (see The Scientific Study of Development)

13.   c is the answer.   Structured observations involve creating a setting and/or tasks that cause a behavior one is interested in studying to occur. Naturalistic observation and participant observation do not involve these contrived settings. Experimentation involves manipulating variables systematically and comparing multiple conditions, not just reactions to a single setting. (see The Scientific Study of Development)

14.   b is the answer.   A negative correlation occurs when two variables are linked in opposite directions. As one variable increases, the other decreases, and vice versa. A positive correlation involves two variables moving together—if one increases, so does the other. (see the Scientific Study of Development)

15.   a is the answer.   The cohort effect is the influence of the fact that people of different ages grew up in different eras and had different experiences. The fact that people who grew up in the Great Depression are generally more frugal complicates one's ability to draw conclusions about why the characteristic of frugality exists. Is it the age of those individuals? Is it their shared experience? Accelerated longitudinal designs can help to tease apart these strands. (see the Scientific Study of Development)

Now turn to the quiz analysis table at the end of this chapter to find which areas you know well and which areas you need to work on. Circle the numbers in the table for items on Quiz 1 that you answered correctly.

Quiz 2

1.   d is the answer.   Middle childhood starts at about at 6 and ends around age 11. (see What Lies Ahead?)

2.   a is the answer.   Socioemotional development involves changes in feelings and motivations, and cognitive development focuses on changes in intellectual abilities, such as thought. (see What Lies Ahead?)

3.   b is the answer.   This question describes how Sam's development has been affected by his interpersonal relationships, his cultural experiences, and the historical period in which he has grown. This illustrates the many layers of his developmental context. (see Why Study Development?)

4.   c is the answer.   Bandura developed social learning theory. Watson was integral to the development of behaviorism; Freud developed psychoanalytic theory, and Piaget the cognitive-developmental theory. (see Theories of Development)

5.   a is the answer.   Assimilation involves fitting new information (in this case, new birds that Molly sees for the first time) to an existing knowledge base ("robin"). Accommodation occurs when Molly realizes that not all birds are robins, and she starts to build new categories, such as cardinal, finch, and so forth. (see Theories of Development)

6.   a is the answer.   The ecological perspective emphasizes context. (see Theories of Development)

7.   c is the answer.   The scientific method begins with formulating a research question, which leads to the development of a hypothesis, which is then tested in a study. Once the study is over, the data are analyzed, and the results are published. (see The Scientific Study of Development)

8.   b is the answer.   Validity is the degree to which the test measures what it claims to measure. Reliability, on the other hand, is the degree of consistency the results provide. (see The Scientific Study of Development)

9.   c is the answer.   Self-reports are not expensive or difficult to administer; in fact, they are relatively inexpensive and easy to administer. (see The Scientific Study of Development)

10. d is the answer.   Naturalistic observation involves watching people in their everyday settings, usually without getting involved. That is what Leia has done. (see The Scientific Study of Development)

11. b is the answer.   A positive correlation occurs when two variables vary in the same direction. In this example, as number of deposits increases, the account balance increases, as well. (see The Scientific Study of Development)

12. c is the answer.   Independent variables are manipulated by the experimenter as certain levels, while dependent variables are measured as a result of the experimental conditions. (see The Scientific Study of Development)

13. a is the answer.   Natural experiments are just for the situation in which one wants to study a particular behavior, but cannot because it would be unethical to randomly assign participants to some of the conditions. A true experiment would involve random assignment to conditions. (see The Scientific Study of Development)

14. d is the answer.   A longitudinal study involves measuring the same individuals over a period of time. Joe has measured the same group of kids for over 12 years, which is what a longitudinal study involves. (see The Scientific Study of Development)

15. d is the answer.   The study of child development helps a variety of people—from parents to teachers, from program developers to policy makers, to business and industry, even health-care professionals. (see Developmental Science in the Real World)

Now turn to the quiz analysis table at the end of this chapter to find which areas you know well and which areas you need to work on. Circle the numbers in the table for items on Quiz 2 that you answered correctly.

For each question you answered correctly, circle its number. (Quiz 1 numbers are not shaded; Quiz 2 numbers are shaded.) Are there patterns in the types of questions or the topics you got wrong that could direct your further study? Did you improve from Quiz 1 to Quiz 2?

QUIZ REVIEW

Topic	Type of Question		
	Definition	**Comprehension**	**Application**
Introductory Section	1		
What Lies Ahead?		2	3
	1	2	
Why Study Development?	4	5	
			3
Theories of Development	7, 10	6, 11	8, 9
	6	4	5
The Scientific Study of Development	13	14	12. 15
	8	7, 9, 12, 13	10, 11, 14
Developmental Science in the Real World			
		15	

Total correct by quiz:

Quiz 1:	
Quiz 2:	

CHAPTER 2

Nature with Nurture

LEARNING OBJECTIVES

1. Show how scientists' views have changed over time regarding genetic and environmental influences on development.

2. Define heritability. How do studies of twins, adopted children, and blended families help us understand heritability?

3. Describe the current epigenetic view of development.

4. Explain the concept of canalization in genetic expression. Give examples of how evolution has helped select for certain highly canalized traits.

5. Describe what genes are. Discuss their structure, components, and arrangement on chromosomes.

6. Define the words genotype and phenotype. Explain why they might be different in a particular individual.

7. Describe the processes of meiosis and mitosis. Show how meiosis helps to account for the differences between people.

8. Define the concepts of dominant genes, recessive genes, and regulator genes. Give examples of each type of gene.

9. Discuss how your genes may affect your vulnerability to environmental influences.

10. Consider Urie Bronfenbrenner's ecological perspective on human development. Explain why it compares the contexts of development to a series of nested Russian dolls. Give an example of a developmental influence found in your own microsystem, mesosystem, exosystem, and macrosystem. Explain how particular situations or institutions in the different contexts of Bronfenbrenner's model may influence each other.

11. Describe the four main types of interaction between genetic and environmental influences on children's development.

12. Explain the idea of reaction range. Give some examples to demonstrate how reaction range works.

OUTLINE

The map of the **human genome** is like the instruction manual for the human species. With its publication, scientists turned toward the goal of determining which genes influence which characteristics. Genes and environment act in concert, with environment influencing the development of genes as well as genes directly influencing behavior.

I.   Nature and Nurture
     In studying the role of heredity and environment in development, four main views have emerged: (1) development is driven by nature; (2) development is driven by nurture; (3)

21

development is part nature, part nurture; and (4) development results from the interaction of nature and nurture. The fourth view is the most recent.

A.   Development is Driven by Nature
      The idea that characteristics are innate is known as *nativism*.

   1.   **Preformationism** is the 17th century idea that embryos are preformed— miniature adults with determined anatomy and behavior. It is accompanied by ideas about human nature. For example, Western culture has typically emphasized the belief that people are innately bad via the concept of original sin.

   2.   Rousseau's Innocent Babes
         a)   Rousseau did not ascribe to preformationism. Rather, he argued that children are innocent at birth and develop according to nature's plan. The environment matters, but not as much as nature, in his view.
         b)   **Genetic determinism** is the idea that human qualities are genetically determined, and unable to be altered by nurture. This belief led to the **eugenics** movement in which some advocated for controlled breeding to produce desirable characteristics and to eliminate undesirable ones by discouraging those individuals with such traits. The Nazis are some of the best known eugenicists. This dark chapter in history led the study of genetic influences to become somewhat disreputable for a number of years.

B.   Development is Driven by Nurture
      Environmentalists believe that an individual's characteristics are entirely the product of experience.

   1.   Philosopher John Locke argued that an infant is like a **tabula rasa**, or blank slate. He saw childhood as a formative period in which parents have a responsibility to teach their children. The success, or failure, of the child then, is the product of those experiences.

   2.   The dominant views on development in the first half of the 20th century— psychoanalytic and behaviorist perspectives—were indeed focused on nurture, not nature. Watson's behaviorism was a revival of Locke's ideas on environmentalism.

C.   Development is Part Nature, Part Nurture
      In the second half of the 20th century, scientists became dissatisfied with nativism and environmentalism, and began to question how much nature versus nurture contributed to different traits.

   1.   Developmentalists began calculating the degree to which different traits were influenced by genetic factors—the **heritability** of the trait. These measures are called the heritability quotient of the trait.

   2.   Studies of heritability employed several designs
         a)   **Twin studies** take advantage of a "natural experiment." **Identical twins** are compared to **fraternal twins**, and if the identical twins are more similar on a trait than fraternal twins are, then the trait is understood to have a high heritability quotient. Twin studies may also examine twins separated at birth.
         b)   **Adoption studies** examine children raised by individuals other than their birth (or biological) parents. The researchers test to see if the children are more similar to their biological parents than their adoptive parents. If children resemble biological parents more, then it suggests a high heritability quotient for the trait in question.

      c)   **Family relatedness studies** examine blended families in which children with different degrees of biological relatedness (e.g., full vs. half vs. step siblings) are raised in the same environment. Individuals raised in blended families usually are more similar to the members to whom they are more closely biologically related.

3.   Research on heritability has shown that most human traits have a strong heritability component; however, that same research also reveals that the environment influences these traits, as well. For example, full siblings raised in the same environment have a **shared environment**, which may contribute to their similarity even as their similar genes do. Siblings also have a **non-shared environment**, in which they have different friends at school, different teachers, and so forth. Both the nature and the nurture (shared and non-shared) influence human development.

4.   Heritability studies have been criticized on three main counts: (1) genetic and environmental influences work together (reciprocally); (2) the impact of genes may vary depending on the quality of the environment; and (3) heritability quotients ignore the facts that human traits are malleable, or changeable.

D.   Development Results from the Interplay of Nature and Nurture
The contemporary view of development emphasizes the interaction of nature and nurture. More than combination, interaction implies that the result of something is quite different than the initial ingredients.

1.   Darwin's **theory of evolution** rests on two main ideas: **survival of the fittest** and **natural selection**. The "fittest" are those organisms best adapted to the situation, which are most likely to survive and then pass on their characteristics. Natural selection is the result of the interplay between a changing environment and the species members. What is adaptive in one environment may not be in the next, so what is most "fit" for survival is changeable.

2.   **Epigenesis** is a gradual process of increasing complexity due to interaction between heredity and environment.

      a)   Most developmental scientists ascribe to the idea of development as epigenesis.

      b)   **Stem cells** illustrate epigenesis. Stem cells are primitive, undifferentiated "pre-cells" found in large numbers in an embryo. They can become anything that the body needs. Some will specialize as brain tissue, others as muscle, and so forth.

II.   What Are Genes, and What Do They Do?
The study of genetics focuses on how genes make humans distinct from other species, and how they explain individual differences within humankind.

A.   Becoming Human
Walking upright on two feet, or **bipedalism**, is a human trait that results from natural selection.

1.   **Canalization**, the degree to which an element of development is dictated by the genetic program all humans inherit, is the phenomena that explain why features such as bipedalism are so pervasive in humans.

2.   One distinctive feature of humans is that we are born "prematurely"—humans are unable to take care of themselves for many years and have prolonged immature appearance and behavior, or **neotony**.

      a)   One reason for this is that humans have evolved to be highly social, and prolonged immaturity promotes social attachments.

        b)   Another reason for prolonged neotony is that humans are highly dependent on learning, and immaturity at birth increases receptivity to environmental learning.

  B.   Human Diversity

    1.   **Chromosomes** are long strands of DNA which contain a complete set of instructions for the development of a unique human being. The DNA "double helix" ladder contains four chemical bases: adenine, which always connects with thiamine, and guanine with cytosine. The order of the **base pairs** determines genetic instructions. **Genes**, segments of chromosomes, are the units of heredity that pass from one generation to the next.

    2.   The 23 pairs of chromosomes one inherits from his or her parents makes up his or her **genotype**; however, one's observable appearance and characteristics, or **phenotype**, depends on experience and environment.

    3.   During ordinary cell reproduction, or **mitosis**, a cell divides into a copy of itself. Reproductive cells, or **gametes**, are different. They reproduce by **meiosis**. Meiosis—the production of sperm and ova—produces cells with only half of a set of chromosomes. At fertilization, the reproductive cells merge and the chromosomes from the mother's ovum link with those from the father's sperm. Each person has two sets of chromosomes and two copies of every gene, called **alleles**.

    4.   Some might call development the transformation of a genotype into a phenotype. The sex of a child is determined by the 23rd pair of chromosomes. In the case of **additive heredity**, the child's phenotype is a mixture of the mother's and father's genes. In contrast, **dominant/recessive heredity** is one version of a gene overriding the other. Regulator genes do not directly affect traits, but turn other genes on or off at different points in the life cycle. The environment is an active partner in these genes actions and interactions.

    5.   Occasionally, copying errors, or **mutations**, do occur.

III. The Importance of Context

  A.   The Ecological Perspective on Development
Bronfenbrenner developed a way of thinking about developmental contexts as nested: a child is nested within the immediate context of whomever he/she interacts with, and that context is nested within the community, the community is nested within the region, and so forth.

  B.   Applying the Ecological Perspective: Understanding the Hispanic-American Dropout Rate
Hispanic teenagers are less likely to graduate from high school than individuals from other ethnic groups. Bronfenbrenner's ecological perspective provides a way to look at this problem from different contextual levels of analysis.

  C.   Microsystems

    1.   A **microsystem** is a setting in which the child interacts with others face-to-face every day (e.g., family, school, day care, etc.). Influences within microsystems are *bidirectional* and relationships within them are *multifaceted*.

    2.   At this level of analysis, one could ask if the reason Hispanic teens are less likely to graduate from high school has to do with the parenting style with which they were raised, the quality of the schools they attend, or the level of achievement their friends seek to attain.

  D.   The Mesosystem

    1.   The **mesosystem** refers to the ways in which microsystems are connected. Two types of connections are important. First, events in one setting may affect

behavior in another setting. Secondly, the characteristics in one microsystem may either conflict with or reinforce the experiences had in another microsystem.

2. At this level of analysis, one could ask if the reason Hispanic teens are less likely to graduate from high school has to do with the conflict between values instilled at home (cooperation) and those operating at school (competition).

E. The Exosystem
1. The **exosystem** comprises the contexts outside the child's immediate, everyday experiences.
2. At this level of analysis, one could ask if the reason Hispanic teens are less likely to graduate from high school has to do with the nature of the neighborhoods in which they tend to live. Are the neighborhoods more stressed? Are the neighborhoods more populated with individuals dealing with unemployment?

F. The Macrosystem
1. The **macrosystem** includes the larger forces that define a society at a given point in time. This includes social and cultural values, political and economic conditions, major historical events, and the like.
2. At this level of analysis, one could ask if the reason Hispanic teens are less likely to graduate from high school has to do with **familism**, which is especially valued in Hispanic cultures and puts pressure on Hispanic children to work to serve their family over working towards their own, individual achievement.

G. Putting It All Together
Although there is evidence to support each of the explanations above for why Hispanic teens are less likely to graduate from high school, it is most likely that it is due to the cumulative effects of many different aspects of life for Hispanic teens. The value of the ecological perspective is that it provides a framework for looking at multiple contextual influences, at different levels of analysis.

IV. The Interplay Between Genes and Context
A. Environmental Effects on Gene Expression
1. Until recently, scientists thought that genes contained a fixed set of instructions and operated on set timetables. However, the ways that genes affect development is through the proteins they "instruct" the body to produce – what scientists refer to as **gene expression**. The gene expression depends not just on the instruction code, but also on the context in which the instructions occur.
2. Manipulating the environment to see what happens to human gene expression is unethical, but has been done with rats. In one study, scientists reared two strains of rats—one group was nurturant mothers, and the other group of rats were not nurturant. The rats born to the "good moms" were less anxious in response to a fearful stimulus, but it was hard to tell if that was because the rats had good genes or favorable experiences. So, scientists transferred rats born to "good moms" to the "bad moms" and vice versa—a practice called **cross-fostering**. The rats with "good genes" that were raised by "bad moms" turned anxious, in spite of their good genes.

B. Environmental Effects on Heritability
1. The heritability of a trait depends on the environment.
2. The way in which the environment changes the heritability of a trait is not always the same.

C. Gene-Environment Interaction
1. How a person's genotype becomes a phenotype depends on **gene-environment interaction**—that is, inherited traits lead to different characteristics in different contexts.

2. The best way to look at inherited traits is as an array of possibilities, not fixed points—what scientists call a **reaction range.**

D. Gene-Environmental Correlations

1. Genotypes can also have an impact on the environment—that is, the developing child can shape his or her world, just by being who he/she is. These relationships refer to correlation, not necessarily causation.

2. **Passive gene-environment correlations** result from the fact that parents provide both genes and environments for their children. This correlation is "passive" in that the child doesn't do anything; both are part of what has been passed down, either through parents' biology or behavior.

3. **Evocative gene-environment correlations** result from the fact that genotypically different individuals elicit different responses from their environments. This correlation is "evocative" in that the child evokes a response from others based on how he/she behaves.

4. **Active gene-environment** correlations occur because children select contexts that they find stimulating and rewarding, a process called **niche-picking.** Children choose to participate in contexts that tend to strengthen the traits that lead them to select those contexts.

5. The importance of these different types of gene-environment correlations changes over the course of development.

KEY TERMS

1. The **human genome** is the complete set of genes for the creation and development of the human organism. (see introductory section)

2. **Preformationism** is the 17th century theory of inheritance that hypothesized that all the organs of an adult were prefigured in miniature within either the sperm or the ovum. (see Development is Driven by Nature)

3. **Genetic determinism** is the idea that human qualities are genetically determined and cannot be changed by nurture or education. (see Development is Driven by Nature)

4. **Eugenics** is a philosophy that advocates the use of controlled breeding to encourage childbearing among individuals with characteristics considered "desirable" and to discourage, or eliminate, childbearing among those with "undesirable" traits. (see Development is Driven by Nature)

5. **Tabula rasa** is the notion, usually associated with the philosopher John Locke, that nothing about development is predetermined, and that the child is entirely a product of his or her environment and experience. (see Development is Driven by Nurture)

6. **Heritability** is the extent to which a phenotypic trait is genetically determined. (see Development is Part Nature, Part Nurture)

7. **Twin studies** are a method for estimating heritability in which the degree of similarity in a trait that is observed among identical twins is compared with that observed among fraternal twins. (see Development is Part Nature, Part Nurture)

8. **Identical twins** are twins born when a single fertilized egg divides, resulting in the birth of two individuals whose genetic makeup is identical. (see Development is Part Nature, Part Nurture)

9. **Fraternal twins** are twins born when two separate eggs are fertilized, who are therefore no more alike genetically than other brothers and sisters. (see Development is Part Nature, Part Nurture)

10. **Adoption studies** are a method for estimating heritability in which similarities between children and their adoptive parents are compared with similarities between children and their biological parents. (see Development is Part Nature, Part Nurture)

11. **Family relatedness studies** are a method for estimating heritability by comparing the similarity of children who vary in their genetic relatedness (e.g., siblings, half-siblings, and stepsiblings). (see Development is Part Nature, Part Nurture)

12. **Shared environment** is, in behavioral genetics, the environment that siblings have in common. (see Development is Part Nature, Part Nurture)

13. **Nonshared environment** is, in behavioral genetics, the environment that siblings do not have in common, such as the peers with whom they are friends. (see Development is Part Nature, Part Nurture)

14. The **theory of evolution** typically refers to Charles Darwin's work, which asserts that organisms evolve and change through the process of natural selection. Other models of evolution have also been proposed. (see Development Results from the Interplay of Nature and Nurture)

15. **Survival of the fittest** is the idea within the theory of evolution that organisms that are best equipped to survive in a given context are therefore more likely to reproduce and pass their genetic material on to future generations. (see Development Results from the Interplay of Nature and Nurture)

16. **Natural selection**, as described in Darwin's theory of evolution, is the process through which adaptive traits that are heritable become more common while maladaptive traits that are heritable become less so. (see Development Results from the Interplay of Nature and Nurture)

17. **Epigenesis** is the gradual process through which organisms develop over time in an increasingly differentiated and complex fashion as a consequence of the interaction between genes and the environment. (see Development Results from the Interplay of Nature and Nurture)

18. **Stem cells** are primitive, undifferentiated cells, or "pre-cells," found in large numbers in the embryo. (see Development Results from the Interplay of Nature and Nurture)

19. **Bipedalism** is being able to stand and walk on two feet. (see Becoming Human)

20. **Canalization** is the degree to which an element of development is dictated by the common genetic program that all humans inherit. (see Becoming Human)

21. **Neotony** is prolonged immature appearance and behavior. (see Becoming Human)

22. **Chromosomes** are strands of DNA that carry genes and associated proteins. (see Human Diversity)

23. **Base pairs** are pairs of adenine and thiamine and of guanine and cytosine that make up the "rungs" of the DNA molecule. (see Human Diversity)

24. A **gene** is a segment of DNA occupying a specific place on a chromosome. (see Human Diversity)

25. A **genotype** is the underlying genetic makeup of an individual organism. (see Human Diversity)

26. **Phenotype** refers to the observable traits and characteristics of an individual organism. (see Human Diversity)

27. **Mitosis** is the process through which all cells other than gametes reproduce, in which a cell divides and each resulting cell receives a full copy of all 46 chromosomes. (see Human Diversity)

28. **Gametes** are reproductive cells (ova, or eggs, in females and sperm in males). (see Human Diversity)

29. **Meiosis** is the process through which gametes (sperm and ova) are produced, in which each resulting gamete has half of the genetic material of the parent cell. (see Human Diversity)

30. **Alleles** are different forms of the same gene occupying the same location on each of the chromosomes that make up a chromosomal pair. (see Human Diversity)

31. **Additive heredity** is the process of genetic transmission that results in a phenotype that is a mixture of the mother's and father's traits. (see Human Diversity)

32. **Dominant/recessive heredity** is the process of genetic transmission where one version (allele) of a gene is dominant over another, resulting in the phenotypic expression of only the dominant allele. (see Human Diversity)

33. **Mutations** are copying errors in the replication of DNA which alter the proteins a gene or chromosome produces. (see Human Diversity)

34. A **micro-system** in Bronfenbrenner's ecological perspective on development is a setting in which the child interacts with others face-to-face, such as a family or classroom. (see Micro-systems)

35. A **mesosystem** in Bronfenbrenner's ecological perspective on development is a system of interconnected micro-systems. (see The Meso-system)

36. An **exosystem** in Bronfenbrenner's ecological perspective on development is the layer of the context that includes the larger settings that the child knows only in part, such as the neighborhood, and settings in which the child herself does not participate, such as the parents' workplace. (see The Exo-system)

37. A **macrosystem** in Bronfenbrenner's ecological perspective on development is the layer of the context that includes the larger forces that define a society at a particular point in time, including culture, politics, economics, the mass media, and historical events. (see The Macro-system)

38. **Familism** is placing high value on the interests of the family rather than the individual. (see The Macro-system)

39. **Gene expression** is the process through which genes influence the production of specific proteins, which in turn influence the phenotype. (see Environmental Effects on Gene Expression)

40. **Cross-fostering** in animal research refers to the process of removing an offspring from its biological parents and having it raised by other adults, often with different attributes than the biological parents. (see Environmental Effects on Gene Expression)

41. **Gene-environment interaction** is the process through which genotypes produce different phenotypes in different contexts. (see Gene-Environment Interactions)

42. **Reaction range** is the array of phenotypic possibilities that a genotype has the potential to produce as a result of the context in which the organism develops. (see Gene-Environment Interactions)

43. **Passive gene-environment correlations** refer to similarity between the results of genetic and environmental influences due to the fact that the same parents provide both genes and environments for their children. (see Gene-Environmental Correlations)

44. **Evocative gene-environment correlations** refer to similarity between the results of genetic and environmental influences due to the fact that genotypically different individuals elicit different responses from their environments. (see Gene-Environmental Correlations)

45. **Active gene-environment correlations** refer to similarity between the results of genetic and environmental influences due to the fact that children select contexts that they find rewarding, and that therefore tend to maintain or strengthen their genetically-influenced traits. (see Gene-Environmental Correlations)

46. **Niche-picking** is the process through which individuals select the environments in which they spend time. (see Gene-Environmental Correlations)

FILL-IN-THE-BLANKS KEY TERMS

This section will help you check your knowledge of the key terms introduced in this chapter. Fill in each blank with the appropriate term from the list of key terms in the previous section.

1. _____ is the idea that all the organs of an adult were miniaturized within either the sperm or ovum.

2. The process through which adaptive traits that are heritable become more common while maladaptive traits that are less heritable become less so is _____.

3. A _____ is the underlying genetic makeup of an individual organism.

4. _____ is prolonged immature appearance and behavior.

5. A setting in which a child interacts with others face-to-face on a daily basis is a _____.

6. _____ are different forms of the same gene occupying the same location on each of the chromosomes that make up a chromosomal pair.

7. Primitive, undifferentiated cells found in large numbers in embryos are _____.

8. _____ is the degree to which an element of development is dictated by the common genetic program that all humans inherit.

9. Placing high value on the interests of the family rather than the individual is known as _____.

10. _____ is the process of genetic transmission that results in a phenotype that is a mixture of the mother's and father's traits.

APPLIED LEARNING AND CRITICAL THINKING

The study of the interplay of nature and nurture in child development is an exciting area. It may not seem like the most "applied" topic you will read about in this course this semester, but there are lots of ways this sort of research is applied in careers and volunteer work. Being able to think carefully about the implications of one's genetic make-up becomes really practical when you start to put that to work in context.

1. If you haven't ever volunteered for a group that is organized around a genetic mutation, consider doing so now. For example, Down Syndrome is a genetic mutation that involves an extra chromosome on the 21st pair. There are a lot of groups devoted to advocacy and volunteerism for this population, including the National Down Syndrome Congress (www.ndsccenter.org) and the Down Syndrome Research Foundation (www.dsrf.org). Explore these or other websites to find ways that you might volunteer to work with a special population of people who have a genetic mutation. As you do your work, notice the wide variability there is in the people who share the same mutation. Reflect on what the sources of that variability are using Bronfenbrenner's levels of analysis. Thinking systematically about the role of each child's micro-, meso-, exo-, and macro systems is an integrative approach to understanding how context affects the expression of a genetic mutation, and volunteering to work with a special population allows you to see that variability up close and personal.

2. If you read an article from one of the academic journals that focuses on child development, which was one of the suggestions in this part of the *Study Guide* in the previous chapter, go back and analyze it using a different lens this time. If you previously analyzed it looking at details that speak to the quality of the research that was done, now consider how that same piece of research speaks to the nature-nurture debate that this chapter focuses on. Do the authors seem to focus more on environmental effects on child development, or on genetic effects? Do they focus on the relationship between those two influences at all? Notice as you go through the article how just bringing a fresh perspective changes what you see in the piece. This is an important part of critical thinking—learning how the same text can reveal different things when you look at it with a different purpose.

3. Genetic counseling is a career path that involves knowledge of both nature and nurture. Genetic counselors are health professionals with specialized graduate training in the areas of medical genetics and counseling. Most come from a variety of disciplines, including biology, genetics, nursing, psychology, public health and social work. Genetic counselors work as members of a health-care team, providing information and support, including some counseling, to families who have members with birth defects or genetic disorders and to families who may be at risk for a variety of inherited conditions. You can find a lot more information on genetic counseling as a career at the website for the National Society of Genetic Counselors (www.nsgc.org), but you may also find it valuable to go to a hospital that supplies genetic counseling to its patients and actually visit with a genetic counselor about their day-to-day work. Going to visit someone on the actual job site is tremendously informative, and just visiting the website can't really substitute for it. Ask the counselor about the tension they may experience as parents who are just receiving a genetic diagnosis for their child seek information and answers. Many parents may press the counselor to predict their child's outcome, so it is helpful to ask how genetic counselors respond to this, given that environmental factors create a reaction range for many genetic mutations.

4. Find out what sorts of research is going on at your own university. Research related to the role of nature and nurture cuts across a variety of disciplines. Individuals in education, biology, psychology, chemistry may all have work related to the role of nature and nurture in child development. You can usually find out who is doing research on what topic by going to each departmental website and finding individual faculty pages. These pages often provide information about that faculty member's current research. If someone's work is related to the interplay of nature and nurture, see if they will let you visit their lab. Find out what sorts of questions they are asking, and what sorts of tools are required to answer them. How do the questions asked and the tools used to answer them vary depending upon the discipline in which the research is conducted?

MULTIPLE-CHOICE QUESTIONS

Quiz 1

1. The 17th century view that infants are miniature adults whose future anatomy and behavior were already determined is known as

    a. epigenesis.
    b. preformationism.
    c. familism.
    d. natural selection.

2. Selective breeding in livestock is similar to _____, which applies the same principles to human populations.

    a. canalization
    b. nativism
    c. eugenics
    d. behaviorism

3. Johnna was adopted as an infant. Her parents allow her to participate in an adoption study. Which of the following questions is most likely to be asked in that study?

    a. Is Johnna more similar to her birth parents or to her biological parents?
    b. Does Johnna have an identical twin?
    c. Does Johnna have a fraternal twin?
    d. How similar is Johnna to her step-siblings?

4. The theory that rests on the ideas of natural selection and survival of the fittest is

    a. nativism.
    b. the ecological perspective.
    c. neotony.
    d. the theory of evolution.

5. A gradual process of increasing complexity due to the interaction between genes and environment is called

    a. epigenesis.
    b. bipedalism.
    c. canalization.
    d. niche-picking.

6. Because all normal infants eventually learn to walk—regardless of the type of environment they grow up in—we say that walking is

    a. highly canalized.
    b. moderately canalized.
    c. not very canalized.
    d. unrelated to canalization.

7. Sarah has brownish hair, but in the summer it turns blonde because she swims a lot and is in the sun a great deal. Sarah's blonde hair in the summer is an example of a(n)

    a. genotype.
    b. phenotype.
    c. meiosis process.
    d. mitosis process.

8. When a child looks like a mixture of his or her parents on a given trait, we can suspect that _____ is(are) at work.

    a. dominant/recessive heredity
    b. alleles
    c. regulator genes
    d. additive heredity

9. A setting in which a child interacts with others daily is called a _____ in the ecological perspective.

    a. microsystem
    b. mesosystem
    c. exosystem
    d. macrosystem

10. Connor knows the neighbors to his right and a few people across the street, but there are 50 families in his neighborhood, and he definitely doesn't know them all. Connor's neighborhood is an example of which level of analysis in Bronfenbrenner's ecological perspective?

    a. microsystem
    b. mesosystem
    c. exosystem
    d. macrosystem

11. Because Eduardo is from a Hispanic background, he is likely to place a great deal of emphasis on

    a. bipedalism.
    b. base pairs.
    c. cross-fostering.
    d. familism.

12. To help determine how genes interact with the environment, scientists may take an animal from its biological parents and have it raised with parents with characteristics quite different from the biological parents', also known as

    a. cross-fostering.
    b. gene expression.
    c. mitosis.
    d. meiosis.

13. Shara's parents are both pretty smart. Her intelligence level is likely to be quite high, though the actual IQ she achieves will likely depend quite a bit on her environment, because intelligence has a fairly broad

    a. gene-environment correlation.
    b. reaction range.
    c. exosystem.
    d. mutation.

14. What is "passive" about a passive gene-environment correlation?

    a. The child doesn't do anything to experience both the parents' genes and the environment the parents provide.
    b. The child passively mimics his or her parents as they interact.
    c. The child evokes a response from his or her parents based on his or her own traits.
    d. None of these

15. Kerry loves sports. She is naturally athletic, and she chooses to play sports almost year round. This makes her even better at sports. Kerry choosing to play sports, which she is already good at, illustrates

    a.   a passive gene-environment correlation.
    b.   an evocative gene-environment correlation.
    c.   niche-picking.
    d.   bipedalism.

Quiz 2

Use this quiz to reassess your learning after taking Quiz 1 and reviewing the chapter.

1. The complete set of genes for building and operating the human body is called the

    a.   chromosome.
    b.   human genome.
    c.   base pair.
    d.   allele.

2. Genetic determinism shares central assumptions with which concept?

    a.   Preformationism
    b.   Behaviorism
    c.   The ecological perspective
    d.   Familism

3. Which trait below has the highest heritability quotient?

    a.   Being right or left handed
    b.   Speaking Spanish or English
    c.   Being moral or immoral
    d.   All of these

4. Mike and Linda are twins. Given only this information, you can guess that they are

    a.   identical twins.
    b.   fraternal twins.
    c.   adopted.
    d.   without step-siblings.

5. Kelly and Kirby grew up in the same household. They have different friends at school, though. Their common experiences at home are called a(n)

    a.   heritability quotient.
    b.   tabula rasa.
    c.   shared environment.
    d.   nonshared environment.

6. Prolonged immature appearance and behavior is called

    a.   heritability.
    b.   canalization.
    c.   bipedalism.
    d.   neotony.

7. _____ look like a twisted ladder, or double helix.

    a.   Base pairs
    b.   Chromosomes
    c.   RNA
    d.   None of these

8.   Making a photocopy is similar to

    a.   meiosis.
    b.   mitosis.
    c.   cross-fostering.
    d.   niche-picking.

9.   Copying errors in the replication of DNA are called

    a.   gametes.
    b.   phenotypes.
    c.   alleles.
    d.   mutations.

10. Trey's parents encourage lots of free exploration and give him lots of unscheduled time. He
    attends a Montessori preschool, which also promotes Trey engaging in discovery based on
    his own explorations. The correspondence between Trey's home and school environments
    speaks to what level of analysis in Bronfenbrenner's ecological perspective?

    a.   Microsystem
    b.   Mesosystem
    c.   Exosystem
    d.   Macrosystem

11. Bronfenbrenner's macrosystem is most similar to which part of an egg?

    a.   The yolk
    b.   The white
    c.   The shell
    d.   None of these

12. _____ is the process through which genes influence the production of specific proteins,
    which in turn influence the phenotype.

    a.   Gene expression
    b.   Mitosis
    c.   Meiosis
    d.   Cross-fostering

13. The process through which genotypes produce different phenotypes in different contexts is
    called

    a.   niche-picking.
    b.   gene-environment interaction.
    c.   familism.
    d.   preformationism.

14. Miranda is very pretty and her parents constantly tell her so. Consequently, Miranda spends
    lots of time fixing her hair and learning how to put make-up on, which elicits further
    compliments from her folks about how beautiful she is. That Miranda's prettiness draws
    compliments from those around her illustrates which type of gene-environment correlation?

    a.   Passive
    b.   Active
    c.   Evocative
    d.   None of these

15. The gist of this chapter could best be summed up as

    a.   Nature predominantly drives development.
    b.   Nurture predominantly drives development.
    c.   Development is part nature, and part nurture.
    d.   Development is the interplay of nature and nurture.

ANSWERS TO FILL-IN-THE-BLANKS KEY TERMS

1. Preformationism (see Development is Driven by Nature)

2. natural selection (see Development Results from the Interplay of Nature and Nurture)

3. genotype (see Human Diversity)

4. Neotony (see Becoming Human)

5. microsystem (see Microsystems)

6. Alleles (see Human Diversity)

7. stem cells (see Development Results from the Interplay of Nature and Nurture)

8. Canalization (see Becoming Human)

9. familism (see The Macrosystem)

10. Additive heredity (see Human Diversity)

ANSWERS TO MULTIPLE-CHOICE QUESTIONS

Circle the question numbers you answered incorrectly.

Quiz 1

1. *b is the answer.*   Preformationism was the belief that infants, indeed even embryos, were miniaturized adults who had future appearance and skills that were set. (see Nature and Nurture)

2. *c is the answer.*   Eugenics is the use of controlled breeding to encourage childbearing among individuals with "desirable" traits, and to discourage breeding among people with "undesirable" traits. (see Nature and Nurture)

3. *a is the answer.*   Adoption studies try to assess how similar a child is to his biological parents relative to how similar he or she is to his or her adoptive parents as a way to determine the heritability of different characteristics. (see Nature and Nurture)

4. *d is the answer.*   The theory of evolution, proposed by Darwin, rests on the ideas of natural selection and survival of the fittest. The former idea is that in nature most organisms do not survive long enough to reproduce, to only the best adapted of a species survive long enough to pass on their genes. As this process iterates over time, certain characteristics are "selected" by nature to be present in a species. (see Nature and Nurture)

5. *a is the answer.*   Epigenesis is the notion that complexity increases gradually as an organism or system interacts with its context. In this view, nothing (or very little) is predetermined, as the environment shapes the way development biologically unfolds. (see Nature and Nurture)

6. *a is the answer.*   Canalization is the degree to which an element of development is dictated by the genetic program that all humans inherit. Because all normally developing infants learn to walk, this suggests that "walking" is genetically programmed rather than environmentally determined (although *when* the infant walks may be influenced by the environmental experiences). (see What Are Genes and What Do They Do?)

7. *b is the answer.*   A phenotype refers to a person's observable characteristics and behavior. Phenotypes depend largely on experiences and context. Sarah's summer hair color is influenced by the experience of swimming and being out in the sunshine. (see What Are Genes and What Do They Do?)

8. *d is the answer.*   Additive heredity occurs when a number of the mother's and the father's genes affect a given trait, and the visible phenotype is a mixture of the two. (see What Are Genes and What Do They Do?)

9. *a is the answer.*   Microsystems refer to situations in which a child interacts face-to-face on a daily basis. (see The Importance of Context)

10. *c is the answer.*   The exosystem refers to settings outside of a child's immediate, everyday experience that he or she may know only in part. A child may interact with neighbors regularly, but not likely all members of the neighborhood. The fact that Connor knows his neighborhood only in part makes it part of his exosystem. (see The Importance of Context)

11. *d is the answer.*   Familism is the importance placed upon family. Hispanic cultures tend to value familism relatively more than other Caucasian or African American cultures. (see The Importance of Context)

12. *a is the answer.*   Cross-fostering of animals involves removing offspring from biological parents to see if the expression of the traits "bred" into the animal genetically are influenced by being part of an environment that may have quite different characteristics in the "new" parents. (see The Interplay Between Genes and Context)

13. *b is the answer.*   Reaction range is the array of possibilities a phenotype can take on based on the genotype. Intelligence can vary depending on the environment, but genetic contributions anchor how far it can vary. (see The Interplay Between Genes and Context)

14. *a is the answer.*   The child passively inherits the parents' biology and behavior—the child doesn't have to do anything to experience these features. A child mimicking a parent is not passive, but active, as is a child evoking a response from his or her parents. (see The Interplay Between Genes and Context)

15. *c is the answer.*   Niche-picking involves selecting contexts that strengthen traits that made those contexts attractive and rewarding in the first place. Kerry is choosing athletic contexts because she finds them rewarding, but by choosing them, she is strengthening her athleticism. (see The Interplay Between Genes and Context)

Now turn to the quiz analysis table at the end of this chapter to find which areas you know well and which areas you need to work on. Circle the numbers in the table for items on Quiz 1 that you answered correctly.

Quiz 2

1. *b is the answer.*   The complete set of genes for building and operating the human body is called the human genome (see introductory section)

2. *a is the answer.*   Preformationism and genetic determinism share the notion that human qualities are genetically determined and cannot be changed by education or nurture. (see Nature and Nurture)

3.   *a is the answer.*   Handedness is hard to "learn," and seems quite driven genetically. In contrast, what language a person speaks or the type of character they develop seems quite malleable in response to environment. (see Nature and Nurture)

4.   *b is the answer.*   Mike (a male's name) and Linda (a female's name) are fraternal twins. They cannot be identical because they are of different sexes. (see Nature and Nurture)

5.   *c is the answer.*   A shared environment is the environment that siblings have in common because of their similar experiences growing up in a shared household. The nonshared portion of their environment includes those experiences that involve parents treating Kelly and Kirby differently from each other, as well as their separate friends at school. (see Nature and Nurture)

6.   *d is the answer.*   Neotony refers to prolonged immature appearance and behavior. (see What Are Genes and What Do They Do?)

7.   *b is the answer.*   Chromosomes are long strands of DNA that look like a twisted ladder, or double helix. Base pairs are the rungs of this ladder, not the ladder itself. RNA serves as the messenger from the ladder. (see What Are Genes and What Do They Do?)

8.   *b is the answer.*   Mitosis, which is ordinary cell reproduction, involves dividing a cell so that the daughter cell is an exact replica. Meiosis is cell production of sperm and ova, and does not involve producing exact replicas. (see What Are Genes and What Do They Do?)

9.   *d is the answer.*   Mutations are copying errors in the reproduction of DNA that alter the protein the gene or chromosome produces. (see What Are Genes and What Do They Do?)

10.   *b is the answer.*   The mesosystem refers to the way in which microsystems are interconnected. Both Trey's school and his home are microsystems because he interacts on a face-to-face basis in each daily, and the connection between the two illustrates the mesosystem. (see The Importance of Context)

11.   *c is the answer.*   The macrosystem in Bronfenbrenner's model is the outer-most layer of context. This is analogous to the shell on an egg because the shell is the outer layer of the egg. (see The Importance of Context)

12.   *a is the answer.*   The process through which genes influence the production of specific proteins is called gene expression. (see The Interplay Between Genes and Context)

13.   *b is the answer.*   Gene-environment interaction is the process through which genotypes produce different phenotypes in different contexts. (see The Interplay Between Genes and Context)

14.   *c is the answer.*   Evocative gene-environment correlations result from the fact that genotypically different individuals elicit different responses from their environments. Miranda's genetics for being pretty elicit compliments from the people she interacts with. (see The Interplay Between Genes and Context)

15.   *d is the answer.*   Although scientists used to debate if development was nature *or* nurture, and then later turned to trying to assess the relative contributions of each to development, we now know that development results from the interaction of nature with nurture. (see The Interplay Between Genes and Context; see also Summing Up and Looking Ahead)

Now turn to the quiz analysis table at the end of this chapter to find which areas you know well and which areas you need to work on. Circle the numbers in the table for items on Quiz 2 that you answered correctly.

For each question you answered correctly, circle its number. (Quiz 1 numbers are not shaded; Quiz 2 numbers are shaded.) Are there patterns in the types of questions or the topics you got wrong that could direct your further study? Did you improve from Quiz 1 to Quiz 2?

QUIZ REVIEW

Topic	Type of Question		
	Definition	Comprehension	Application
Introductory Section	1		
Nature and Nurture	1, 5	2, 4	3
		2, 5	3, 4
What Are Genes, and What Do They Do?		6, 8	7
	6, 9	7	8
The Importance of Context	9		10, 11
		11	10
The Interplay Between Genes and Context	12	13, 14	15
	12, 13	15	14

Total correct by quiz:

Quiz 1:	
Quiz 2:	

CHAPTER 3

Conception, Prenatal Development, and Birth

LEARNING OBJECTIVES

1. Describe the processes of conception and implantation.

2. Describe the factors that cause infertility and the treatments for infertility.

3. Explain the development of the embryo.

4. Describe the physical development of the fetus.

5. Describe the cognitive development of the fetus.

6. Explain the process of sexual development from conception through birth.

7. List some of the chromosomal and genetic abnormalities that may affect an unborn child.

8. Describe techniques used to monitor fetal health.

9. Describe the effects of the mother's age, diet, and stress level on her unborn child.

10. Define teratogen. List the different types of teratogens and their potential effects on the fetus.

11. Describe the psychological effects of pregnancy on the parents-to-be.

12. Describe the process of delivery.

13. Explain some possible medical complications that may affect birth, and describe how they are handled.

14. List some of the dangers that premature babies face.

15. Explain how the Apgar test and Neonatal Behavioral Assessment Scale are used to rate the health and well-being of newborns.

OUTLINE

I. The First Nine Months
The period of development from conception to birth is known as **gestation**, and it last about 280 days. It is divided into three main stages of development: The period of the zygote, the period of the embryo, and the period of the fetus.

    A. Conception and the Zygote: The First Two Weeks
        1. When a woman experiences **ovulation**, her ovaries release a mature **ovum** which begins to journey down the fallopian tube toward the uterus. During intercourse, a male ejaculates over 500 million sperm into the female's vagina, which swim up through the cervix, the uterus, and the fallopian tubes. Not all sperm can make the journey, and of the ones that do only one can fertilize the egg. **Fertilization** occurs if the intercourse takes place on or a few days prior to the day of ovulation.

2. The ovum and sperm unite to form a new cell called a **zygote**. As the zygote travels towards the uterus, it begins to differentiate into cells with specialized roles, with the outer cells to become the **placenta** and the inner cells the embryo. Once the zygote reaches the uterus, **implantation** may occur.

3. Some couples have difficulty conceiving. **Infertility** is failure to conceive after having unprotected intercourse for 12 months. Primary factors influencing risk for infertility are the couple's age, lifestyle, and overall health. Infertility is treatable, and distinct from sterility.

4. If the infertility is due to the female's failure to ovulate regularly, **fertility drugs** can stimulate ovulation. If the infertility is due to the male, then **artificial insemination** may be helpful. **In vitro fertilization (IVF)** is helpful in more complex cases of infertility. Occasionally, this may also require a **surrogate mother** if the infertile mother cannot sustain the pregnancy. In most cases, the surrogate carries an embryo that has the **gametes** of the individuals who he or she will call "parents."

5. The main risk for reproductive technologies is multiple births. Birth defects are not more likely. Another risk is that the procedure will not work, and the cycles of trying and failing can be very disappointing for would-be parents.

B. The Embryo: Weeks Three through Eight

1. After implantation, the embryo's cells form specialized layers. The **ectoderm** will become skin, nerves, and sense organs. The **mesoderm** will become muscle, bones, circulatory system, and some organs. The **endoderm** will become digestive system, lungs, urinary tract, and glands. The **amniotic sac** cushions the embryo.

2. During the embryonic period, the basic structure of a human being appears and organs begin to function. **Neurogenesis** begins.

3. By the end of the embryonic period, all the major organ and body parts have formed.

C. The Fetus: Week Eight to Birth

1. During the fetal period, the primitive organ and body parts develop and grow.

2. Neurogenesis is typically complete by the end of the sixth month, and the brain begins to organize itself, allowing some neurons to die off while others make new connections.

3. The fourth month of pregnancy is the time of **quickening**, when mothers feel their baby move for the first time.

4. Fetal behavior becomes increasingly organized. At three months the fetus swallows, urinates, hiccups, blinks and yawns. At six months, the fetus breathes, cries, and has distinct sleep-wake patterns. By seven or eight months, the fetus is less active but more vigorous, mostly due to space constraints in the womb.

5. Evidence suggests that fetuses are able to learn to recognize familiar sounds and rhythms. Variability is also observable prenatally, with **temperament** being related to the level of fetal activity observed.

D. Boy or Girl?

1. Sex differentiation begins at conception, with girls having two X chromosomes and boys an X and a Y chromosome.

2. Prenatal sex development can be divided into four stages. During the first month and a half, the embryo is "unisex"; at about seven weeks, the Y chromosome and testosterone stimulate the development of the physiological sex differences; at about two and a half to three months, external genitalia forms; and finally testosterone inhibits the rhythmic cycles of the hypothalamus and pituitary gland to suppress ovulation in male fetuses.

3. The basic plan of nature is female, as the Y chromosome must trigger the development of male sex characteristics. In **Turner's Syndrome**, the fetus has only one X chromosome. In the absence of the Y, female characteristics develop. Testosterone is also required to stimulate male development.

4. Sex differentiation can be seen as a series of gates that cannot be re-opened. For women who took DES during pregnancy, that drug stimulated testosterone, which resulted in masculine-looking external genitalia in genetically female infants.

5. Sex differences are not merely anatomical, and are related to how people treat the infant. However, people treat an infant in particular ways based on their anatomical structures, allowing both social and physiological factors to influence gender development.

II. Monitoring Prenatal Development
Ultrasound imaging is the predominant way in which prenatal development can be monitored today. Most babies are healthy at birth, as nature eliminates most malformed fetuses prior to birth. Most disorders that a fetus might have are **multifactoral disorders,** having to do with interactions among multiple genes, and between genes and the environment.

A. Chromosomal and Genetic Abnormalities
1. Chromosomal abnormalities are often caused by mutations during *meiosis*. Down syndrome is the most common example. Children with Down syndrome have smaller heads, unusual facial features, are short and stocky, and tend to be exceptionally cheerful. They have severe learning difficulties, and many have other health problems. Most are able, though, to attend public school and live into adulthood.

2. Most genetic disorders are carried on a recessive gene. Sickle cell anemia is one such example. Children who inherit the gene for this disease from both parents suffer shortness of breath, fatigue, pain, and some fatal crises related to organ failure. Other disorders are sex-linked, such as colorblindness or hemophilia.

3. The *founder effect* underlies the frequency of genetic disorders amongst the Amish.

B. Genetic Counseling
1. Genetic counseling helps couples understand the effects heredity might have on their children. A genetic counselor starts with a history, and then a **karyotype,** which is useful in identifying recessive genetic defects. These processes help a couple understand the likelihood of a genetic defect in their offspring.

2. If both partners carry an abnormal recessive gene or if the mother is over 35, the couple has several options, none of which are easy. If a fetus is identified as abnormal, they may consider abortion. Other couples may prefer not to risk an abnormal child, and adopt or conceive through IVF with donor eggs or sperm. Genetic counselors help parents understand the risks associated with each of these choices.

C. Prenatal Testing
1. Some genetic defects can be identified before birth. Couples using IVF may seek a **preimplantation genetic diagnosis** to select an embryo free of identifiable genetic defects.

2. The most common prenatal screening is **amniocentesis**. Using a needle, the doctor withdraws a small amount of amniotic fluid from the mother's uterus. These cells are then cultured for 10–12 days, and then tested for chromosomal abnormalities. Unfortunately, these results are usually not available until the 5th

month of the pregnancy, which (if there is an abnormality) presents a difficult decision.

3. **Chorionic villi sampling (CVS)** allows earlier results in the third month. But neither CVS nor amniocentesis is foolproof, and both tests carry some risks to the pregnancy and the fetus.

III. Protecting the Fetus

A. Maternal Characteristics

1. Both older and younger mothers are more at risk for problems in pregnancy and birth. Younger mothers tend to wait longer to seek prenatal care and are at risk for preterm delivery. Older mothers have more birth complications.

2. The quality of maternal nutrition impacts the health of the fetus. Malnutrition in early pregnancy, particularly lack of folic acid, increases risk for birth defects such as **spina bifida** or **anencelapathy**. Malnutrition later in pregnancy is associated with lower birth weight, although the effects can be overcome by quality nutrition after birth in a stable, supportive environment.

3. High stress in pregnancy increases the risk for premature birth.

B. Outside Influences

1. A **teratogen** is any substance that can have a negative impact on fetal development. Most of these can be avoided if the mother is aware of the problems.

2. The placenta protects the fetus from many bacteria but not viruses. **Rubella** contracted during the first three months of pregnancy can be devastating for the fetus. **HIV**, the virus that causes **AIDS**, is a major threat today. About 1 in 4 infants affected with HIV develops AIDS symptoms shortly after birth. An HIV-positive mother can protect her fetus by taking AZT and other drugs that slow the HIV duplication.

3. Many medications can be harmful to a fetus. Pregnant women should take no drugs or vitamins without consulting their physician.

4. **Fetal alcohol syndrome (FAS)** is a pattern of mental disabilities and facial abnormalities found in infants with alcoholic mothers. FAS babies typically have some degree of mental retardation, short attention span, and emotional/behavioral disorders. Babies that have some of the problems of FAS, but not all, have **Fetal Alcohol Effects (FAE)**. While FAS is linked to alcohol abuse, alcohol consumption in any amount can be unsafe for the fetus, reducing IQ or increasing risk for attention deficits.

5. Nicotine may or may not harm the fetus, but smoking clearly does.

6. Babies born to heroin-addicted mothers are themselves addicted, and go through withdrawal. Cocaine exposure for fetuses is linked to low birth weights, small head circumference and length, irritability, hypersensitivity, lack of muscle tone and mood control, and increased risk for **SIDS**. Long-term problems are not well understood, but likely involve problems with language and cognitive development.

7. The environmental toxins most known for adversely affecting fetal development include lead, mercury, DDT, and PCB. Air pollution can also affect cognitive development of the fetus.

C. The Importance of Timing

1. The impact of outside substances on fetal development depends on the timing and duration of the exposure. Exposure during a **sensitive period** may alter anatomy or function irreversibly.

2. Although some environmental factors have immediate effects, others have **sleeper effects** which do not emerge until later in development.

D. Pregnancy and Parents-to-Be
   1. Early in the pregnancy, a woman tends to concentrate on her own well-being. By the third trimester, though, she feels more of a bond with her baby.
   2. Pregnancy presents a series of social and emotional challenges for the mother—a transformation of her identity to "mother," loss of freedom, changes in relations with her partner, and changes in her body. Feeling that the pregnancy was a choice helps with these challenges.

IV. Birth
   A. Labor and Delivery
      1. The pituitary gland releases **oxytocin**, which triggers uterine contractions, which ultimately push the baby into the world.
      2. During the first half of labor, the uterine contractions pull and tug the cervix open. During the second stage, the contractions push the baby into the birth canal. During the third stage, contractions expel the placenta, fetal membranes, and the remainder of the umbilical cord.
   B. Birth Complications and Controversies
      1. Some complications are positional, such as a *breech* or *hammock* position.
      2. **Anoxia** is one of the most significant complications. It can be caused by the umbilical cord being pinched, or because of a *placental abruption* or *placenta previa*. Short-term anoxia is usually not a problem, but long-term oxygen loss can cause brain damage.
      3. If the baby is threatened by a circumstance during delivery, the physician may perform a **Cesarean section (c-section)**. Like any surgery, the c-section carries some risk for the mother and the baby. In addition to these problems, it can create problems in managing pain following the surgery for the mother.
      4. Natural childbirth has increased in popularity, particularly the Lamaze method.
   C. Newborns at Risk
      1. **Preterm babies** are born before 37 weeks gestation. **Low birth weight** babies weigh less than 5.5 pounds, and very low birthweight is below 2.5 pounds.
      2. The reasons for preterm birth are numerous, including structural abnormalities to the uterus, maternal age, lack of spacing between a previous pregnancy, or maternal or fetal distress.
      3. Preterm babies often suffer from **respiratory distress syndrome (RDS)**, and are vulnerable to infection. They usually are fed intravenously or by feeding tube, and are at risk for brain hemorrhaging.
      4. Today the survivability of preterm infants is surprisingly high. Ninety percent of infants weighing less than 5.5 pounds survive; 67% of those weighing between 1.65 and 2.2 pounds survive, and 33% of those weighing 1.1 to 1.65 pounds survive. However, they often struggle with developmental delays for many years after their preterm birth.
   D. Infant Assessment
      1. The **Apgar test** is given to newborns at 1 minute after birth and 5 minutes after birth. The test scores the infant on appearance, pulse, grimace, activity, and respiration. Scores above 7 indicate a healthy baby, and below 4 a baby in critical condition.
      2. The **Neonatal Behavioral Assessment Scale** uses reflexes and social interaction to assess the newborn's overall well-being, including motor capabilities, state changes, and central nervous system stability.

KEY TERMS

1. **Gestation** is the period from conception to birth that lasts about 280 days, counting from the mother's last menstrual period. (see The First Nine Months)

2. The **ovum** (or plural, **ova**)   refers to female sex cells (egg). Girls are born with about 2 million ova. (see The First Nine Months)

3. **Ovulation** is an event that occurs about every twenty-eight days for women, in which a follicle in one of the ovaries ruptures, releasing a mature ovum to begin its four- to five-day journey down a fallopian tube toward the uterus. (see The First Nine Months)

4. **Fertilization** is insemination of an ovum by a sperm. (see The First Nine Months)

5. The **zygote** is the new cell created when the sperm and egg fuse. (see The First Nine Months)

6. The **placenta** is the support system that—via the umbilical cord—provides food and oxygen to the developing child and carries waste products away. (see The First Nine Months)

7. **Implantation** refers to the process, upon reaching the uterus, of the zygote embedding in the uterus's nutrient-rich lining (or endometrium), like roots of a growing plant into soil. (see The First Nine Months)

8. **Infertility** is failure to conceive a child after 12 months of sexual intercourse without birth control. (see The First Nine Months)

9. **Fertility drugs** are hormone-based agents that enhance ovarian activity. (see The First Nine Months)

10. **Artificial insemination** is the most common treatment for male infertility, which involves inserting sperm directly into the woman's uterus with a syringe. (see The First Nine Months)

11. **In Vitro Fertilization (IVF)** is the best-known and most common advanced reproductive technology procedure in which the woman takes fertility drugs so that her body releases more than one egg, her ova are surgically extracted at ovulation, and then are mixed with her partner's sperm in a laboratory dish. (see The First Nine Months)

12. A **surrogate mother** is the woman who is impregnated with a male's sperm through artificial insemination or with the couple's embryo, conceived in vitro. (see The First Nine Months)

13. **Gametes** are sex cells, the male sperm and female ova. (see The First Nine Months)

14. The **ectoderm** is the outer layer of an embryo's cells that will become fetal skin, nerves, and sense organs. (see The First Nine Months)

15. The **mesoderm** is the middle layer of an embryo's cells that will become muscle, bones, the circulatory system, and some organs. (see The First Nine Months)

16. The **endoderm** is the inner layer of an embryo's cells that will become the digestive system, lungs, urinary tract, and glands. (see The First Nine Months)

17. The **amniotic sac** is a protective membrane filled with warm liquid that cushions the embryo. (see The First Nine Months)

18. **Neurogenesis** is the production of neurons or nerve cells. (see The First Nine Months)

19. The **quickening** refers to the first fetal movements the mother can feel. (see The First Nine Months)

20. **Temperament** refers to a child's emotional and behavioral predispositions. (see The First Nine Months)

21. **Turner's syndrome** is a condition in which the embryo's cells have only one (X) chromosome. (see The First Nine Months)

22. **Ultrasound imaging** is a technology that provides a living picture of prenatal development (including sex differentiation). (see Monitoring Prenatal Development)

23. **Multifactoral disorders** are disorders that result from interactions among multiple genes and between genes and the environment. (see Monitoring Prenatal Development)

24. A **karyotype** is a picture of an individual's chromosomes. (see Monitoring Prenatal Development)

25. A **preimplantation genetic diagnosis** is a screening technique that involves removing cells from a test-tube embryo to determine if the cell contains genes linked to fatal childhood disorders. (see Monitoring Prenatal Development)

26. **Amniocentesis** is a prenatal test in which, using ultrasound as a guide, the doctor inserts a thin needle through the woman's abdomen into the uterus to withdraw amniotic fluid that contains skin cells from the fetus. (see Monitoring Prenatal Development)

27. **Chorionic villi sampling** is a fetal test that involves removal of a small piece of the villi, extensions that attach the amniotic sac to the wall of the uterus. (see Monitoring Prenatal Development)

28. **Spina bifida** is a developmental condition in which the spinal cord does not close completely. (see Protecting the Fetus)

29. **Anencelapathy** is a developmental condition in which part of the brain does not develop. (see Protecting the Fetus)

30. A **teratogen** is any environmental substance that can have a negative impact on fetal development and possibly result in birth defects or even death. (see Protecting the Fetus)

31. **Rubella** is German measles, a disease that can be devastating for the fetus if the mother contracts it during the first three months of pregnancy. (see Protecting the Fetus)

32. **HIV** is the human immunodeficiency virus that causes AIDS. (see Protecting the Fetus)

33. **AIDS** is acquired immunodeficiency syndrome. (see Protecting the Fetus)

34. **Fetal alcohol syndrome** refers to a pattern of disabilities found in babies and children of mothers who consumed alcohol during pregnancy. (see Protecting the Fetus)

35. **Fetal alcohol effects** are fetal deformities that are the result of significant (but not chronic) prenatal exposure to alcohol. (see Protecting the Fetus)

36. **Sudden infant death syndrome** is unexplained death, usually during the night, of an infant under one year old. (see Protecting the Fetus)

37. A **sensitive period** is a time in development during which the organism is especially vulnerable to experience. (see Protecting the Fetus)

38. The **sleeper effect** is an outcome that is displaced in time from a cause. (see Protecting the Fetus)

39.   **Oxytocin** is a maternal pituitary gland hormone that triggers uterine contractions. (see Birth)

40.   **Anoxia** is cutoff of the supply of oxygen through the umbilical cord before the baby can breathe independently. (see Birth)

41.   A **cesarean section** (or **C-section**) is a method of delivering a baby surgically through an incision in the mother's abdomen. (see Birth)

42.   **Preterm** babies are born before the thirty-seventh week of pregnancy. (see Birth)

43.   **Low birth weight** babies are born weighing less than 5.5 pounds (2,500 grams). (see Birth)

44.   **Respiratory distress syndrome** is a condition common to preterm babies whose lungs do not produce enough surfactant that helps to carry oxygen into and carbon dioxide out of the lungs. (see Birth)

45.   The **Apgar test** is a delivery room test that assesses a newborn with a score of 0, 1, or 2 on each of five measurements: **A**ppearance, **P**ulse, **G**rimace, **A**ctivity, and **R**espiration. (see Birth)

46.   The **Neonatal Behavioral Assessment Scale** is a test for newborns that uses reflexes and social interaction to assess their overall well-being, including motor capabilities, state changes, attention, and central nervous system stability. (see Birth)

FILL-IN-THE-BLANKS KEY TERMS

This section will help you check your knowledge of the key terms introduced in this chapter. Fill in each blank with the appropriate term from the list of key terms in the previous section.

1.   A prenatal test in which, using ultrasound as a guide, the doctor inserts a thin needle through the woman's abdomen into the uterus to withdraw amniotic fluid that contains skin cells from the fetus is _____.

2.   _____ is a maternal pituitary gland hormone that triggers uterine contractions.

3.   The first fetal movements the mother can feel are called the _____.

4.   _____ is a developmental condition in which part of the brain does not develop.

5.   A delivery room test that assesses a newborn with a score of 0, 1, or 2 on appearance, pulse, grimace, activity, and respiration is called the _____.

6.   The best-known and most common advanced reproductive technology procedure in which the woman takes fertility drugs so that her body releases more than one egg, her ova are surgically extracted at ovulation, and then are mixed with her partner's sperm in a laboratory dish is called _____.

7.   _____ is a condition common to preterm babies whose lungs do not produce enough surfactant that helps to carry oxygen into and carbon dioxide out of the lungs.

8.   A pattern of disabilities found in babies and children of mothers who consumed alcohol during pregnancy is called_____.

9.   _____ refers to the process, upon reaching the uterus, of the zygote embedding in the uterus's nutrient-rich lining.

10. A technology that provides a living picture of prenatal development is called_____.

APPLIED LEARNING AND CRITICAL THINKING

Prenatal development is one of those periods of child development during which it seems somewhat more difficult to access in a context-rich way. The fetus' development isn't visible with mere observation, after all. Yet there are creative ways to gain a window into prenatal development through service, work, and research. Here are just a few ideas.

1. Physicians and mothers alike have been subject to criticism for scheduling ostensibly unnecessary Cesarean section deliveries. Collaborate with a professor to develop a survey to measure percentage of deliveries in your community that are c-sections. Be sure to measure the gestational age of the fetus on such deliveries. Are the babies that are born by c-section on average arriving earlier than those that are delivered vaginally? Be sure to ask if the c-section was elective or not, and include that information in your analysis of gestational age at delivery. If you have access to a collaborator in another country, see if you can work together to collect the same data from another culture, to add another layer of analysis to your study. Be sure to get IRB approval for such a study before you proceed with data collection.

2. Sadly, some families receive a prenatal diagnosis that indicates that the baby's condition will not be compatible with life. For couples in this situation, many may decide to terminate their pregnancy, but many others elect to extend their baby's life for as long as possible. For couples making the latter choice, perinatal hospice programs provide enormous emotional support. Go to www.perinatalhospice.org and locate a perinatal hospice organization near your community. See if there is any volunteer work that they might need done, and spend some time there doing it. Some of these families may want to share their stories, and you might be able to help them record these events.

3. Most children's and other hospitals have genetic counseling clinics. Do a little research online at www.nsgc.org about this career. Then find a genetic counselor in your area and conduct an informational interview. If you've never done this type of interview, the following website has a tutorial for everything from how to find people to interview, to what questions to ask, to how to dress and conduct yourself while on an informational interview: http://www.quintcareers.com/informational_interviewing.html.

4. Maternal nutrition is one of the key factors that will influence the health and well-being of the baby. Talk to an OB/GYN in your area and ask them what sorts of resources are available to support high-quality maternal nutrition in at-risk populations. If they feel that the resources are insufficient, consider writing a grant to an organization whose mission is to improve the health of babies, like the March of Dimes (www.marchofdimes.com). Many of these organizations have "community grants" or "program services grants" that will fund work that focuses on promoting maternal nutrition as a means to promote the health of babies. There may even be a Grants and Sponsored Programs Office on your campus at which the staff can help you identify potential funding streams for such work.

MULTIPLE CHOICE QUESTIONS

Quiz 1

1. The period from conception to birth is called
   a. gestation.
   b. fertilization.
   c. ovulation.
   d. artificial insemination.

2. The event that occurs approximately every 28 days in women in which the ovaries release an egg is called

   a. gestation.
   b. ovulation.
   c. implantation.
   d. in vitro fertilization.

3. Megumi and Kashima have been trying to have a baby for the past year. Megumi is really frustrated because she still isn't pregnant. They consult a specialist, and find out that her fallopian tubes are blocked and that she will need a surgery to be able to conceive. Megumi is

   a. sterile.
   b. pregnant.
   c. infertile.
   d. preterm.

4. During the first two weeks of pregnancy, the product of fertilization is called a

   a. fetus.
   b. embryo.
   c. zygote.
   d. surrogate mother.

5. The success rate of IVF is

   a. nearly 90%.
   b. about 50%.
   c. less than 40%.
   d. less than 30%.

6. The layer of cells of the embryo that will become skin, nerves, and sense organs is called the

   a. ectoderm.
   b. endoderm.
   c. mesoderm.
   d. amniotic sac.

7. Disorders that are a result of interactions among genes or between genes and the environment are called

   a. Turner's Syndrome.
   b. spina bifida.
   c. multifactoral disorders.
   d. anoxia.

8. Christiana and Hans are using IVF. Before they insert the embryos for implantation, Christiana and Hans ask the doctor to test the embryo for genes related to fatal childhood disorders, and the genes for breast cancer. They want the doctor to not implant those embryos. Christiana and Hans are asking for

   a. a surrogate mother.
   b. a preimplantation genetic diagnosis.
   c. a karyotype.
   d. chorionic villi sampling.

9. Which maternal nutritional deficit has been linked to neural tube defects such as spina bifida?

   a. Vitamin C
   b. Lead
   c. Calcium
   d. Folic Acid

10. Which of the following is an example of a teratogen?

    a. Rubella
    b. DES
    c. Alcohol
    d. All of these

11. Which of the following is NOT a way a mother can pass on HIV to her baby?

    a. During pregnancy
    b. During labor/delivery
    c. Through breastfeeding
    d. None of these, as all of these are ways that a mother can pass on HIV.

12. Laraine is devastated. She rocked her newborn to sleep and when she went in to check on her a few hours later, the baby wasn't breathing. None of the doctors can explain to her why her baby died. Laraine's baby was a victim of

    a. rubella.
    b. SIDS.
    c. spina bifida.
    d. anencelapathy.

13. When Nduta's son was born, her home country was war-torn, and it was hard to find enough food to eat. She relocated to a safer country, and her son was raised there. Throughout his childhood and adolescence, he seemed fine, but as an adult he was diagnosed with mental illness. It turns out that many of the children in his situation are at elevated risk for mental illness because of the prenatal malnutrition they experienced. This is an example of

    a. a sleeper effect.
    b. a sensitive period.
    c. FAS.
    d. FAE.

14. When Kelly was born, her umbilical cord was squeezed during delivery and her oxygen supply was cutoff. The doctor's quick delivery through an emergency c-section prevented any lasting brain damage due to the

    a. anoxia.
    b. respiratory distress syndrome.
    c. karyotype.
    d. mesoderm.

15. The soapy substance that helps infants carry oxygen into and carbon dioxide out of the lungs is called

    a. quickening.
    b. ova.
    c. surfactant.
    d. amniocentesis.

Quiz 2

Use this quiz to reassess your learning after taking Quiz 1 and reviewing the chapter.

1. Girls are born with about_____ ova.

    a. 300,000
    b. 500,000
    c. 1,000,000
    d. 2,000,000

2.   When is fertilization most likely to be successful?

   a.   If a couple has intercourse a week before ovulation
   b.   A few days before ovulation
   c.   A few days after ovulation
   d.   A week after ovulation

3.   The prenatal support system that provides oxygen and nutrients to the developing child via the umbilical cord is called the

   a.   placenta.
   b.   zygote.
   c.   embryo.
   d.   fetus.

4.   Which of the following is artificial insemination?

   a.   Giving a woman drugs to stimulate ovulation
   b.   Mixing a woman's ova and with sperm in a lab dish
   c.   A woman sustaining a pregnancy for a friend who can't carry to term
   d.   Inserting sperm into a woman's uterus directly with a syringe

5.   Greta's friend, Kerry, has had several miscarriages. Kerry's doctor feels that she will be unable to sustain a pregnancy to term. So Kerry and her husband have her egg mixed with his sperm in a test tube, and the resulting embryo is implanted in Greta's womb. Greta is

   a.   a gamete.
   b.   a nanny.
   c.   a surrogate mother.
   d.   an endoderm.

6.   Johanna is pregnant and is really excited that she is going to learn the sex of her baby today at her

   a.   ultrasound.
   b.   amniocentesis.
   c.   chorionic villi sampling.
   d.   in vitro fertilization.

7.   After learning that their baby has a fatal genetic flaw, Bryan and Lisa want to find out what the odds are that their next child will inherit this flaw. A genetic counselor is working with them to determine their risk for this to happen again. To do so, the counselor takes a family history for each of them and then does a

   a.   preimplantation genetic diagnosis.
   b.   karyotype.
   c.   neurogenesis.
   d.   gestation.

8.   If a couple wants results of a prenatal genetic test most quickly, which test should they do?

   a.   Ultrasound imaging
   b.   Amniocentesis
   c.   Chorionic villi sampling
   d.   All of these are equally speedy genetic tests.

9.   A developmental condition in which part of the brain does not develop is called

   a.   anoxia.
   b.   anencelapathy.
   c.   rubella.
   d.   Fetal Alcohol Syndrome.

10. During what stage of pregnancy is rubella most likely to cause serious harm to the fetus?

    a. First trimester

    b. Second trimester

    c. Third trimester

    d. Rubella is equally devastating at all stages of pregnancy.

11. What amount of alcohol consumption has been proven safe for pregnant mothers and their fetus?

    a. A glass of wine a day

    b. A glass of wine each week

    c. A shot of whiskey each night

    d. No amount of alcohol has been proven safe during pregnancy.

12. The time during which a developing fetus is more vulnerable to teratogens is called

    a. gestation.

    b. implantation.

    c. a sensitive period.

    d. quickening.

13. What gland releases the hormone that triggers uterine contractions?

    a. Pituitary

    b. Adrenal

    c. Hypothalamus

    d. Oxytocin

14. The survival rate for preterm infants

    a. is 90%.

    b. is 67%.

    c. is 33%.

    d. depends on the baby's birth weight and gestational age.

15. Which test would best assess if a newborn required immediate assistance or intervention without measuring overall well-being?

    a. The Apgar test

    b. The Neonatal Behavioral Assessment Scale

    c. Ultrasound imaging

    d. Amniocentesis

ANSWERS TO FILL-IN-THE-BLANKS KEY TERMS

1. amniocentesis (see Monitoring Prenatal Development)

2. Oxytocin (see Birth)

3. quickening (see The First Nine Months)

4. Anencelapathy (see Protecting the Fetus)

5. Apgar test (see Birth)

6. in vitro fertilization (see The First Nine Months)

7. Respiratory distress syndrome (see Birth)

8. fetal alcohol syndrome (see Protecting the Fetus)

9. Implantation (see The First Nine Months)

10. ultrasound imaging (see Monitoring Prenatal Development)

ANSWERS TO MULTIPLE-CHOICE QUESTIONS

Circle the question numbers you answered incorrectly.

Quiz 1

1. *a is the answer.*   Gestation is the period from birth to conception. (see The First Nine Months)

2. *b is the answer.*   Ovulation occurs about every 28 days in women. During ovulation, a follicle in one of the ovaries ruptures, releasing a mature egg. (see The First Nine Months)

3. *c is the answer.*   Megumi is infertile. Sterility occurs when someone is permanently unable to conceive. Megumi's doctor indicated he thinks she can conceive if her fallopian tube blockage is removed. (see The First Nine Months)

4. *c is the answer.*   During the first two weeks of pregnancy, the product of fertilization of the egg is a one-celled organism called the zygote. Over the two weeks, the zygote divides and begins to differentiate, and ultimately may implant in the uterus. (see The First Nine Months)

5. *d is the answer.*   The success rate of in vitro fertilization (IVF) is less than 30%, and often only after several attempts. (see The First Nine Months)

6. *a is the answer.*   The outer layer of the embryo cells will become skin, nerves, and sense organs. The outer layer is called the ectoderm. (see The First Nine Months)

7. *c is the answer.*   Multifactoral disorders have multiple causes from interactions among genes and between genes and the environment. (see Monitoring Prenatal Development)

8. *b is the answer.*   Preimplantation genetic diagnosis is a screening in which one or two cells are removed from three-day old embryos prior to implantation and tested for genes linked to fatal childhood disorders, and possibly other diseases. (see Monitoring Prenatal Development)

9. *d is the answer.* Folic acid deficiency in pregnant mothers has been linked to neural tube defects. (see Protecting the Fetus)

10. *d is the answer.*   A teratogen is any environmental substance that can have a negative impact on fetal development. Viruses (e.g., rubella), drugs (e.g., DES and alcohol) and environmental pollutants all fall into this category. (see Protecting the Fetus)

11. *d is the answer.*   A mother can pass HIV on to her child in pregnancy, during labor and delivery, or through breastfeeding. (see Protecting the Fetus)

12. *b is the answer.*   SIDS is the unexplained death, usually during the night, of an infant under one year old. (see Protecting the Fetus)

13. *a is the answer.*   A sleeper effect occurs when an outcome is displaced in time from its cause. The outcome of Nduta's son's mental illness as an adult is temporally distant from its imputed cause, maternal malnutrition during pregnancy.   (see Protecting the Fetus)

14. *a is the answer.*   Anoxia is a serious birth complication that involves cutoff of the oxygen supply via the umbilical cord before the baby can breathe independently. (see Birth)

15.   *c is the answer.*   Surfactant is the soapy substance that helps carry oxygen into and carbon dioxide out of the lungs.   (see Birth)

Now turn to the quiz analysis table at the end of this chapter to find which areas you know well and which areas you need to work on. Circle the numbers in the table for items on Quiz 1 that you answered correctly.

Quiz 2

1.   *d is the answer.*   Girls are born with about 2 million ova. (see The First Nine Months)

2.   *b is the answer.*   Fertilization is most likely if a couple has intercourse on or a few days before ovulation. (see The First Nine Months)

3.   *a is the answer.*   The placenta is the support system to babies in utero. It delivers oxygen and food via the umbilical cord, and also carries waste products away. (see The First Nine Months)

4.   *d is the answer.*   Artificial insemination is inserting sperm directly into a woman's uterus with a syringe. (see The First Nine Months)

5.   *c is the answer.*   A surrogate mother is impregnated with a male's sperm via artificial insemination or with the embryo of a couple conceived in vitro. Kerry and her husband conceived an embryo in vitro which was then used to impregnate Greta. (see The First Nine Months)

6.   *a is the answer.*   Ultrasound imaging is used to monitor prenatal development, including determining the sex of the baby at about 3 months. Although amniocentesis can determine sex as well, Johanna would not have those results available on the same day of the test. (see Monitoring Prenatal Development)

7.   *b is the answer.*   A karyotype is a picture of the man's and woman's chromosomes that is useful in identifying recessive genetic defects. (see Monitoring Prenatal Development)

8.   *c is the answer.*   Chorionic villi sampling provides faster genetic results than amniocentesis. Ultrasound does not provide genetic testing. (see Monitoring Prenatal Development)

9.   *b is the answer.*   Anencelapathy is a developmental condition in which part of the brain does not develop. (see Protecting the Fetus)

10.   *a is the answer.*   Rubella causes the greatest amount of harm during the first three months of pregnancy, also known as the first trimester. (see Protecting the Fetus)

11.   *d is the answer.*   No amount of alcohol consumption has been proven safe during pregnancy. (see Protecting the Fetus)

12.   *c is the answer.*   A sensitive period is a time when the developing fetus is particularly vulnerable, or sensitive, to teratogens. (see Protecting the Fetus)

13.   *a is the answer.*   The pituitary gland releases the hormone oxytocin, which triggers uterine contractions. (see Birth)

14.   *d is the answer.*   Ninety percent of babies weighing over 2.2 pounds but under 5.5 pounds survive; 67% of babies weighing 1.65-2.2 pounds survive, and 33% of babies weighing 1.1-1.65 pounds survive. The rate of survival depends on the weight of the preemie, and on his or her gestational age at birth. (see Birth)

15. *a is the answer.*   The Apgar test assesses appearance, pulse, grimace, activity, and
respiration. Problems with both pulse and respiration are clear indicators if a
newborn needs intervention. The Neonatal Behavioral Assessment Scale, on the
other hand, assesses overall well-being. (see Birth)

Now turn to the quiz analysis table at the end of this chapter to find which areas you know well
and which areas you need to work on. Circle the numbers in the table for items on Quiz 2 that you
answered correctly.

For each question you answered correctly, circle its number. (Quiz 1 numbers are not shaded;
Quiz 2 numbers are shaded.) Are there patterns in the types of questions or the topics you got
wrong that could direct your further study? Did you improve from Quiz 1 to Quiz 2?

QUIZ REVIEW

Topic	Type of Question		
	Definition	Comprehension	Application
The First Nine Months	1, 2	4, 5, 6	3
	3, 4	1, 2	5
Monitoring Prenatal Development	7		8
		8	6, 7
Protecting the Fetus		9, 10, 11	12, 13
	9, 12	10, 11	
Birth	15		14
		13, 14, 15	

Total correct by quiz:

Quiz 1:
Quiz 2:

CHAPTER 4

Physical Development in Infancy

LEARNING OBJECTIVES

1. Describe the general principles of growth (directionality, independence of systems, and canalization) that apply to child development.

2. Explain how environmental factors influence individual growth.

3. List the order of development of the central nervous system.

4. Describe the anatomy of brain cells.

5. Define the processes of synaptogenesis, synaptic pruning, and myelination.

6. List a few examples of the methods used by neuroscientists to study brain cells.

7. Define plasticity, including an explanation of its dual-directionality.

8. Describe the activity of the autonomic nervous system in infancy, in terms of its cycles and states.

9. List the basic reflexes of an infant.

10. Describe the sequence of motor development in infancy, and explain how this process may be affected by cultural expectations.

11. Explain the development of an infant's sensory capabilities.

12. Explain how environmental influences can affect the development of an infant's sensory and perceptual capabilities.

OUTLINE

I.   Physical Growth
    A.   General Principles of Physical Growth
        1.   **Directionality** refers to how body proportions change. Change is generally *cephalocaudal* (from head to tail) and *proximodistal* (moves from the center of the body outward).
        2.   **Independence of systems** asserts that different parts of the body will develop according to different timetables.
        3.   **Canalization** refers to genetic forces that guide development along a normative course.
    B.   Norms and Individual Differences
        1.   **Norms** are average outcomes, not actual or ideal ones. **Individual differences** refer to variation among persons on a given characteristic.
        2.   Development can follow different paths to the same or different ends.
        3.   Physical growth is influenced by genetic and cultural factors, such as race, nutritional availability, and so forth.
II. The Development of the Central Nervous System

The **central nervous system** consists of the brain and spinal cord. It processes information and directs behavior.

A. The Brain
1. **Subcortical structures** in the brain control the state of arousal and develop first. Components of the **limbic system** regulate emotion and develop next. The **cortex** and **association areas** control awareness, attention, memory, and integration, and develop last.
2. The brain's two **hemispheres** are connected by the **corpus callosum**.
3. Different areas of the cortex have special functions. The **visual cortex** regulates sight; the **auditory cortex** regulates hearing, the **sensorimotor cortex** regulates touch, and the **motor cortex** processes voluntary movement. The **frontal cortex** is the brain's "command center" and is responsible for higher cognitive functions. In the left cortex, two small areas are responsible for language comprehension (**Wernicke's area**) and language production (**Broca's area**).

B. Brain Cells
1. **Neurons** are the cells that carry information across the body and the brain, as well as back and forth within the brain. Each neuron has a cell body, an axon, and dendrites. The **dendrites** pick up signals from other neurons. The **cell body** keeps the cell alive and determines if it will "fire" or not. The **axon** carries fired signals away from the cell body toward other neurons.
2. The connection between neurons is a tiny gap called a **synapse**. Chemicals called **neurotransmitters** cross the synapse when the neuron fires an **action potential**.
3. Through **synaptogenesis** more and more connections are made between neurons. This is important in early brain development, and the more a synapse is used the stronger that connection becomes. Synaptogenesis peaks around age 1.
4. **Synaptic pruning** is a complementary process to synaptogenesis. It eliminates unused and unnecessary synapses. Pruning makes the brain more efficient, but both synaptic pruning and synaptogenesis are important to brain **plasticity**.
5. Myelination is another key process to brain development. **Myelin** is a white fatty tissue that encases cell axons and speeds neural transmission. The parts of the brain involved with vision and movement are myelinated before other parts (e.g., the **cerebellum** becomes fully myelinated by age 4). **Multiple sclerosis** occurs when the autoimmune system strips neurons of myelin.
6. The transmission of information between cells is initially *diffuse*, but over time and with experience becomes more *phasic*.

C. Cell Activity
1. **Microelectrode recording** is a way to measure the activity of individual brain cells. Using this technology, scientists have discovered that some brain cells seem to be "prewired" to perform in certain ways, even without experience.
2. **Electroencephalograph (EEG) recordings** measure (using sensors) electrical activity of masses of cells. EEG research shows that by age 2, children's EEG recordings look much more similar to adult recordings than they did at birth.
3. Using the EEG technology, scientists can study **event-related potentials (ERPs)** in the brain waves. ERPs are specific patterns of brain activity evoked by specific stimuli. Such responses become more rapid and focused as children grow older. More mature auditory ERPs at birth predict language skills at age 3.

D. Brain Plasticity

1. **Experience-expectant processes** are those in which brain cells are prewired to engage. **Experience-dependent processes** involve the active formation of new synapses based on individual experience.
2. Experience-dependent processes combined with active exploration of one's environment underlie brain plasticity.
3. Although certain cells are prewired, many of them are able to be modified through experience. This **modifiability** sometimes occurs during **sensitive periods**.
4. Beyond modifiability, another type of plasticity is **compensation**. Compensation occurs when cells substitute for each other when one sort of cell is damaged or lost. Embryonic **stem cells** are maximally capable of compensation.

III. The Autonomic Nervous System
   A. The **autonomic nervous system (ANS)** regulates those bodily activities that are not under voluntary control. Many systems governed by the ANS **cycle** on a regular basis, but the different systems are not coordinated in the newborn. These cycles help promote rest from activity with the complementary stimulation activity provides.
   B. Arousal states are not regular during infancy and there is great variability in when infants gain the ability to regulate such states. State regularity reveals the maturity of the infant's nervous system.
   C. Infants who receive more sensitive caregiving tend to spend more time in quiet sleep. Experiences such as whether the infant co-sleeps or not can also influence the timing of the child's maturing abilities in state regulation.

IV. Reflexes and Motor Development
   A. Reflexes
      1. **Reflexes** are simple, involuntary reactions to certain stimuli. They often have *adaptive significance* and can be divided into three types: *approach, avoidance,* and *other*.
      2. Newborn reflexes are usually present before birth and last for about four months after birth, before disappearing. The disappearance of the reflexes signals the development and emergence of higher-level cognition.
   B. Motor Development
      1. Motor development during infancy depends both on physical maturation and experience. Motor development follows a fairly predictable pattern, with most infants sitting up around 6 months of age, crawling by 8–10 months, followed by cruising with the average infant walking for the first time around age 1. There is great range in what is considered "normal" for achieving these milestones.
      2. Cultural and parental expectations can influence motor milestones, too. American mothers tend to value crawling and most American infants do crawl. Mali and Jamaican mother do not see this as necessary, and many of their infants skip crawling.
      3. **Dynamic systems theory** asserts that change in one area of development affects other areas of development. For example, even though infants have depth perception well before they crawl, it is only once they begin crawling that they show a fear of heights.

V. Sensing and Perceiving
   The five senses achieve maturity at different times, allowing the infant to "concentrate" on one area of development at a time.
   A. Seeing
      1. Newborns can see and actively seek visual stimulation, focusing on the boundaries of patterns they are shown. Visual acuity is poor at birth, but near

adult levels by 6 months of age. Infants show a preference for looking at faces and can imitate facial expressions.

2. Scientists use the visual cliff to test infants' depth perception. Very few infants aged 6–14 months will crawl across the cliff to their mother, suggesting they have some fear of falling. Other research indicates babies perceive depth long before they show a fear of falling. *Kinetic cues* help us see depth, and infants as young as one month blink in response to the cue of a rapidly approaching object.

3. By age 3 and a half months, infants recognize different directions of motion, and by 5 months they discriminate rotation from oscillation. Using tests like the point-light walker display to animate a pattern of lights moving as a human would move, the pattern in still form is uninterpretable, but animated is easily identified as a human moving. Infants show the ability to discriminate this as well by 5 months.

4. By 2 months, infants see colors well. By 4 months, they perceive qualitatively different hues much as adults do.

B. Hearing

1. Infants can hear quite well at birth and can discriminate melodies by age 6 months. At that age they can also locate sound as well as an adult can.

2. Infants very quickly begin to apply their hearing to deciphering speech. Adults tend to use **infant-directed speech** when speaking with babies. Infant-directed speech involves exaggerated tones, sing-song rhythms, simple and repeated words, and abbreviated utterances. Infants prefer this, even if the language spoken is not their own.

3. Infants are initially able to discriminate sounds that are not part of their native language, but with repeated exposure to their native language, they slowly lose the ability to distinguish non-native sounds.

C. Touching

1. Touch is important to an infant's ability to learn about the world. Babies hold (or fail to drop or push away) new objects more than familiar ones and study complex objects longer than simpler ones. They will change an object's orientation to study it further.

2. Touch is also vital to establishing emotional intimacy. Harlow's research on monkeys demonstrated that contact comfort is a stronger motivator than food.

D. Tasting and Smelling

1. Infants show different facial expressions for sweet, sour, salty, and bitter flavors. They prefer sweet tastes, which promotes receptivity to breastfeeding, as breast milk is slightly sweet.

2. Smell is well-developed at birth. Newborn preferences for odor mirror those of adults. Newborns that breastfeed are able to identify their mother's odor.

VI. Multimodal and Cross-Modal Perception

A. Sensory systems do not function in isolation. **Multimodal perception** refers to perception of objects and events in the world that stimulate many senses at once. Learning about something via one sense is enhanced experiencing it in another as well.

B. An example of this cross-modal communication occurred in a study in which infants were able to identify by sight an object (pacifier) they had experienced only by sucking on it previously.

C. This type of perception illustrates the beginnings of self-knowledge. For example, infants show the rooting reflex if their cheek is stroked by someone else or a pacifier, but not as much if the stroke comes from their own hand.

VII. Experience and Early Perceptual Development

Although infants' perceptual abilities are relatively well organized at birth, perceptual experience is very important as well. For example, infants whose mothers smiled a lot at them showed more sensitivity to smiling faces in a laboratory setting, too. What is in place at birth allows the infant to seek additional perceptual stimulation unique to his or her environment.

KEY TERMS

1. **Directionality** is a principle of development that refers to how body proportions change; *cephalocaudal* means advancing from head to tail, and *proximodistal* means progressing from the center of the body outward. (see Physical Growth)

2. **Independence of systems** is a principle of development that asserts that not all parts of the body develop along the same timetable. (see Physical Growth)

3. **Canalization** refers to genetic forces that guide development along a normative course. (see Physical Growth)

4. **Norms** are average outcomes rather than actual or even ideal ones. (see Physical Growth)

5. **Individual differences** refer to the variation among individuals on a characteristic. (see Physical Growth)

6. The **central nervous system (CNS)** is the division of the nervous system, consisting of the brain and spinal cord, which processes information and directs behavior. (see The Development of the Central Nervous System)

7. **Subcortical structures** are brain components that control state of arousal. (see The Development of the Central Nervous System)

8. The **limbic system** is the part of the nervous system that manages emotions. (see The Development of the Central Nervous System)

9. The **cortex** refers to the thin layers of outer tissue that cover the brain. (see The Development of the Central Nervous System)

10. The **association areas** are the parts of the brain concerned with awareness, attention, memory, and the integration of information. (see The Development of the Central Nervous System)

11. **Hemispheres** are the two halves of the brain. (see The Development of the Central Nervous System)

12. The **corpus callosum** is the connection between the two halves or hemispheres of the brain. (see The Development of the Central Nervous System)

13. The **visual cortex** is the part of the brain that regulates sight. (see The Development of the Central Nervous System)

14. The **auditory cortex** is the part of the cortex that monitors hearing. (see The Development of the Central Nervous System)

15. The **sensorimotor cortex** is the part of the brain concerned with touch. (see The Development of the Central Nervous System)

16. The **motor cortex** is the part of the brain that controls voluntary movement. (see The Development of the Central Nervous System)

17. The **frontal cortex** is the brain's command central responsible for thinking, planning, initiative, impulse control, and creativity. (see The Development of the Central Nervous System)

18. **Wernicke's area** is the region of the left cortex dedicated to language or speech comprehension. (see The Development of the Central Nervous System)

19. **Broca's area** is the region of the left cortex dedicated to language production or speech. (see The Development of the Central Nervous System)

20. **Neurons** are cells that carry information across the body and brain. (see The Development of the Central Nervous System)

21. **Dendrites** are branched extensions of a neuron that act like antennas that pick up signals from other neurons. (see The Development of the Central Nervous System)

22. The **cell body** is the part of the cell that contains the nucleus and biochemical mechanisms to keep the cell alive and determine whether the cell will fire. (see The Development of the Central Nervous System)

23. **Axons** are the part of the cell that carries signals away from the cell body toward other neurons. At their tips, axons divide into many axon terminals. (see The Development of the Central Nervous System)

24. A **synapse** is the connection between one neuron's axon and another neuron's dendrite. (see The Development of the Central Nervous System)

25. **Neurotransmitters** are electrochemicals through which neurons intercommunicate. (see The Development of the Central Nervous System)

26. An **action potential** is the form an electrical charge takes inside the neuron. (see The Development of the Central Nervous System)

27. **Synaptogenesis** is the development of connections between neurons through the growth of axons and dendrites. (see The Development of the Central Nervous System)

28. **Synaptic pruning** refers to the process of elimination of unused and unnecessary synapses. (see The Development of the Central Nervous System)

29. **Plasticity** is the capacity of the brain to be modified by experience. (see The Development of the Central Nervous System)

30. **Myelin** is the white fatty tissue that encases cell axons. (see The Development of the Central Nervous System)

31. The **cerebellum** is the part of the brain associated with balance and control of body movements. (see The Development of the Central Nervous System)

32. **Multiple sclerosis** is a disease in which the autoimmune system strips neurons of myelin, leading to loss of motor control. (see The Development of the Central Nervous System)

33. **Microelectrode recording** is a technique used to measure the activity of individual cells. (see The Development of the Central Nervous System)

34. **Electroencephalographic (EEG) recordings** are measurements acquired with sensors that show electrical activity of masses of individual cells. (see The Development of the Central Nervous System)

35. **Event-related potentials (ERPs)** are specific patterns of brain activity evoked by a specific stimulus. (see The Development of the Central Nervous System)

36. **Experience-expectant processes** are prewired processes in the brain. (see The Development of the Central Nervous System)

37. **Experience-dependent processes** are brain processes that involve the active formation of new synaptic connections in response to the individual's unique experience. (see The Development of the Central Nervous System)

38. **Modifiability** is a principle of development that asserts that, although cells are predestined for specific functions, they can be changed. (see The Development of the Central Nervous System)

39. **Sensitive periods** are times in development when the organism is especially open to environmental influence. (see The Development of the Central Nervous System)

40. **Compensation** is a kind of plasticity in which cells substitute for others, permitting recovery of function after loss or damage. (see The Development of the Central Nervous System)

41. **Stem cells** are the newest, youngest, and least developed cells that can be grafted to repair damaged parts of the CNS or replace cells that have died. (see The Development of the Central Nervous System)

42. The **autonomic nervous system (ANS)** is the division of the nervous system that regulates many body activities without our voluntary control, such as breathing, blood flow, or digestion. (see The Autonomic Nervous System)

43. **Cycle** refers to moving in an identifiable and predictable rhythm. (see The Autonomic Nervous System)

44. **Reflexes** are simple, involuntary responses to certain stimuli that have (or had) adaptive significance. (see Reflexes and Motor Development)

45. **Dynamic systems theory** is a theory that asserts that change in one area of development impacts others. (see Reflexes and Motor Development)

46. **Infant-directed speech** is a special speech register reserved for babies that simplifies normal adult-directed speech in many ways. (see Sensing and Perceiving)

47. **Multimodal perceptions** are perceptions of information about objects and events in the world that stimulate many senses at once. (see Multimodal and Cross-Modal Perception)

FILL-IN-THE-BLANKS KEY TERMS

This section will help you check your knowledge of the key terms introduced in this chapter. Fill in each blank with the appropriate term from the list of key terms in the previous section.

1. A technique used to measure the activity of individual cells is called _____.

2. _____ is a special speech register reserved for babies that simplifies normal adult-directed speech in many ways.

3. A principle of development that refers to how body proportions change is_____.

4. _____ refers to how perceptions of information about objects and events in the world stimulate many senses at once.

5. Simple, involuntary responses to certain stimuli that have (or had) adaptive significance are called _____.

6. Moving in an identifiable and predictable rhythm is called_____.

7. _____ are processes that are prewired in the brain.

8. The development of connections between neurons through the growth of axons and dendrites is called_____.

9. _____are average outcomes, not actual or ideal ones.

10. The newest, youngest, and least developed cells that can be grafted to repair damaged parts of the CNS or replace cells that have died are called_____.

APPLIED LEARNING AND CRITICAL THINKING

Physical development in infancy presents an astonishing array of changes in both physical growth and brain development.

1. Sleep training for infants differs from family to family and culture to culture. If you are studying abroad and have the opportunity to get to know some of the local people, take it! Talk to them about how they try to get infants to sleep. Do they allow the babies to co-sleep? Do they "wear" their babies using a sling or other baby-holder throughout the day? Or does the infant sleep alone in a crib? How do their practices differ from your own families? Do you think that the differences are more familial or cultural? Why?

2. Multiple sclerosis (MS) is a devastating disease that can afflict children. Many communities hold a walk or a bike ride to raise money for research on MS. For a service project, see if you can pull a team together to participate in one of these events. As you do, look around at the other families you see. Many of them may have stories they are willing to share about someone they've loved who has died from MS. Getting to know someone for whom the disease is quite personal is an important way to learn about the effects of MS.

3. Infant-directed speech is a fascinating phenomenon, in part because it seems widespread across cultures. Collaborate with a professor at your university to study the phenomenon in your own community using an observational design. Identify different "types" of public locations where parents and infants are more or less likely to interact. For example, you would expect to see lots of mothers and babies shopping together at a "Babies R Us" superstore, but fewer at high-end department stores. Then conduct some observations there of the kind of speech you hear directed towards infants at those sites. Does the specific context seem to be related to the type of speech people use with babies? Do you think it has to do with the type of person you see in those settings, or with features specific to that place? What sort of evidence would make you lean towards one explanation over another? As always, seek IRB approval prior to collecting your data.

4. Compensation is a type of brain plasticity in which cells substitute for one another after loss or damage. Many hospitals and research centers conduct research using stem cells, either embryonic or adult. See if you can get an interview with one of the researchers on these projects and ask for their opinion on the ethics behind this hot-button topic. If they are using only adult stem cells, ask them why they aren't using the embryonic kind? If they are willing to use embryonic stem cells, ask them how they justify the ethics of that as well? Do you think that their opinion (in either direction) is well justified? Why or why not? Would you be willing to be a research assistant on a project using embryonic stem cells? How did the interview change your perspective on this matter?

MULTIPLE-CHOICE QUESTIONS

Quiz 1

1. The fact that children learn to hold their heads up before they learn to sit up, and learn to sit up before they learn to stand, illustrates

    a. directionality.
    b. canalization.
    c. independence of systems.
    d. maturation.

2. Average outcomes are represented by

    a. individual differences.
    b. norms.
    c. canalization.
    d. cycling.

3. Which part of the brain develops first in the embryo?

    a. Subcortical structures
    b. Limbic system
    c. Cortex
    d. Association areas

4. Which part of the neuron is responsible for *sending* messages?

    a. Dendrite
    b. Cell body
    c. Axon
    d. Corpus callosum

5. Neurotransmitters cross the

    a. corpus callosum.
    b. synapse.
    c. association area.
    d. cerebellum.

6. At what age does the rate of synaptogenesis peak?

    a. Three months before birth
    b. At birth
    c. Around 6 months of age
    d. Around age 1

7. Plasticity depends on

    a. synaptogenesis.
    b. synaptic pruning.
    c. Both A and B
    d. None of these

8. Which technology would help measure the activity of individual cells in the brain?

    a. Event-related potentials
    b. Electroencephalograph recording
    c. MRI
    d. Microelectrode recording

9.   As Jiang learns a new gymnastics routine, her brain forms new synapses the more she repeats the routine. This development in her brain based on her experience is

   a.   experience-expectant.
   b.   experience-dependent.
   c.   compensation.
   d.   a dynamic system.

10. Which cells are maximally flexible with respect to the ability to compensate?

   a.   Neurons
   b.   Adult stem cells
   c.   Embryonic stem cells
   d.   Neurotransmitters

11. When a baby dies of SIDS, it is because he or she stopped breathing (usually in the nighttime) for an unknown reason. Which part of the nervous system is responsible for regulating the baby's breathing?

   a.   Corpus callosum
   b.   Cortex
   c.   Limbic system
   d.   Autonomic nervous system

12. Which of the following is an example of an *approach* reflex?

   a.   Blinking
   b.   Rooting
   c.   Coughing
   d.   Sneezing

13. Which tool is used to study depth perception in infants?

   a.   The visual cliff
   b.   Event-related potentials
   c.   Dynamic systems
   d.   Habituation task

14. In Harlow's research with monkeys, the importance of touch was demonstrated through the construct of

   a.   contact comfort.
   b.   tactile exploration.
   c.   visual cliff.
   d.   cross-modal perception.

15. Baby Shawn is playing with her mom on the floor. Her mom gets out a ball and rolls it to her. Shawn looks at the ball, watches it roll, and picks it up and feels it. Both her vision and her tactile experience with the ball inform her understanding of what a "ball" is. This illustrates

   a.   multimodal perception.
   b.   touching.
   c.   seeing.
   d.   infant-directed play.

Quiz 2

Use this quiz to reassess your learning after taking Quiz 1 and reviewing the chapter.

1.   Connor was born at 25 weeks gestation—a full 15 weeks preterm. At birth, he only weighed two pounds, which was not even on the growth chart. By his second birthday he had caught up to most kids his age and was at the 40th percentile on the growth chart. Connor's catch up illustrates the principle of

   a.   directionality.
   b.   independence of systems.
   c.   canalization.
   d.   dynamic systems.

2.   Caden walked at age 8 months. Connor walked at 19 months. Adam walked at 14 months. They are all within "normal" range for walking. The differences in when they each actually reached this motor milestone illustrates_____ within the normal range.

   a.   norms
   b.   individual differences
   c.   canalization
   d.   directionality

3.   Cassie is a first grader who has enormous difficulty managing her own emotions. Which part of her nervous system is most likely responsible for her struggling with this difficulty?

   a.   Limbic system
   b.   Subcortical structures
   c.   Corpus callosum
   d.   Autonomic nervous system

4.   Kaleb is an infant. He is at the age where he should begin to demonstrate understanding of language, but he shows no signs of this. Which area of his brain might be responsible for his problem?

   a.   Wernicke's area
   b.   Broca's area
   c.   Motor cortex
   d.   Limbic system

5.   Neurotransmitters are

   a.   electrical.
   b.   spiritual.
   c.   chemical.
   d.   both A and C.

6.   Synaptic pruning helps make the brain more

   a.   connected.
   b.   efficient.
   c.   retarded.
   d.   both A and B.

7.   Cara's baby has just been diagnosed with a disease that strips her baby's neurons of myelin. What is likely to happen to Cara's baby?

   a.   He will have advanced intelligence.
   b.   He will lose motor control.
   c.   He will have trouble with emotional regulation.
   d.   He will have difficulty with language comprehension.

8. ERP's rate of development is slowest in
    a. infancy.
    b. early childhood.
    c. middle childhood.
    d. adolescence.
9. A principle of development that asserts that, although cells are predestined for specific functions, they can be changed, is called
    a. canalization.
    b. directionality.
    c. modifiability.
    d. compensation.
10. Every three hours or so, Shara's infant starts rooting around and sucking on her hand. Shara looks at this as a cue that the baby is hungry and starts to nurse her. The fact that the baby does this reliably every three hours illustrates
    a. cycling.
    b. association areas.
    c. compensation.
    d. modification.
11. Which infant will most likely have the greatest difficulty regulating her state?
    a. Xiao-ping, who was born at 27 weeks gestation
    b. Federica, who has parents who are very sensitive to her
    c. Mary Ann, who was born at 38 weeks gestation
    d. It is impossible to predict who will have difficulty regulating her state.
12. Learning to crawl often helps infants become better at assessing distances. The fact that a motor skill like crawling affects a cognitive skill like assessing distances supports
    a. experience-expectancy.
    b. experience-dependency.
    c. stem-cell compensability.
    d. dynamic systems theory.
13. When Brandy talks to baby Carter, she uses a sing-song voice and repeats herself a lot. Brandy is using
    a. cycling.
    b. dynamic systems.
    c. infant-directed speech.
    d. directionality.
14. Which taste preference common in newborns promotes receptivity to breastfeeding?
    a. Salty
    b. Sweet
    c. Sour
    d. Bitter
15. Introducing an interesting object into an otherwise bland environment will have what impact on an infant's visual attentiveness?
    a. No impact
    b. Decrease it
    c. Slightly increase it
    d. Nearly double it

ANSWERS TO FILL-IN-THE-BLANKS KEY TERMS

1. microelectrode recording (see The Development of the Central Nervous System)

2. Infant-directed speech (see Sensing and Perceiving)

3. directionality (see Physical Growth)

4. Multimodal perception (see Multimodal and Cross-modal Perception)

5. reflexes (see Reflexes and Motor Development)

6. cycling (see The Autonomic Nervous System)

7. Experience-expectant processes (see The Development of the Central Nervous System)

8. synaptogenesis (see The Development of the Central Nervous System)

9. Norms (see Physical Growth)

10. stem cells (see Monitoring Prenatal Development)

ANSWERS TO MULTIPLE-CHOICE QUESTIONS

Circle the question numbers you answered incorrectly.

Quiz 1

1. *a is the answer.* Directionality is a principle of physical growth that refers to how body proportions change. The change described here of development beginning with the head and proceeding down towards the tail and legs illustrates the directional principle of development as cephalocaudal, that is, proceeding from head to tail. (see Physical Growth)

2. *b is the answer.* Norms represent average outcomes, not actual or ideal ones. (see Physical Growth)

3. *a is the answer.* Subcortical structures develop first, followed by limbic system, with the cortex and association areas developing last. (see The Development of the Central Nervous System)

4. *c is the answer.* The axon sends messages; the dendrites receive messages that have been sent from other neurons. (see The Development of the Central Nervous System)

5. *b is the answer.* Neurotransmitters cross the synapse, which is the tiny space between the axon of the neuron sending a signal and the dendrite of the receiving neuron. (see The Development of the Central Nervous System)

6. *d is the answer.* The rate of synaptogenesis peaks at around age 1, and decreases across early childhood although it continues throughout life. (see The Development of the Central Nervous System)

7. *c is the answer.* Both synaptogenesis and synaptic pruning are necessary for brain plasticity. Just as a bush must be pruned to grow, the brain must be pruned to create new connections through synaptogenesis. (see The Development of the Central Nervous System)

8. *d is the answer.*   Microelectrode recording measures individual cell activity. Electroencephalograph (EEG) recordings measure electrical activity of masses of cells in the cortex. Event-related potentials are responses the brain makes to specific stimuli, and are observable on EEG output. (see The Development of the Central Nervous System)

9. *b is the answer.* Jiang's experience with the routine is actively forming new synapses. Experience-dependent processes involve the active formation of new synapses in response to unique experiences. This is exactly what is happening to Jiang's brain with her practice. (see The Development of the Central Nervous System)

10. *c is the answer.*   Embryonic stem cells are the newest, youngest, and least developed of all cells. They are presently considered the ultimate version of compensation. (see The Development of the Central Nervous System)

11. *d is the answer.*   The autonomic nervous system is responsible for regulating involuntary actions such as breathing. (see The Autonomic Nervous System)

12. *b is the answer.*   Rooting is an approach reflex because it allows the infant to seek out and ingest food. Coughing, blinking, and sneezing all help an infant avoid a stimulus. (see Reflexes and Motor Development)

13. *a is the answer.*   The visual cliff is a Plexiglas table with protective sides and a checkerboard surface below the glass in one half of it, and a "deep" side with the checker pattern several feet below the glass. The infant that recognizes depth and fears heights is reluctant to crawl off the "cliff" towards his or her mother. (see Reflexes and Motor Development)

14. *a is the answer.*   Contact comfort was operationalized by covering a "wire" mother with a soft cloth, and comparing how the monkeys responded to a stressor. They could either seek the contact comfort of the mother with the soft cloth, or go to a wire mother (not covered) who had a bottle. They preferred to cling to the soft cloth mother, seeking contact comfort. (see Sensing and Perceiving)

15. *a is the answer.*   Multimodal perception refers to information about events that stimulates many senses at once. This question describes multiple senses being stimulated at the same time based on an environmental experience. (see Experience and Early Perceptual Development)

Now turn to the quiz analysis table at the end of this chapter to find which areas you know well and which areas you need to work on. Circle the numbers in the table for items on Quiz 1 that you answered correctly.

Quiz 2

1. *c is the answer.*   Canalization is a principle of physical growth that asserts that if anything happens to direct development off course (e.g., in this case, a preterm birth), genetic forces will make a correction as soon as possible. Connor's weight gain and "catch up" to his same-age peers illustrates this sort of correction. (see Physical Growth)

2. *b is the answer.* Individual differences are variations among individuals on a characteristic. In this case, the characteristic is achievement of the motor milestone of walking. The three boys described in this question achieved it at quite different times, but all are considered "normal." (see Physical Growth)

3. *a is the answer.* The limbic system is the part of the nervous system responsible for managing emotions. (see The Development of the Central Nervous System)

4. *a is the answer.*   Wernicke's area is a portion of the association cortex in the left hemisphere that is responsible for language comprehension. (see The Development of the Central Nervous System

5. *d is the answer.*   Neurotransmitters are electrochemical. (see The Development of the Central Nervous System)

6. *b is the answer.*   Synaptic pruning is associated with the brain's efficiency. In contrast, synaptogenesis is associated with increasing the number of connections. (see The Development of the Central Nervous System)

7. *b is the answer.*   Cara's baby has probably been diagnosed with multiple sclerosis, a disease in which the neurons are stripped of myelin. The consequences of MS are that the baby will lose motor control, have decreased speech and vision, and may die in early childhood. (see The Development of the Central Nervous System)

8. *a is the answer.*   ERP's have a simple form and develop slowly during infancy, but develop quickly and become more complex as the child matures. (see The Development of the Central Nervous System)

9. *c is the answer.*   Modifiability is the principle of development that asserts that cells predestined for a particular function can be modified, and take on an alternate function. (see The Development of the Central Nervous System)

10. *a is the answer.*   Cycling is behavior that occurs in an identifiable and predictable temporal rhythm. The baby's feeding cues occur every three hours, which is identifiable and predictable. (see The Autonomic Nervous System)

11. *a is the answer.*   Infants who are born preterm tend to have poor state regulation. Infants who have sensitive parents tend to have better state regulation. (see The Autonomic Nervous System)

12. *d is the answer.*   Dynamic systems theory asserts that change in one area of development will affect other areas of development. (see Reflexes and Motor Development)

13. *c is the answer.*   Infant-directed speech uses a sing-song rhythm, simplified grammar, lots of repetition, and shorter words and phrases. (see Sensing and Perceiving)

14. *b is the answer.*   Newborns show a preference for sweet tastes, and breast milk tastes slightly sweet. (see Sensing and Perceiving)

15. *d is the answer.*   Research on institutionalized infants indicates that introducing a visually interesting object into an otherwise bland environment nearly doubles the infant's visual attentiveness and visually directed reaching. (see Experience and Early Perceptual Development)

Now turn to the quiz analysis table at the end of this chapter to find which areas you know well and which areas you need to work on. Circle the numbers in the table for items on Quiz 2 that you answered correctly.

For each question you answered correctly, circle its number. (Quiz 1 numbers are not shaded; Quiz 2 numbers are shaded.) Are there patterns in the types of questions or the topics you got wrong that could direct your further study? Did you improve from Quiz 1 to Quiz 2?

QUIZ REVIEW

Topic	Type of Question		
	Definition	**Comprehension**	**Application**
Physical Growth	2		1
			1, 2
The Development of the Central Nervous System	4, 5	3, 6, 7, 8, 10	9
	5, 9	6, 8	3, 4, 7
The Autonomic Nervous System			11
			10, 11
Reflexes and Motor Development		13	12
			12
Sensing and Perceiving		14	
		14	13
Multimodal and Cross-Modal Perception			15
Experience and Early Perceptual Development			
		15	

Total correct by quiz:

Quiz 1:	
Quiz 2:	

CHAPTER 5

Cognitive Development in Infancy

LEARNING OBJECTIVES

1. Explain how researchers use habituation and novelty responsiveness to determine what a baby is thinking.

2. Describe what Piaget meant when he said that infants "actively construct knowledge."

3. Describe Piaget's process of adaptation, and how assimilation and accommodation help children understand the world.

4. Describe the six stages of the sensorimotor period of infancy.

5. Describe the major challenges to Piaget's theory of development.

6. Explain how infants use categorization to make sense of the world.

7. Describe the ways in which play changes during infancy and explain how play helps infants to understand life.

8. Describe the research methods used to assess the intelligence of infants, and explain how we measure the quality of these assessments.

9. Explain how social and cultural factors influence the intelligence of infants.

10. Define phonology, semantics, and syntax.

11. Describe the methods used to study language development in infants.

12. Explain how infant-directed speech, turn-taking, and gestures contribute to language development during infancy.

13. List the stages of sound production in infancy.

14. Explain how infants solve the immediate reference problem and the extension problem as they're learning to understand spoken language.

15. Compare and contrast B. F. Skinner's and Noam Chomsky's views on how children learn grammar.

OUTLINE

I. How Scientists Know What Babies Know
    A. Scientist's strategies for asking infant's questions rely on **habituation** and **novelty responsiveness**. Habituation occurs when an infant begins to be bored with a stimulus, which indicates that they have formed some mental representation of it. Novelty responsiveness refers to the infant's interest in new stimuli more than ones that are shown repeatedly. These processes indicate that the baby can tell the difference between old and new stimuli.
    B. A second strategy, also based on habituation and novelty responsiveness, asks yes-no questions, such as, "Can an infant tell the difference between a smiling and frowning face?" Researchers might show a picture of a person smiling repeatedly until the baby

habituates to that picture, and then show the smile and frown pictures together. If the baby looks more at the frown picture because it is novel, it indicates the baby can tell the difference.

C.   A third strategy involves putting a baby in a crib with a mobile overhead and taking baseline measures of how often the baby kicks. Then, the researchers attach the mobile to the infant's foot so that the kick will move the mobile. The baby quickly learns that kicking moves the mobile and kicks more often. If you wait and repeat this in a few days, the infant learns the same thing much faster the second time than the first, indicating some memory involved in the infant's learning process.

D.   A fourth strategy involves performing a sequence of events in front of an infant, and then giving the infant the opportunity to do the same. If the infant repeats the order of events, then the infant can remember a sequence of events.

II.   Piaget and Infant Cognition

Piaget studied his own three children primarily, and developed a stage theory of infant cognition. Piaget believed that infants construct their understanding of the world based on their own motor activity and interactions with the world.

A.   Assimilation and Accommodation
      Adaptation is the process whereby knowledge is altered by experience. Piaget argued that adaptation involves both **assimilation** (information processes according to what the infant already knows) and **accommodation** (infant must change cognitive understanding to process new information).

B.   Stage Theory
      1.   Infancy encompasses Piaget's **sensorimotor period** of development. During this stage, "thinking" consists of coordinating sensory information with motor activity.
      2.   Major advances in the sensorimotor period include developing an understanding of *causality* and **object permanence**. The latter advance is the first step towards being able to hold **mental representations** of objects.

C.   Challenges to Piaget
      1.   Some scientists have pointed out that Piaget overemphasized the importance of motor activity in infant cognition, noting that limbless infants are capable of learning even with severely limited motor activity.
      2.   Other research suggests that the development of object permanence and the capacity for mental representations develops much earlier than Piaget believed. For example, infants can imitate faces relatively early in life, indicating they have a mental representation of the face they use as a model to imitate. They can also imitate model's actions after a delay, also suggesting mental representation.

III. Mental Representation in Infancy
      A.   **Categorization** involves grouping objects into a set according to some rule. It simplifies and organizes the infant's world by allowing the infant to store more information about one object in a single "file" and by helping the infant understand that knowledge about one category exemplar will apply to other category members.
            1.   Habituation and novelty responsiveness illustrate infants' categorization abilities. Infants respond more to novel stimuli from a totally new category than they do to novel stimuli from the same category as the object they habituated to.
            2.   Observational studies of infant play also suggest that infants categorize. Infants given objects from two categories (e.g., animals vs. vehicles) tend to touch objects within a category more frequently than across categories.
      B.   Remembering

1. For many years, infants were believed to be unable to remember anything. Freud called this **infantile amnesia**. Piaget also held this view, although we now know it is inaccurate.

2. Habituation studies that involve testing infants immediately after habituation measure *short-term memory* while studies that impose a delay between habituation and the test assess *long-term memory*.

3. Infants' ability to remember improves with age. Studies of **deferred imitation** indicate that 6-month-old infants perform the modeled sequence the poorest after a 24-hour delay, with increases in performance up through the end of infancy.

C. Playing

1. Piaget argued that play becomes more sophisticated as children age. Play begins as **exploratory play** in which infants simply engage in sensorimotor manipulation of objects.

2. In the second year of life, infants advance to **symbolic play** in which children enact simple make-believe scenarios. Most children follow this sequence, although there is great variability in what percent of time two-year olds spend in symbolic play.

3. Adult social interaction with infants during play increases the sophistication of the play, particularly when it is encouraging or affirming rather than disapproving.

4. Culture influences the ways in which parents play with their children. Japanese mothers engage in more symbolic play with infants, while mothers in the United States engage in more exploratory play. These patterns are consistent with cultural emphases on interpersonal connection that underlies symbolic play, which is emphasized more in Japan than the U. S.

IV. Infant Intelligence

A. Infant Tests

1. The Bayley Scales of Infant Development are the most widely used assessments of infant development.

2. The degree to which an intelligence test actually measures what it is intended to measure refers to the tests **validity**. It is difficult to validate an infant intelligence test because the criterion for intelligence at that age cannot be identified with a definitive index of achievement. Infant tests can be correlated with later tests taken in adulthood to establish **predictive validity**, but the Bayley Scales do not correlate with other measures of intelligence taken at age 18 in longitudinal studies.

3. Scales like the Bayley are useful, though, in identifying developmental problems and predicting developmental delay.

4. The lack of predictive validity could be due to several factors. First, it could reflect a genuine discontinuity in intellectual development. Alternately, it could be because the tests themselves over-rely on sensorimotor skills and not truly "cognitive" skills like paying attention and memory. Tests that focus on cognitive skills might correlate more significantly with later indicators of intelligence.

B. Infant Mental Development in Social Context

1. The *ecological perspective* takes into account both *proximal* and *distal* factors' influence on infant mental development. For example, socioeconomic status (a distal factor) influences infant development, but it is largely through the fact that fewer educated parents live in poverty, and less educated parents provide less verbal stimulation. The parenting is the proximal factor. Additionally, infants and parents jointly influence this process.

2.   As children grow and mature, parents provide **scaffolding** to help the child advance. Scaffolding strategies include *joint attention*, *parental responsiveness*, and the specific *toys and books* that the parents actually provide.

3.   Parental belief systems are called **ethnotheories**, and these determine how parents interact with their infants. They underlie differences in scaffolding strategies observed around the world.

V.   Language Development in Infancy
Phonology is production and perception of sound. **Semantics** are the meanings of words and **syntax** refers to grammar. All of these skills must be mastered in infancy.

A.   Language Norms and Methods of Study
1.   During the first month of life, infants tend to merely coo and babble, but by age 24 months, they generate grammatically correct sentences.

2.   Although early infant speech may sound like the infant fails to distinguish certain sounds, special recordings reveal that they do make such distinctions, but often not to the degree that adults can hear them. This suggests that infant language acquisition cannot be solely due to adult reinforcement, as the adult cannot hear the behavior needing to be reinforced.

3.   Parent reports provide another way to study infant language development, using either diaries or checklists.

B.   Language Comprehension and Production
Comprehension is understanding language; **production** is making the sounds of language. Comprehension nearly always precedes production in language development.

C.   Individual Variation in Language Development
1.   Children of the same age vary greatly in language development. Using **morphemes** to measure mean length of utterance, scientists can index individual children's verbal growth to measure this.

2.   Although there is variability across children, the pattern within individuals is similar in that infants who know more words at one year tend to know more at two years as well.

3.   In addition to quantitative measures like number of words or mean length of utterance, children's language development differs qualitatively, with some children having vocabularies that are quite **referential** and others' vocabularies being more **expressive**.

D.   The Building Blocks of Language
One of the main achievements in language development in infancy is to become a conversational partner.

1.   **Infant-directed speech** is a special dialect that adults adopt when interacting with infants that involves rhythm and tone, simplification, redundancy, special forms (e.g., mama, not Mother), and content restricted to the child's world. It is helpful in developing the infant as a conversationalist, and it is nearly universal.

2.   Turn-taking is important to adult dialogue, and infants and their mothers engage in turn-taking to a greater degree than speaking at the same time.

3.   Gestures help children acquire conversational and pragmatic language skills. Pointing and labeling help infants pay attention to and remember objects better.

E.   Making and Understanding Sounds
1.   The auditory system is well developed at birth, but babies are especially appreciative of human speech over other sounds. They perceive and categorize speech sounds which facilitate language development.

2. Babies begin their vocalization with prelinguistics of crying and babbling. Even deaf babies babble, so hearing vocalization is not essential to making attempts to produce sound. Infants use both others' speech and feedback from their own speech in learning to speak. Early babblings are influenced by the language spoken around the infant.

F. How Infants Learn Words

1. When infants learn their first word around 12 months, they tend to use that word for many purposes. This is called **holophrasis.**

2. Frequency of hearing a word is not always a predictor of what words an infant will learn. For example, "you" is frequently heard in the English language but rarely amongst an infant's first words. However, frequency does help an infant acquire a word in his or her vocabulary.

3. Word learning may occur through **induction**. Induction requires that the infant work through the *immediate reference problem* and the *extension problem*. Infants manage to do this rapidly, which is called **fast-mapping**.

4. Infants use rules like the **whole object assumption** and a bias towards **mutual exclusivity** to help them discern the meaning of words.

5. Parents who are lower in **socioeconomic status (SES)** talk less than parents from affluent homes. Thus, infants from lower SES homes tend to talk less and later than their more affluent peers. More important to language development than the amount of speech, though, is the verbal responsiveness of the parent to the infant.

G. How Infants Learn Grammar

1. **Grammar** refers to rules for combining words into meaningful and interpretable communications. Skinner argued this occurred as children learned *transitional probabilities* among words, and were reinforced by adults for using them to construct their own grammatically correct sentences.

2. Chomsky felt this view was too simplistic, and argued that **universal grammar** existed in all children within the brain. Like a heart, Chomsky believed that language would develop in all children given basic preconditions.

3. If language is like a heart, one might look in the brain for the structure there responsible for language development. Although no such singular structure has been identified, both **Broca's area** and **Wernicke's area** are essential to language production and comprehension, respectively.

4. Although it would be unethical to perform an experiment involving deprivation of language exposure to see what "natural" language develops, natural experiments using deaf children whose parents were unable to learn sign language reveal that these children develop their own vocabulary and grammar patterns. The deaf children's first words tend to appear around the same age as non-deaf children—12 months.

KEY TERMS

1. **Habituation** is the process in which a baby compares each new stimulus with a developing memory of the stimulus based on previous exposures, thus becoming accustomed to the stimulus. (see How Scientists Know What Babies Know)

2. **Novelty responsiveness**, which occurs following habituation, is the process in which a baby looks more at a new stimulus than at one shown previously. (see How Scientists Know What Babies Know)

3.   **Adaptation** is the process whereby knowledge is altered by experience. Adaptation involves two complementary processes: assimilation and accommodation. (see Piaget and Infant Cognition)

4.   **Assimilation** is the process by which information can be incorporated according to what the infant already knows. Assimilation allows the infant to use existing understanding to make sense of the world. (see Piaget and Infant Cognition)

5.   **Accommodation** is the process by which the infant changes to reach new understanding; that is, the modification of existing understanding to make it apply to a new situation. (see Piaget and Infant Cognition)

6.   The **sensorimotor period** is a developmental time, consisting of a six-stage sequence, when thinking consists of coordinating sensory information with motor activity. (see Piaget and Infant Cognition)

7.   **Object permanence** is the understanding that an object continues to exist, even though it cannot be sensed. (see Piaget and Infant Cognition)

8.   **Mental representation** is the ability to hold in the mind an image of objects (and people) that are not physically present. (see Piaget and Infant Cognition)

9.   **Categorization** is a process that involves grouping separate items into a set according to some rule. (see Mental Representation in Infancy)

10. **Infantile amnesia** is the adult recollection of almost nothing of events that took place before the age of three or four. (see Mental Representation in Infancy)

11. **Deferred imitation** involves reproducing a series of actions seen at an earlier time. (see Mental Representation in Infancy)

12. **Exploratory play** refers to children's play in which activities are tied to the tangible properties of objects. (see Mental Representation in Infancy)

13. **Symbolic play** refers to children's play that enacts activities performed by the self, others, and objects in pretend or make-believe scenarios. (see Mental Representation in Infancy)

14. **Validity** is the degree to which a test measures what it was designed to measure. (see Infant Intelligence)

15. **Predictive validity** is established when performance at one time relates meaningfully to performance at a later time. (see Infant Intelligence)

16. **Scaffolding** is providing learning opportunities, materials, hints, and clues when a child has difficulty with a task. (see Infant Intelligence)

17. **Ethnotheories** are parents' belief systems that motivate them to behave in the ways they do. (see Infant Intelligence)

18. **Phonology** refers to sounds in the language that are produced and perceived. (see Language Development in Infancy)

19. **Semantics** are the meaning of words and sentences, or the content of speech. (see Language Development in Infancy)

20. **Syntax** refers to the rules that define the ways in which words and phrases are arranged to ensure correct and meaningful communication. Also called grammar. (see Language Development in Infancy)

21. **Comprehension** is understanding language. (see Language Development in Infancy)

22. **Production** refers to speaking the language. (see Language Development in Infancy)

23. **Morphemes** are meaningful units of sound in a language. (see Language Development in Infancy)

24. **Referential** is a linguistic style hallmarked by vocabularies that include a high proportion of nouns and speech that provides information and refers to things in the environment. (see Language Development in Infancy)

25. **Expressive** is a linguistic style hallmarked by early vocabularies that have relatively more verbs and speech that uses social routines to communicate feelings and desires. (see Language Development in Infancy)

26. **Infant-directed speech** is a special speech register reserved for babies that simplifies normal adult-directed speech in many ways. (see Language Development in Infancy)

27. **Holophrasis** is the use of a single word for many things. (see Language Development in Infancy)

28. **Induction** is the process of using a limited set of examples to draw conclusions that permit inferences about new cases. (see Language Development in Infancy)

29. **Fast mapping** is a phenomenon that refers to how easily children pick up words they have heard only a few times. (see Language Development in Infancy)

30. **Whole object assumption** is a concept that refers to children's belief that a novel label refers to the "whole object" and not to its parts, substance, or other properties. (see Language Development in Infancy)

31. **Mutual exclusivity** is a concept that refers to an infant's assumption that any given object has only one name. (see Language Development in Infancy)

32. **Socioeconomic status (SES)** is the education, occupation, and income of householders. (see Language Development in Infancy)

33. **Grammar** refers to the rules that define the ways in which words and phrases are arranged to ensure correct and meaningful communication. Also called syntax. (see Language Development in Infancy)

34. **Universal grammar** is Chomsky's term for aspects of syntax that are thought to be innate and built into every infant's brain. (see Language Development in Infancy)

35. **Broca's area** is the area in the left frontal lobe concerned with producing fluent speech and comprehending syntactic structure. (see Language Development in Infancy)

36. **Wernicke's area** is the area in the left temporal lobe that is concerned with comprehension generally and fluent but relatively meaningless speech. (see Language Development in Infancy)

FILL-IN-THE-BLANKS KEY TERMS

This section will help you check your knowledge of the key terms introduced in this chapter. Fill in each blank with the appropriate term from the list of key terms in the previous section.

1. Meaningful units of sound in a language are called _____.

2. _____ is the process in which a baby compares each new stimulus with a developing memory of the stimulus based on previous exposures, thus becoming accustomed to the stimulus.

3.   Parents' belief systems that motivate them to behave in the ways that they do are called_____.

4.   _____ refers to adult recollection for few events that occur prior to the age of 3 or 4.

5.   Use of a single word for many things is called_____.

6.   A linguistic style hallmarked by vocabularies that include a high proportion of nouns and speech that provides information and refers to things in the environment is called_____.

7.   _____ is children's play that enacts activities performed by the self, others, and objects in pretend or make-believe scenarios.

8.   _____ is established when performance at one time relates meaningfully to performance at a later time.

9.   _____ refers to aspects of syntax that are thought to be innate and built into every infant's brain.

10. Sounds in the language that are produced and perceived are called_____.

APPLIED LEARNING AND CRITICAL THINKING

During infancy, cognitive development occurs at an astonishing rate. Particularly visible is the explosion of language development. Many real-world contexts provide venues in which you might study these developments more closely rather than merely reading about them. Finding those opportunities to apply the information you learn as you read your text will give you a means to test the limits of your new knowledge.

1.   When scholars have the kind of enormous impact that Piaget had, or that Chomsky has, it can be quite interesting to visit the sites at which much of their work was conducted. Chomsky's work was conducted largely in Cambridge, Massachusetts, at MIT in the linguistics department. Piaget's work occurred in several European countries, including France, Switzerland, and Germany. If you are studying abroad, consider visiting some of the sites where Piaget might have worked. If study abroad is not in your plans, consider a visit to Cambridge, Massachusetts, to explore the place where Chomsky was inspired to do his ground-breaking research. How do you think the social and physical context where these men worked influenced their thinking?

2.   If you need part-time work, day-care centers provide the student of developmental psychology wonderful opportunities to work with children and observe their play. Infant rooms usually require much more staff than rooms that cater to older children, so the opportunities there may well be easily available if you are qualified. If you decide to pursue such a part-time position, use the opportunity to observe how infants play. Can you distinguish between exploratory and symbolic play? Does the age at which you see children increase symbolic play correspond to the descriptions in this text? If not, what reasons might explain that discrepancy?

3.   Many research projects that focus on infant cognition will use the Bayley Scales of Infant Development. See if you can work with a professor in your department who studies child development and train to administer this test, and perhaps others designed to measure infant cognition. What sorts of research questions does actually administering the test raise for you that you would not have considered if you had not actually administered the test to children yourself?

4.   *Success by 6* is a United Way program that is available in many communities. Find out if your community has one and see if you can volunteer with their professional staff. Rather

than working directly with children (although that may occur, too), *Success by 6* often aims to address more systemic issues that affect children under the age of 6. One of those areas may be addressing the availability of high-quality, affordable infant day care. If you are able to volunteer with this organization or a similar one in your community, find out what the availability of infant day care is in your area. What steps are needed to increase its availability, quality, and affordability?

MULTIPLE-CHOICE QUESTIONS

Quiz 1

1. Baby Josephine's mother ties a string connecting her foot to her mobile in her crib. When Josephine wiggles, the mobile jiggles and Josephine cackles with delight. It takes her a few minutes to figure out that she is moving the mobile, but once she realizes it, she wiggles constantly! Josephine's mom then removes the string for a few days, and reattaches it after the third day. Based on the research described in your text, which of the following is most likely to happen the second time Josephine has a string attaching her to her mobile?

    a. Josephine will take longer to re-learn that the new string will wiggle the mobile.
    b. Josephine will re-learn that the new string wiggles the mobile faster this time.
    c. Josephine will throw a tantrum because her mom had taken it away before.
    d. Josephine will re-learn that the string wiggles the mobile at the same rate.

2. The process whereby knowledge is altered by experience is called

    a. assimilation.
    b. adaptation.
    c. accommodation.
    d. habituation.

3. Which of the following best describes how Piaget conceived of "thinking" for infants in the sensorimotor period?

    a. Remembering and comparing recent experiences
    b. Analyzing events
    c. Exploring objects by touching and mouthing them
    d. Both A and B

4. Baby Jackson is in an experiment. He is presented a series of pictures of the same cat, and after a while, he doesn't spend as much time looking at them. Then, he is presented with two pictures to look at: a DIFFERENT cat than he had been seeing and a dog. Based on the research on categorization described in your text, which of the two pictures will Jackson spend more time looking at?

    a. The different cat picture
    b. The dog picture
    c. Both pictures equally
    d. Neither picture because he is tired of the whole experiment

5. Maya is watching her mother clap her hands and then slap her knees in time to the music. Maya doesn't do any of these actions right then, but a few days later her mom walks into her room and Maya is singing a little tune and clapping her hands and slapping her knees in time. This illustrates

    a. object permanence.
    b. categorization.
    c. infantile amnesia.
    d. deferred imitation.

6.   The average one-year-old spends_____ of his or her time in symbolic play.

    a.   0%

    b.   15%

    c.   33%

    d.   50%

7.   Providing learning opportunities, materials, hints, and clues when a child has difficulty with a task is called

    a.   scaffolding.

    b.   predictive validity.

    c.   ethnotheory.

    d.   phonology.

8.   Who would most likely argue that children's brains are biologically wired to learn language?

    a.   Skinner

    b.   Steinberg

    c.   Chomsky

    d.   Obama

9.   _____ is to looking at and understanding a piece of visual art, as _____ is to being able to produce a piece of art.

    a.   Comprehension; production

    b.   Production; comprehension

    c.   Semantics; syntax

    d.   Syntax; semantics

10.   Molly's first word was "up," which she combined with her arms raised to indicate she wanted to be carried. Most of the words she acquired thereafter were helpful to her in communicating her wishes (e.g., "I hungry" or "I tired" or "Go swimming"). Molly's vocabulary is largely

    a.   expressive.

    b.   referential.

    c.   exploratory.

    d.   symbolic.

11.   Connor talks to his baby sister with a sing-song rhythm, really short words, and lots of inflection. Connor is engaged in

    a.   morphemes.

    b.   holophrasis.

    c.   fast-mapping.

    d.   infant-directed speech.

12.   The process of using a limited set of examples to draw conclusions about a new case is called

    a.   scaffolding.

    b.   accommodation.

    c.   fast mapping.

    d.   induction.

13.   John points to the wheel of his tractor and says "wheel" to his infant daughter, Rachel. Rachel, however, assumes he is talking about the whole tractor, and starts calling the tractor "wheel." This illustrates the

    a.   mutual exclusivity bias.

    b.   whole object assumption.

    c.   deferred imitation.

    d.   predictive validity.

14. The education, occupation, and income of householders is referred to as

   a.   socioeconomic status.
   b.   ethnotheory.
   c.   universal grammar.
   d.   None of these

15. Broca's area is located in the

   a.   left temporal lobe.
   b.   left frontal lobe.
   c.   right temporal lobe.
   d.   right frontal lobe.

Quiz 2

Use this quiz to reassess your learning after taking Quiz 1 and reviewing the chapter.

1. The process by which, following habituation, infants look more at new stimuli than the previously shown stimulus is called

   a.   novelty responsiveness.
   b.   adaptation.
   c.   assimilation.
   d.   accommodation.

2. Nine-month-old Frankie knows that if he drops his rattle it will fall to the floor. When he drops his cheerios, he understands that these, too, will fall to the floor. Frankie's new experience with the cheerios is

   a.   assimilated.
   b.   accommodated.
   c.   habituated.
   d.   deferred.

3. Terrell is 9 months old. When his dad shows him an old cell phone, Terrell is fascinated and reaches for it. Terrell's dad then hides it in his lap. Terrell giggles and searches for the phone more. Terrell's behavior illustrates the cognitive achievement of

   a.   holophrasis.
   b.   object permanence.
   c.   categorization.
   d.   exploratory play.

4. Adult recollection for almost nothing of events taking place prior to age 3–4 is called

   a.   validity.
   b.   deferred imitation.
   c.   infantile amnesia.
   d.   object permanence.

5. McKenzie is playing with a toy that requires her to push a button to make something "pop out" of the toy. McKenzie is engaged in_____ play.

   a.   symbolic
   b.   exploratory
   c.   referential
   d.   expressive

6. Which of the following statements about the predictive validity of the Bayley Scales of Infant Development when given at age 3–4 is true?

    a. It has no relation to intelligence at age 18.
    b. It is moderately related to intelligence at age 18.
    c. It is inversely related to intelligence at age 18.
    d. None of these is true.

7. Parent belief systems that motivate them to behave in particular ways are called

    a. scaffolding.
    b. phonology.
    c. holophrasis.
    d. ethnotheories.

8. Grammar is to_____, as meaning is to_____ .

    a. syntax; semantics
    b. semantics; syntax
    c. induction; deduction
    d. deduction; induction

9. In terms of infant language acquisition, which typically comes first?

    a. Production
    b. Comprehension
    c. Deferred imitation
    d. All of these occur together at equivalent times.

10. Zhou's vocabulary at 20 months is rich in words that describe objects in his environment. He can name every brand of car that there is, and he knows the difference between lots of different types of clocks (grandfather clock, alarm clock, etc.). Zhou's vocabulary is

    a. expressive.
    b. referential.
    c. exploratory.
    d. symbolic.

11. Shahariah's first word is *doggie*. She calls every animal she sees a "doggie." Shahariah's use of "doggie" for all animals illustrates

    a. morphemes.
    b. fast mapping.
    c. holophrasis.
    d. universal grammar.

12. When infants are able to pick up on the meaning of a word after only hearing it a few times, we call this phenomenon

    a. holophrasis.
    b. induction.
    c. mutual exclusivity.
    d. fast mapping.

13. Usain's dad points to a "cup" and calls it a "glass." Usain is confused because he doesn't understand how something can be both a "cup" and a "glass" as it violates his bias towards

    a. whole object assumption.
    b. extension.
    c. immediate reference.
    d. mutual exclusivity.

14. Aspects of syntax thought to be innate and built into every infant's brain are called

    a. grammar.
    b. universal grammar.
    c. phonology.
    d. induction.

15. Injury to Wernicke's area tends to cause problems in

    a. fluency.
    b. fast mapping.
    c. comprehension.
    d. memory.

ANSWERS TO FILL-IN-THE-BLANKS KEY TERMS

1. morphemes (see Language Development in Infancy)

2. Habituation (see How Scientists Know What Babies Know)

3. ethnotheories (see Infant Intelligence)

4. Infantile amnesia (see Mental Representations in Infancy)

5. holophrasis (see Language Development in Infancy)

6. referential (see Language Development in Infancy)

7. Symbolic play (see Mental Representation in Infancy)

8. Predictive validity (see Infant Intelligence)

9. Universal grammar (see Physical Growth)

10. phonology (see Language Development in Infancy)

ANSWERS TO MULTIPLE-CHOICE QUESTIONS

Circle the question numbers you answered incorrectly.

Quiz 1

1. *b is the answer.* Based on her previous experience, Josephine will learn faster the second time around that the string wiggles the mobile. This indicates that Josephine, on some level, remembers her experience the first time around. (see How Scientists Know What Babies Know)

2. *b is the answer.* Adaptation is the process whereby knowledge is altered by experience. It is based on both accommodation and assimilation processes. (see Piaget and Infant Cognition)

3. *c is the answer.* Piaget argued that infants in the sensorimotor period "thought" by coordinating sensory experience with motor activity. Touching an object is a motor activity, and both that and mouthing the object provide sensory inputs. (see Piaget and Infant Cognition)

4. *b is the answer.* Categorization research of this kind shows that Jackson will likely spend more time looking at the picture from the *new* category rather than the new picture of something from the *same* category previously viewed. (see Mental Representations in Infancy)

5.   *d is the answer.*   Deferred imitation is reproduction of a series of actions seen at an earlier time. Maya is reproducing her mother's actions from a few days prior. (see Mental Representations in Infancy)

6.   *b is the answer.*   The average 1-year-old spends 15% of the time in symbolic play, although this varies widely, with some spending no time in symbolic play and others up to 50% of their time in such play. (see Mental Representations in Infancy)

7.   *a is the answer.*   Scaffolding involves providing assistance to children when they have difficulty with a task. The assistance can involve providing materials, hints, clues, or other opportunities. (see Infant Intelligence)

8.   *c is the answer.*   Chomsky argued that language was too complex to be learned through simple reinforcement processes, which was what Skinner had believed. Instead, Chomsky felt that children were biologically prepared to acquire language. (see Language Development in Infancy)

9.   *a is the answer.*   Comprehension refers to understanding language, and production refers to being able to produce language. It is analogous to the distinction between understanding/appreciating art, and being able to create artwork oneself. (see Language Development in Infancy)

10.   *a is the answer.*   Molly's vocabulary has lots of verbs that she uses to *express* her desires and to plug into social routines. It is not *referential*, or based heavily on nouns to *refer* to objects in her environment. (see Language Development in Infancy)

11.   *d is the answer.*   Connor's inflection, rhythm, and simplicity in speech when addressing his baby sister is consistent with the description of infant-directed speech. (see Language Development in Infancy)

12.   *d is the answer.*   Induction is the process of using a limited set of examples to draw conclusions that permit inferences about a new exemplar. (see Language Development in Infancy)

13.   *b is the answer.*   The whole object assumption is the tendency for infants to think that a label an adult provides to an object refers to the whole object, not to its parts, substance, or other properties. (see Language Development in Infancy)

14.   *a is the answer.*   Socioeconomic status refers to the education, occupation, and income of members of a household. (see Language Development in Infancy)

15.   *b is the answer.*   Broca's area is in the left frontal lobe. This area of the brain is responsible for producing fluent speech. (see Language Development in Infancy)

Now turn to the quiz analysis table at the end of this chapter to find which areas you know well and which areas you need to work on. Circle the numbers in the table for items on Quiz 1 that you answered correctly.

Quiz 2

1.   *a is the answer.*   Novelty responsiveness occurs when infants respond more to novel stimuli than to stimuli to which they have grown habituated. (see How Scientists Know What Babies Know)

2.   *a is the answer.*   Assimilation occurs when an infant is able to fit new experiences into existing knowledge structures. Frankie fit the experience of dropping the cheerios into the same knowledge structure he had from previously dropping his rattle. (see Piaget and Infant Cognition)

3. *b is the answer.* Object permanence is the ability to understand that an object continues to exist even when it cannot be seen. (see Piaget and Infant Cognition)

4. *c is the answer.* Infantile amnesia is adult failure to remember events from their own lives prior to the age of 3 or 4. (see Mental Representation in Infancy)

5. *b is the answer.* Exploratory play focuses on extracting information from the object itself—what it does, what qualities it has, what effects it produces, and so on. McKenzie is learning that the object has the effect of something "popping up" when she presses a certain button. (see Mental Representation in Infancy)

6. *a is the answer.* The Bayley Scales of Infant Development are unrelated to intelligence at age 18. (see Infant Intelligence)

7. *d is the answer.* Ethnotheories are parental belief systems that underlie their behaviors. (see Infant Intelligence)

8. *a is the answer.* Syntax refers to grammar while semantics refers to the underlying meaning of words. (see Language Development in Infancy)

9. *b is the answer.* Comprehension of language spoken usually precedes an infant producing language himself or herself. (see Language Development in Infancy)

10. *b is the answer.* Zhou's vocabulary tends to *refer* to objects in his environment. It is a referential vocabulary as it is described in this question. (see Language Development in Infancy)

11. *c is the answer.* Holophrasis is the use of a single word for many meanings. Shahariah is using the word "doggie" to refer to many animals. (see Language Development in Infancy)

12. *d is the answer.* Fast mapping refers to an infant's ability to pick up on the meaning of a word after only hearing it a few times. (see Language Development in Infancy)

13. *d is the answer.* Mutual exclusivity is the bias for a child to believe that any given object can have only one name. (see Language Development in Infancy)

14. *b is the answer.* Universal grammar was Chomsky's term for aspects of syntax, or grammar that he thought were built into every infant's brain. (see Language Development in Infancy)

15. *c is the answer.* Damage to Wernicke's area tends to cause poor language comprehension, and fluent (but meaningless) speech. (see Language Development in Infancy)

Now turn to the quiz analysis table at the end of this chapter to find which areas you know well and which areas you need to work on. Circle the numbers in the table for items on Quiz 2 that you answered correctly.

For each question you answered correctly, circle its number. (Quiz 1 numbers are not shaded; Quiz 2 numbers are shaded.) Are there patterns in the types of questions or the topics you got wrong that could direct your further study? Did you improve from Quiz 1 to Quiz 2?

QUIZ REVIEW

Topic	Type of Question		
	Definition	**Comprehension**	**Application**
How Scientists Know What Babies Know			1
	1		
Piaget and Infant Cognition	2	3	
			2, 3
Mental Representation in Infancy		6	4, 5
	4		5
Infant Intelligence	7		
	7	6	
Language Development in Infancy	12, 14	8, 9, 15	10, 11, 13
	12, 14	8, 9, 15	10, 11, 13

Total correct by quiz:

Quiz 1:	
Quiz 2:	

CHAPTER 6

Socioemotional Development in Infancy

LEARNING OBJECTIVES

1. Explain the difference between primary and secondary emotions, and give examples of each.

2. List the order in which infants typically express particular emotions, and describe the expression of these emotions.

3. Describe the normal progression of an infant's understanding of the emotional expressions of others.

4. Define social referencing and give an example of the phenomenon.

5. Define temperament and describe the different temperaments.

6. Describe the biological and experiential foundations of temperament.

7. Explain how researchers measure temperament in infants.

8. Explain how the "goodness of fit" between a child's temperament and the demands of his or her environment affects that child's long-term adjustment.

9. Define attachment and explain its evolutionary advantages.

10. Describe the four phases of infant-parent attachment identified by John Bowlby.

11. Describe Mary Ainsworth's Strange Situation technique for studying attachment and the four classifications of infants' attachment security.

12. Describe the aspects of parent-child interactions that affect attachment.

13. Explain how Harry Harlow's experiment on Rhesus monkeys demonstrated the importance of contact comfort in normal development.

14. Describe the differences in how typical mothers and fathers interact with their infants, and explain the developmental consequences for infants reared by only one parent.

15. Describe the eight criteria for ensuring high quality infant care specified by the National Center for Infants, Toddlers, and Families.

16. Describe the affects of infant day care on the children's attachments to their parents and on their individual socioemotional development.

17. Describe the gender-stereotyped ways in which infants are treated beginning at birth, and explain how these behaviors might influence the development of the children's gender identities.

OUTLINE

Developmental scientists are interested in infants' **emotions, temperament,** and **attachments**. Emotions provide cues as to the infant's current state. Temperament refers to stable, biologically-based differences in behavior that impact the child's interactions in his or her environment. Attachments are specific, lasting, social relationships with others.

I. Infants' Emotions
    Because infants cannot communicate verbally, deciphering their emotions can be challenging. There are two sides to emotional behavior: **emotional expression** and **emotional understanding**.

    A. Development of Emotional Expressions
        1. **Primary emotions** are the first emotions infants express. These feelings, including joy, surprise, sadness, anger, fear and shyness, are rooted in human biology. **Secondary emotions** like embarrassment or envy do not emerge until the second or third year of life and depend on higher mental capacities.
        2. Some emotions, like an infant crying, are adaptive as they encourage others to respond.
        3. Researchers measure facial expression of emotion in infants in a variety of ways. MAX, for example, codes infant facial patterns alone and in combination to identify 27 distinct patterns. Other systems measure how an infant responds to stimuli in the environment.
        4. Infants express emotion vocally, and with gestures and movements, as well. They are still when interested, turn away from scary stimuli, and show a slumped posture when sad. Fear and anger occur as early as 3–4 months and increase after 6 months. Sadness occurs as early as 2 and a half months. Infants vary in their level of sadness, and infants of depressed mothers are at special risk.
        5. Infants also express positive emotions. Social interaction can elicit smiles during the infant's first month of life. Joy is observed as early as 3–4 months, and by six months infants laugh when engaged in social play.
        6. Infants' emotional development is closely intertwined with cognitive development. For example, peek-a-boo won't elicit much emotion from a child who lacks object permanence, but between 6–12 months when that ability emerges, peek-a-boo elicits laughter.
        7. Social experiences themselves influence infants' emotional development. Infants with mothers who smile more tend to smile more themselves.
        8. As infants develop self-awareness, secondary emotions emerge. Infants who recognize themselves in a mirror, for example, are more likely to exhibit embarrassment when effusively praised by an adult.
    B. The Development of Sensitivity to Emotional Signals
        1. To read an emotional signal, an infant first must be able to see it. Around 2 months, infants begin to have the visual acuity necessary to discriminate facial expressions and can even distinguish intensity in facial expressions.
        2. Infants respond to emotional expression by matching the expression. This reaction is supported by **mirror neurons**.
        3. Around 8–9 months of age, infants begin to engage in **social referencing**.
        4. As infants become more skilled at perceiving emotional expressions in others, this lays the groundwork for the emergence of *prosocial* behavior during the second year of life.
        5. Emotional differences in infants are the beginnings of individuality which is expressed as an infant's temperament.
II. Infant Temperament
    The biological origins of temperament are observed in twin studies. Traits such as activity level and sociability (which are part of temperament) are highly heritable. However, these traits are affected by experience.

A.   Measuring Infant Temperament
1.   Scientists can measure infant temperament by either asking people who know the infant well, or by directly observing infant behavior.
2.   Parent reports can provide insight into infant temperament, but are highly subjective and potentially biased. Alternately, observation may be less biased but are based on limited sampling, observer effects, context effects, and other problems.
B.   Approaches to Characterizing Infant Temperament
1.   **Positive affectivity** and **negative affectivity** have been consistently studied as important dimensions of infant temperament.
2.   **Inhibited children** and **difficult children** are both high in negative affectivity, and can create challenges for parents. Inhibited children are fearful, wary and shy as infants. **Difficult children** are irritable and negative as infants, and those difficulties tend to persist.
C.   Does Temperament Matter
1.   Temperament can influence cognitive development. More sociable infants tend to do better on standardized tests than difficult infants do.
2.   The reasons underlying this relationship may be that more positive infants approach cognitive tasks more constructively, or the effect may be indirect. Positive infants may elicit more interaction from adults, and thus gain better cognitive skills, or they may just tolerate a stranger giving the test better than difficult children do.
3.   Temperament lays the foundation for personality, although this connection is not immutable.
D.   Context Matters
1.   One of the reasons the temperament-personality connection is not immutable is because the context in which the infant develops highly influences personality. Parents who respond to difficult infants with firm parental control without physical coercion tend to promote self-regulation in these infants. In contrast, parents who react to difficult infants with hostility tend to see the child have greater maladaptive behavior in the future.
2.   **Goodness of fit** refers to the fit between the child's temperament and the demands of the environment. This match has a large impact on a child's adjustment.
III.   Attachment and Infant Social Development
Environment of evolutionary adaptedness is the context of the environment in which our species evolved. It is perhaps the most popular explanation of the attachment process. Infants benefit from having adults want to care for them, as they require it for survival and they are unable to cling to an adult themselves. Infants develop signals (like cries) to attract adults, and adults are predisposed to respond to such signals.

A.   Phases of Social Development
1.   From 1–2 months, infants exhibit indiscriminate social responsiveness. They use signals like cries to draw adults to them, and they seem satisfied by whomever responds to their cries.
2.   From 2–7 months, infants engage in discriminating sociability. They recognize and prefer important people in their lives, and tend to exhibit greater behavioral coordination.
3.   Between 7–24 months, the first infant-adult attachments are thought to form. Babies respond with **separation protest** when the people to whom they are attached leave.

4.   From age 3 onward, attachment relationships are characterized by goal-corrected partnerships in which children take their parent's needs into account in interacting with them.

B.   How Do Attachments Form?
1.   The presence and availability of adults during a **sensitive period** (birth to 6 months) in infancy determines to whom the infant will become attached. Both Bowlby and Ainsworth argued attachments form hierarchically, typically first with the mother and father and later with other primary caregivers.
2.   Although there is a minimum amount of time required for attachments to form, developmental scientists have not identified a set number of hours. The quality of interaction is also very important to attachment.
3.   Although it is somewhat adaptive to be cautious with strangers, the **stranger wariness** infants show does diminish rapidly over time, allowing infants to interact in a friendly manner with nonattachment figures.

C.   How Is Infant Attachment Measured?
1.   The Strange Situation is the most popular strategy for measuring infant attachment. It has seven episodes that expose the infant to increasing amounts of mild stress.
2.   The Strange Situation begins with the parent and infant alone in a room (1st episode), and then a stranger appears (creating the 2nd episode). The parent departs (3rd episode), and then returns (4th episode). The parent then departs and returns again (5th and 7th episode).
3.   Typically responding infants tend to use their parents as a base from which to explore, to react to the stranger's initial entrance with inhibition, and then their parent's departure with crying or searching, followed by attempts to re-engage in interaction (including seeking comfort) when the parent returns. These responses intensify with the repeated departure and return. These infants are designated as *Type B*, and are *securely attached*.
4.   Some children react in another way, characterized as *insecure-resistant* and *insecure-ambivalent (Type C)*. They are distressed by their parent's departure, but react ambivalently upon their return.
5.   Infants classified as *Type A* exhibit *insecure-avoidant* attachments. They actively avoid their parents when they return to the room.
6.   A very small group of infants (*Type D*) behave in a *disorganized* manner, displaying contradictory behavior patterns, appearing confused or apprehensive about approaching their parents.
7.   Infants' attachment classification tends to be consistent across time. When they are not, it tends to be predictable based on changes in family stress levels or the birth of a second child—both events that tend to lessen the security of the attachment.

D.   Parent-Child Interaction and Attachment Security
1.   Through play with parents and repeated distress-relief sequences, infants learn both **reciprocity**, **effectance**, and **trust**. These are major steps in the process of becoming social.
2.   Individual differences in trust levels are rooted in the level of sensitivity and responsiveness of the adults in the infant's life. Infants count on attachment figures to be accessible when they need them and to protect them, and so use such figures as a **secure base** from which to explore the environment. Securely attached infants tend to explore the environment more readily than those who are insecurely attached.

3. Infant temperament affects the quality of the parent-child interaction, which in turn has an influence on the way infants respond in the strange situation and become classified in it.

4. Infant attachment is of interest because it can to some degree predict future behavior. Securely attached infants tend to be more cooperative with a friendly stranger and have better social relationships with siblings and peers. Securely attached infants also show better problem-solving skills when they reach pre-school.

5. Most babies in most cultures are securely attached, but the distribution across the attachment categories varies cross-culturally. For example, Japanese, Israeli, and Indonesian infants tend to show more stress in the separation phase of the strange situation, perhaps because they have less experience with separations.

IV. Parental Behavior and Interaction with Infants

One of the critical features of parent-child interaction is **contact comfort**, demonstrated in Harlow's classic study of motherless monkeys. These monkeys strongly preferred the cloth "mother" to the wire one, even though both provided food. Removal from their mothers, however, severely stunted their social development. During the first year of life, human babies' relations with their parents become increasingly *object-oriented*, incorporated the outside world into their interactions.

A. Mothers and Fathers

1. Mothers tend to kiss, hug, and talk while fathers tend to be more rambunctious with their infants in play. This pattern persists even when the father is the primary caregiver and the mother is the individual who works outside of the home.

2. In most countries, mothers spend a much greater amount of time with infants than fathers. However, infants do become attached to fathers, indicating that there must be sufficient quality interaction in spite of the lower quantity.

3. Infants from two-parent families tend to fare better in their social development and self-control than those from one-parent families where presumably the familial stress is greater. Stress inhibits the parents' ability to interact effectively with the child.

B. Nonparental Care

1. Most children in the U. S. now experience some form of nonparental care. It is impossible to generalize about the effects of nonparental child care because these situations vary widely, and because children are not assigned randomly to child care situations.

2. Eight criteria have been identified as important to supporting high-quality day care that will promote socioemotional development. These are: health/safety, small group size, each infant has a primary caregiver, continuity in care, responsive caregiving, meeting individual needs in the larger group context, ensuring cultural/linguistic continuity, and providing a stimulating physical environment.

3. Infants are often distressed when they start day care. However, research indicates no difference in the proportion of secure attachments between children in day care and those who stay home with their mothers. Maternal sensitivity did increase the probability that a child would achieve a secure attachment regardless of their care situation.

4. When infants spend many hours in day care, maternal sensitivity declines, which may risk the infant becoming insecurely attached. Parents need to insure they have high-quality interactions at home when the infant is not in day care.

5. Relationships with nonparental caregivers influence socioemotional development, too. Attachment to early day care providers can predict school-age children's relationship quality with their teacher.

6. The broader ecology influences the child care situation. Infants in non-industrialized countries tend to spend most of their time with their parents as their parents work.

C. Gender and Infant Socioemotional Development

1. Mothers and fathers treat their infants differently based on the child's gender. From birth onward, fathers tend to interact preferentially with their sons and mothers with their daughters.

2. Children, especially boys, tend to show preferences for gender-stereotypical toys as early as the second year of life. Research shows that children tend to have more same-sex-typed toys at home than cross-sex-typed, and they prefer same-sex-typed typed toys.

3. These toy preferences are supported by the child's social environment from very early in life. Parent expectancy contributes to such gender differences, with mothers overestimating how well their sons will do on a motor task and underestimating how well their daughters will do. In actuality, no gender differences in performance on the motor task were observed.

KEY TERMS

1. **Emotions** are feelings that give strong and informative cues about one's current state. (see introductory section)

2. **Temperament** is the biologically based source of individual differences in behavioral functioning. (see introductory section)

3. **Attachments** are infants' specific, lasting, social relationships with others, especially parents and other caregivers. (see introductory section)

4. **Emotional expression** is the communication of feelings to others through facial expressions, gestures, and vocalizations. (see Infants' Emotions)

5. **Emotional understanding** is the interpretation (reading) of the emotional expressions of others. (see Infants' Emotions)

6. **Primary emotions** are the feelings of joy, surprise, sadness, anger, fear, and shyness that appear to be deeply rooted in human biology and develop early in life. (see Infants' Emotions)

7. **Secondary emotions** are the feelings of embarrassment, pride, guilt, shame, and envy that emerge in the second and third years of life. (see Infants' Emotions)

8. **Mirror neurons** are the cells in the brain that are activated both when we do something and when we see someone else do the same thing. (see Infants' Emotions)

9. **Social referencing** is the tendency to use others' emotional expressions to interpret uncertain or ambiguous events. (see Infants' Emotions)

10. **Positive affectivity** is a dimension of behavior that reflects the extent to which a person feels enthusiastic and alert (e.g., cheerful, outgoing, etc.). (see Infant Temperament)

11. **Negative affectivity** is a dimension of behavior that reflects the extent to which a person feels distressed (e.g., sad, angry, guilty). (see Infant Temperament)

12. **Inhibited children** are children who are characteristically shy, fearful, and timid. (see Infant Temperament)

13. **Difficult children** are children who are easily irritated and hard to soothe. (see Infant Temperament)

14. **Goodness of fit** is a concept that refers to a match between the interaction of the child's temperament and the demands of the environment. (see Infant Temperament)

15. The **environment of evolutionary adaptedness** is the context of the environment in which our species evolved. (see Attachment and Infant Social Development)

16. **Separation protest** refers to a signal, characterized by crying, that is aimed at making attachment figures return. (see Attachment and Infant Social Development)

17. A **sensitive period** is a time in development during which the organism is especially vulnerable to experience. (see Attachment and Infant Social Development)

18. **Stranger wariness** is the hesitancy that infants show at around ten months when they are approached by unfamiliar people. (see Attachment and Infant Social Development)

19. The **Strange Situation** is an experimental paradigm that reveals a child's security of attachment. (see Attachment and Infant Social Development)

20. **Reciprocity** is a lesson in social interaction in which partners take turns acting and reacting to the other's behavior. (see Attachment and Infant Social Development)

21. **Effectance** is a lesson in social interaction that involves learning that one's behavior can affect the behavior of others in a consistent and predictable fashion. (see Attachment and Infant Social Development)

22. **Trust** is a lesson in social interaction that involves learning that another person can be counted on to respond when signaled. (see Attachment and Infant Social Development)

23. A **secure base** is the trustworthy place infants count on for protection and accessibility when needed as they explore and interact with other people. (see Attachment and Infant Social Development)

24. **Contact comfort** refers to the gratification derived from touch. (see Parental Behavior and Interaction with Infants)

FILL-IN-THE-BLANKS KEY TERMS

This section will help you check your knowledge of the key terms introduced in this chapter. Fill in each blank with the appropriate term from the list of key terms in the previous section.

1. Infants' specific, lasting, social relationships with others, especially parents and other caregivers, are called _____.

2. _____ is a lesson in social interaction that involves learning that another person can be counted on to respond when signaled.

3. A dimension of behavior that reflects the extent to which a person feels enthusiastic and alert is called_____.

4. _____ is a concept that refers to a match between the interaction of the child's temperament and the demands of the environment.

5. The tendency to use others' emotional expressions to interpret uncertain or ambiguous events is called _____.

6.   The context of the environment in which our species evolved is called the_____.

7.   The_____ is an experimental paradigm that reveals a child's security of attachment.

8.   _____ is a lesson in social interaction that involves learning that one's behavior can affect the behavior of others in a consistent and predictable fashion.

9.   ____ are the feelings of joy, surprise, sadness, anger, fear, and shyness that appear to be deeply rooted in human biology and develop early in life.

10. The gratification derived from touch is called_____.

APPLIED LEARNING AND CRITICAL THINKING

As infants mature over the first two years of life, parents and others involved in their lives take great joy in watching their individuality emerge. Emotions, temperament, and attachment are all part of that bundle of what makes each infant unique. Below are some ways that you can apply and investigate a little further what you've learned about in this chapter in real-world contexts that afford interaction with these budding individuals we know as infants.

11. If you will be traveling to other countries during the course of your university studies, use that opportunity to study the child-care situations that are common in the culture(s) you visit. Nonparental care, while relatively common in the United States, is relatively rare in nonindustrialized nations in which parents take their children with them as they work. If you have the opportunity to see such a practice in person, take some time to reflect on the pros and cons of each approach. While sending a child to child care certainly offers benefits to the parents by allowing them to focus on their work and to the child by allowing them to engage in "developmentally appropriate" activities, it also creates a situation in which the child is not connected closely to the fabric of the adult culture of work. And while nonindustrialized nations certainly maintain this close connection, infants may be exposed to things that in the United States would be considered unsafe or developmentally inappropriate. What are the costs and benefits of the different cultural traditions regarding child care as an influence on socioemotional development in infancy?

12. If you can find work in a child-care situation or engage in much babysitting, you may well have the opportunity to run into a child with a difficult or inhibited temperament. As you get to know these children and their parents, what sorts of observations can you make about the relationship between the child's temperament and the parental interaction style? How does the child's broader social context seem to influence the nature of his or her temperament? Is there a good fit between his or her context and temperament, or does this seem to be a source of conflict? How can you help create an environment in the child-care situation that will be a good fit to his or her temperament?

13. The study of infant emotion is largely accomplished through the use of coding systems for facial expressions and body language. What developmental scientists learn about infant emotion is largely dependent on what the coding system actually "captures." Your text describes two such coding systems—MAX and BabyFACS. Work with one of your professors on a literature review of coding systems for infant emotion, including these two, and compare and contrast the information such systems provide. Do you notice any gaps in terms of what these systems theoretically *should* attempt to measure and what they actually *do* measure? Is one coding system superior to others? If you think so, articulate why.

14. Some religious organizations provide child care during their worship services for infants. If you are part of such a group, consider volunteering your services to work in the nursery from time to time. For many infants whose parents opt to use these services, they are being

dropped off in the care of someone whom they may not know well. As such, the situation approximates the "strange situation" used to study infant attachment. While volunteering in the nursery is hardly a research setting, it will give you a chance to make some observations about how infants behave when they arrive at a new, relatively unfamiliar setting with a stranger, and how they react both when their parents leave and ultimately return. Given what you have learned about the strange situation in your reading, are you able to apply that to informally "classify" the infants in the nursery? It is often much harder to actually categorize infants than one might think upon initially reading the attachment categories!

MULTIPLE-CHOICE QUESTIONS

Quiz 1

1. Emotions are
   a. biologically based sources of individual differences in behavioral functioning.
   b. strong, informative cues about one's state.
   c. specific, lasting social relationships with others.
   d. the gratification derived from touch.

2. Anna is a very easy baby for her mom to "decipher." She gives strong cues as to how she is feeling. Her mom can easily tell from her facial expression and body language if she is happy, sad, hungry, or angry. Anna is good at
   a. emotional expression.
   b. emotional understanding.
   c. temperament.
   d. attachment.

3. Who is most likely to experience a secondary emotion?
   a. 6-month-old Alex
   b. 2-month-old Jada
   c. 1-year-old Angie
   d. 2-year-old Kenny

4. MAX is a system for coding facial expressions in infants. How many different distinct patterns can it identify?
   a. 12
   b. 27
   c. 63
   d. 92

5. Eva is watching her 18-month-old daughter Bailey walk on a rail at the park. Eva looks fearful, and Bailey stops walking on the rail and sits down, reaching for her mother because she is now feeling scared, too. Bailey has engaged in
   a. mirror neurons.
   b. positive affectivity.
   c. social referencing.
   d. reciprocity.

6. Andrew is a very fussy baby. He is easily over-stimulated and displays fear over the smallest incidents. Andrew is high on
   a. positive affectivity.
   b. negative affectivity.
   c. effectance.
   d. social referencing.

7. Children who are characteristically shy, fearful, or timid are
   a. difficult children.
   b. inhibited children.
   c. securely attached.
   d. disorganized in their temperament.

8. Which of the following is NOT an explanation offered by your text for temperament's influence on cognitive development?
   a. Infants who are temperamentally positive approach tasks more constructively.
   b. Parents interact more positively with more sociable infants, which promotes their cognitive development.
   c. Sociable infants tolerate strange examiners better, thus scoring higher on cognitive tests.
   d. Smarter parents tend to have more sociable infants.

9. The environmental context in which our species evolved is called by Bowlby the
   a. environment of evolutionary adaptedness.
   b. goodness of fit.
   c. secure base.
   d. sensitive period.

10. At what age do infants typically begin to show stranger wariness?
    a. 2 months
    b. 6 months
    c. 10 months
    d. 18 months

11. Nancy is an infant participating in a study of attachment. The experimenter is using the Strange Situation to measure Nancy's attachment to her mom. When Nancy and her mom first come into the room, Nancy explores it and sticks a little closer to mom when the stranger enters the room. When her mom leaves the room, Nancy cries and bangs on the door her mom left through. When her mom returns, she wants to be cuddled. When her mom leaves again, Nancy cries harder and when she comes back the second time, Nancy is more vehement in her desire to be held and cuddled by her mother. Nancy probably has a(n) _____ attachment.
    a. secure
    b. insecure-ambivalent
    c. insecure-avoidant
    d. disorganized

12. When an infant learns that a caregiver can be counted on to respond when given a signal, the infant has established
    a. secondary emotions.
    b. goodness of fit.
    c. reciprocity.
    d. trust.

13. The gratification derived from touch is called
    a. effectance.
    b. social referencing.
    c. attachment.
    d. contact comfort.

14. Which of the following is true about the effects of day care on attachment?

    a.   The proportion of secure attachments is higher for children who stay home with their mothers than who go to day care.

    b.   The proportion of secure attachments is lower for children who stay home with their mothers than who go to day care.

    c.   Mothers whose infants spend long hours in day care tend to be more sensitive to their child's needs when they are with the child.

    d.   Mothers whose infants spend long hours in day care tend to be less sensitive to their child's needs when they are with the child.

15. All things equal, which of the following activities is a father most likely to do with his infant son rather than infant daughter?

    a.   Snuggle and read a book

    b.   Tickle and giggle

    c.   Peek-a-boo

    d.   Shop for clothes

Quiz 2

Use this quiz to reassess your learning after taking Quiz 1 and reviewing the chapter.

1. Biologically based sources of individual differences in behavioral functioning in infants are called

    a.   temperament.

    b.   attachment.

    c.   emotions.

    d.   mirror neurons.

2. Which of the following is an example of a primary emotion?

    a.   Guilt

    b.   Sadness

    c.   Embarrassment

    d.   Envy

3. Which of the following behaviors signals infant interest?

    a.   Slumped posture

    b.   Turning away

    c.   Trying to duplicate an experience

    d.   Sitting very still

4. Cells in the brain that are activated when we do something and when we see someone else do the same thing are called

    a.   inhibited.

    b.   secure.

    c.   mirror neurons.

    d.   evolutionarily adapted.

5. Which of the following is NOT one of the benefits of using parental report as a measure of infant temperament?

    a.   They are highly insightful reports.

    b.   They are highly detailed reports.

    c.   They are highly unbiased reports.

    d.   They are based on long-term experience with the child.

6. What percent of difficult infants go on to develop behavior problems later in childhood?
    a. 18%
    b. 30%
    c. 50%
    d. 70%

7. The match between a child's temperament and his or her environmental demands is called
    a. social referencing.
    b. goodness of fit.
    c. effectance.
    d. a strange situation.

8. Two-year-old Royce's mother is leaving for work. When she gets ready to walk out the door and leave him with his nanny, he cries and calls for "Mommy." Royce is engaged in a(n)
    a. stranger wariness.
    b. separation protest.
    c. attachment crisis.
    d. social referencing.

9. What is the earliest age at which an infant might likely begins discriminating the attachment figure by whom they prefer to be comforted?
    a. 1 month
    b. 2 months
    c. 6 months
    d. 7 months

10. Kendall's mother has just left him in the Strange Situation. He doesn't seem to mind her leaving, and when she returns, he won't let her hold him. In fact, he actively ignores her. Kendall may have a(n)_____ attachment.
    a. secure
    b. insecure-ambivalent
    c. insecure-avoidant
    d. disorganized

11. Learning that one's behavior can affect the behavior of others in a consistent and predictable fashion is called
    a. effectance.
    b. reciprocity.
    c. trust.
    d. contact comfort.

12. Valerie is a 19-month-old infant who is in a new doctor's office with her mother. Valerie toddles around and looks at magazines and other objects in the office, returning to her mother from time to time to show her something or share a smile. Valerie is using her mother as a(n)
    a. contact comfort.
    b. mirror neuron.
    c. secure base.
    d. point of separation.

13. In Harlow's classic study of motherless monkeys, what finding was observed?
    a. The monkeys preferred the wire mother because she had the bottle.
    b. The monkeys preferred the contact comfort of the cloth mother.
    c. The monkeys preferred the wire and cloth mother equally.
    d. The monkeys developed normal social skills.

14. The amount of time that mothers spend with infants is

   a.   greater than the amount of time that a father is likely to spend with his infant child.
   b.   equal to the amount of time that a father is likely to spend with his infant child.
   c.   less than the amount of time that a father is likely to spend with his infant child.
   d.   greater than the amount of time a father will spend in individualist cultures only.

15. Why do psychologists believe that self-control is better in children who are raised in a home with their two biological parents than in homes with step-parents or single parents?

   a.   Two biological parents love the child more and invest more time in him or her.
   b.   Two biological parents are more disciplined than step-parents or single parents.
   c.   The amount of stress is greater in households with step- or single-parents.
   d.   All of these

ANSWERS TO FILL-IN-THE-BLANKS KEY TERMS

1. attachments (see introductory section)

2. Trust (see Attachment and Infant Social Development)

3. positive affectivity (see Infant Temperament)

4. Goodness of fit (see Infant Temperament)

5. social referencing (see Infants' Emotions)

6. environment of evolutionary adaptedness (see Attachment and Infant Social Development)

7. Strange Situation (see Attachment and Infant Social Development)

8. Effectance (see Attachment and Infant Social Development)

9. Primary emotions (see Infants' Emotions)

10. contact comfort (see Parental Behavior and Interaction with Infants)

ANSWERS TO MULTIPLE-CHOICE QUESTIONS

Circle the question numbers you answered incorrectly.

Quiz 1

1. *b is the answer.*   Emotions are strong, informative cues as to one's current state. (see introductory section)

2. *a is the answer.*   Emotional expression is the ability to communicate how one is feeling using facial expressions, gestures, and vocalizations. Anna is good at conveying how she is feeling to her mom. (see Infants' Emotions)

3. *d is the answer.*   Secondary emotions rely on higher mental functioning and thus tend not to emerge until the second or third year of life. Kenny is the oldest child in this list, and he is only 2 years old, so he is the most likely to feel a secondary emotion. (see Infants' Emotions)

4. *b is the answer.*   MAX allows users to identify 27 distinct facial patterns either alone or in combination. (see Infants' Emotions)

5. *c is the answer.*   Social referencing is the ability to use another's emotional expressions to interpret ambiguous events. Bailey didn't realize that climbing on the rail and walking on it were scary, but her mom's expression signaled that to her. At that point, Bailey also interpreted the activity as scary. (see Infants' Emotions)

6.   *b is the answer.*   Negative affectivity is a dimension of behavior that indicates the degree to which a person feels distressed. Andrew displays fear and upset easily, which indicates that he is distressed easily.   (see Infant Temperament)

7.   *b is the answer.*   Inhibited children are characteristically shy, fearful or timid. (see Infant Temperament)

8.   *d is the answer.*   There is no evidence cited in your text to suggest that smart parents have more sociable children. (see Infant Temperament)

9.   *a is the answer.*   The environment of evolutionary adaptedness refers to the environmental context in which our species evolved. (see Attachment and Infant Social Development)

10.   *c is the answer.*   Infants usually begin to show stranger wariness around 10 months of age. (see Attachment and Infant Social Development)

11.   *a is the answer.*   Secure attachments are categorized as such in the Strange Situation when the infant uses the parent as a secure base from which to explore the environment, drawing closer to the parent in the presence of the stranger, seems sad to have the parent leave and happy to have them return. Nancy has displayed all of these patterns. (see Attachment and Infant Social Development)

12.   *d is the answer.*   Trust is established when the infant learns that the caregiver will respond when signaled. (see Attachment and Infant Social Development)

13.   *d is the answer.*   The gratification derived from touch is called contact comfort (see Parental Behavior and Interaction with Infants)

14.   *d is the answer.*   Although the proportion of secure attachments is similar for children in day care versus those who stay home with their mothers, long hours in day care do seem to adversely affect the sensitivity of the parenting. (see Parental Behavior and Interaction with Infants)

15.   *b is the answer.*   Fathers tend to play more boisterous activities with their sons than their daughters. Tickling is the most "boisterous" activity on this list. (see Parental Behavior and Interaction with Infants)

Now turn to the quiz analysis table at the end of this chapter to find which areas you know well and which areas you need to work on. Circle the numbers in the table for items on Quiz 1 that you answered correctly.

Quiz 2

1.   *a is the answer.*   Temperament refers to those biologically based sources of individual differences in behavioral functioning. (see introductory section)

2.   *b is the answer.* Sadness is the only example that is a primary emotion. The other examples—embarrassment, envy, and guilt—all involve understanding another person's perspective (e.g., that they see you and think you look funny, that you did something wrong, etc.). Emotions that require those higher cognitive skills are considered secondary. (see Infants' Emotions)

3.   *d is the answer.* Infants tend to sit very still when they are interested in an event. (see Infants' Emotions)

4. *c is the answer.*   Mirror neurons are in the brain and they are activated both when we perform an action, and when we observe someone else perform that same action. (see Infants' Emotions)

5. *c is the answer.*   Parents can provide detailed, insightful descriptions of their child's temperament that are grounded in long-term experience, but the down side of using such measures is that parental report can be biased. Unbiased reporting is not a benefit of using parental reports as measures of temperament. (see Infant Temperament)

6. *d is the answer.*   Seventy percent of difficult infants go on to develop behavior problems later in childhood. (see Infant Temperament)

7. *b is the answer.*   Goodness of fit refers to the match between a child's temperament and his or her environmental demands. (see Infant Temperament)

8. *b is the answer.*   Separation protest is characterized by crying, and is aimed at making attachment figures return. Royce cries and calls for his mother *before* she leaves with the intent that she will hear his protests and not leave for work, thus returning to him. (see Attachment and Infant Social Development)

9. *b is the answer.*   Between 2 and 7 months of age infants begin to discriminate in their sociability, recognizing specific people and preferring their familiar caregivers. Two months would be the earliest age at which such discrimination is likely. (see Attachment and Infant Social Development)

10. *c is the answer.*   Kendall likely has an insecure-avoidant attachment. Such an attachment is characterized in the Strange Situation by little concern with the parent's absence, and actively avoiding and ignoring the parent upon return. (see Attachment and Infant Social Development)

11. *a is the answer.*   Effectance is the lesson in social interaction that one's behavior can affect the behavior of others in a predictable fashion.

12. *c is the answer.*   A secure base is a trustworthy place, or person, that infants can access as needed when they are engaged in exploration. Valerie is exploring the new doctor's office, and accessing her mother periodically for reassurance. (see Attachment and Infant Social Development)

13. *b is the answer.*   Although both the wire and cloth mother had bottles in this study, the monkeys strongly preferred the cloth mother and spend much of their time clinging to it. (see Parental Behavior and Interaction with Infants)

14. *a is the answer.*   Almost anywhere in the world, mothers are likely to spend more time with their infants than fathers do. (see Parental Behavior and Interaction with Infants)

15. *c is the answer.*   Stress is posited to be the underlying cause for self-control being better in children who are raised with two biological parents. Such households likely have lower stress levels than households with step parents or single parents. Stress can undermine these parents' abilities to interact with infants in healthy ways that promote the development of self-control.

Now turn to the quiz analysis table at the end of this chapter to find which areas you know well and which areas you need to work on. Circle the numbers in the table for items on Quiz 2 that you answered correctly.

For each question you answered correctly, circle its number. (Quiz 1 numbers are not shaded; Quiz 2 numbers are shaded.) Are there patterns in the types of questions or the topics you got wrong that could direct your further study? Did you improve from Quiz 1 to Quiz 2?

QUIZ REVIEW

Topic	Type of Question		
	Definition	**Comprehension**	**Application**
Introductory section	1		
	1		
Infants' Emotions		4	2, 3, 5
	4	2, 3	
Infant Temperament	7	8	6
	7	5, 6	
Attachment and Infant Social Development	9, 12	10	11
	11	9	8, 10, 12
Parental Behavior and Interaction with Infants	13	14, 15	
		13, 14, 15	

Total correct by quiz:

Quiz 1:	
Quiz 2:	

CHAPTER 7

Physical Development in Early Childhood

LEARNING OBJECTIVES

1. Describe normative development (the typical body size and physical skills) in early childhood.

2. Explain how heredity, nutrition, physical health, and exercise influence physical development in early childhood.

3. Explain how synaptogenesis, synaptic pruning, and myelination contribute to the development of the brain in early childhood.

4. Describe how mirror neurons help young children to learn new skills.

5. List the order in which different structures develop in the brain during early childhood, and explain how their development affects children's abilities and behaviors.

6. Describe how the stage of brain development makes it possible for a child to experience something new, and how the experience itself influences further brain development.

7. Describe the nature, nurture, and interactionist views of motor development in children.

8. Show how maturation and environmental factors contribute to the development of gross motor skills.

9. Describe how fine motor skills such as drawing and writing develop throughout early childhood.

10. Show how culture affects a child's acquisition of fine motor skills.

11. List the most common causes of illness, injury, and death in early childhood.

12. Describe the interventions that would be most likely to reduce worldwide child mortality.

13. Explain the functions of sleep.

14. List children's most common sleep problems, and the steps parents can take to help their children get a good night's sleep.

15. Discuss how children's temperaments, attachment styles, and environments affect their stress levels, and explain how physiological stress levels are measured in children.

16. Explain how abuse in early childhood affects children's ability to read and process emotions.

17. Explain how severe neglect in early childhood affects children's ability to read and process emotions.

18. Describe the range of autism spectrum disorders.

OUTLINE

I. Physical Growth and Development
    The rate of growth slows from infancy into early childhood.

105

A.   Pattern of Normative Growth

1.   Early studies of physical growth established **norms,** or standards, for what is typical size for different ages. These study results were used to create *growth curve tables* of **normative development**, which establish growth in early childhood as slow but steady, a pattern that persists across cultures.

2.   Although the growth curve is smooth on average, examination of individual growth patterns is a stop-and-start proposition. Periods of growth alternate with periods of little to no growth.

B.   **Individual Differences**

1.   Although healthy babies all look relatively similar in size and shape, during early childhood we see more variance in physical development.

2.   The **Body Mass Index (BMI)** helps to discern if a child is over or under weight. It is calculated by taking the child's weight (in kilograms) and dividing it by the child's height (in meters). An average child's BMI is at the 50th percentile. Children in the 85th–94th percentile are considered "overweight," and those over the 95th percentile are considered obese. Children in the 5th percentile or lower are considered underweight for their height.

3.   Heredity plays a big role in a person's BMI, but another significant influence is the role of diet and nutrition. Improvements in diet and nutrition account for increases in weight and height over the past 100 years.

C.   Diet and Nutrition

1.   During early childhood, children's appetites decrease, and they graduate to adult food from baby food.

2.   Preschoolers can be very picky eaters, but they usually will accept new foods within 8 to 15 exposures. How much they eat at each meal can also vary widely. Asking a child to clean his/her plate can simply train them not to reflect on their own internal hunger cues.

3.   The danger of not attending to hunger cues is overeating, ultimately leading a child to become **obese**. Childhood obesity is troubling because increasingly related health problems are occurring in younger kids.

4.   Parents can minimize the chances of childhood obesity in their offspring by offering healthy meal and snack times, not pressuring kids to eat, not using food as a bribe or entertainment source, encouraging active play and limiting sedentary play, and serving as a good role model.

II.   Brain Development

During early childhood, the brain matures in structure and function. By way of review, the brain is composed of **neurons,** which have both **axons** and **dendrites**, which help to bridge the **synapses**. As messages travel to the end of the synapse, chemicals called neurotransmitters are released.

A.   Improvement in the Brain's Communication Network

1.   **Synaptogenesis**, the creation of new synapses, peaks at age 1 but continues into childhood.

2.   The selective elimination of some synapses, called **synaptic pruning**, peaks during early childhood and helps make the brain more efficient.

3.   **Myelination** also improves connections and communication within the brain. **Myelin** is the white, fatty substance that wraps around axons and speeds neural transmission. Myelination during early childhood focuses on connections of the cerebellum to the cerebral cortex, which accounts for the improvement in balance and coordination in children as they mature in early childhood. The same is true for the areas of the brain that govern hand-eye coordination, as well.

B.   Mirror Neurons
Mirror neurons are neurons that fire when action is performed as well as when one observes an action being performed. The presence of these neurons helps explain how one can learn effectively through observation.

C.   Brain Anatomy
1.   **Lateralization** occurs as the two hemispheres of the brain not only control different sides of the body, but actually specialize in separate functions. The left hemisphere is especially active during early childhood, corresponding to the development of language. At the same time, the **corpus callosum** develops rapidly during early childhood, allowing the two hemispheres to communicate and coordinate more effectively.
2.   Handedness, which usually emerges by five years of age, is a sign of lateralization.
3.   The **frontal lobes** are the area of the brain that develops the most during early childhood. This area is responsible for "executive function"—planning, organizing, problem-solving, regulating emotion, and so forth.
     a)   The Go/No-Go task illustrates the development of the frontal lobes at different ages during early childhood. The child is instructed to push a green "Go" button if they see a picture of something specific, and to not push the button (the "No-Go" response) if they do not see the picture of that (similar to Simon Says).
     b)   At the beginning of early childhood, toddlers have difficulty suppressing the "Go" response. By the end of early childhood, most children may make a few mistakes, but understand and are able to suppress the "Go" response when appropriate.
     c)   Ability to suppress an initial response and choose another response is called **effortful processing**. This skill noticeably emerges during early childhood, supported by frontal lobe development.

D.   Brain Plasticity
1.   **Brain plasticity** is the degree to which the brain can be altered by experience. Plasticity varies greatly over the lifespan, with the effects of experience on the brain depending on the age at which that experience occurs.
2.   **Sensitive periods** illustrate this shifting relationship. For example, consider the condition of **strabismus**, which occurs when eyes are not aligned properly at birth. It can be corrected with eye-glasses up to the age of 4 or 5, but after that, it cannot be corrected and normal three-dimensional depth perception does not develop. Language development illustrates another sensitive period, with early and middle childhood being the times the brain is most ripe to acquire language.
3.   Experience does not just happen, but interacts with the brain itself. For example, a 2-year-old reading a book enjoys picture recognition, while a 5-year-old reading the same book may be sounding out the printed letters.
4.   **Hemispherectomy**, a surgery in which half of the brain is removed, illustrates plasticity, as well. Most patients for this surgery are very young, and go on to live relatively normal lives. Although a significant "experience," the brain is plastic enough at a young age to cope with and adapt to the changes the surgery entail.

III.   Motor Development
Gross motor skills require large movements of the arms, legs, and feet or the whole body (e.g., running). **Fine motor skills** require smaller movements of the hands and fingers (e.g., tying shoes). Development of both sets of skills is linked to perception and cognition.

A. Theories of Motor Development
   1. Arnold Gesell held that development was the result of **maturation**, with the emergence of new skills following a genetic timetable and blueprint.
   2. In contrast, learning theory proponents such as John B. Watson argued that development was the result of learning experiences.
   3. Myrtle McGraw argued that both were important. This interactionist perspective saw experience as valuable when it matched the neurological and muscular maturity of the child.
B. Gross Motor Skills
   1. Arnold Gesell and his colleagues were the first to catalog the development of gross motor skills in childhood and develop normative standards. Physical therapists use these standards to assess if a child is developing normally. Although tests of gross motor skills (such as the Bayley Scales of Infant Development) do not predict later achievement, low scores can indicate a developmental problem.
   2. Like physical growth charts, gross motor development charts appear as a smooth curve, but individual development may straddle two stages of skill acquisition, and even revert backwards from time to time.
   3. Motor development must be studied in context. The environment in which a child develops determines the challenges he or she will have access to, and can support or impede the acquisition of gross motor skills.
C. Fine Motor Skills
   Like gross motor development, fine motor development depends in part on culture and experience.

   1. Drawing
      a) Drawing is a fine motor skill that emerges in early childhood in many cultures. Toddlers seem to focus on the activity of drawing itself rather than the product of drawing. Around age 3, children begin to try to draw recognizable objects. By age 5 or 6, the drawings are more detailed and accurate.
      b) Some developmentalists argue that drawing is a natural activity—wired into the brain. Others argue drawing takes practice and instruction.
      c) Interest in drawing usually fades within middle childhood, as children become increasingly aware of the importance of "getting it right" and at the same time lack the training to do so.
   2. Writing is another fine motor skill that emerges in early childhood. It begins as scribbles, but by age four a child can pay attention to the printed word, distinguish writing from non-writing, and recognize and copy individual letters.
IV. Physical Health
   A. Injuries and Illness
      1. Unintentional injury is the leading cause of death in early childhood in the United States, with drowning leading the list. Although accidents may be part of childhood, death and serious injury from such accidents are avoidable with proper precautions. Adequate supervision coupled with the appropriate safety equipment has dramatically decreased the number of deaths due to unintentional injury during early childhood.
      2. Unintentional injury is a leading cause of death in part because immunization programs in the United States have almost eliminated diseases like polio and measles that used to result in children's deaths. Yet these programs are not being adequately maintained, with noticeable income disparities between those

children who are fully immunized and those who are not. Parents may fail to immunize their children because of lack of healthcare, or because they believe the immunizations may be dangerous.

3. Minor illnesses are part of childhood, although rarely serious. Minor infections are often spread by contact with other children, as in a childcare setting. These exposures can serve to boost immunity, however. A major risk of the common upper respiratory infection is that it will result in a middle ear infection, called *otitis media*. Such infections can make hearing difficult, leading to social isolation. Hand washing with soap and water is the best defense against these minor illnesses of childhood.

B. Mortality and Malnutrition

1. Childhood mortality is relatively low in the United States, but quite high in developing nations, often due to preventable and treatable infections.

2. In 2000, the United Nations Millennium Declaration set goals for reducing childhood mortality using well-known, cost-effective strategies such as immunizations. Some progress has been made, yet wide disparities still exist.

3. Malnutrition is one of the underlying causes of death of children under the age of five. Malnutrition is not just lack of food. **Kwashiorkor** involves not receiving enough protein or calories, but **marasmus** involves sufficient calories but insufficient protein. Failure to get other micronutrients can also result in malnutrition.

4. Poverty is also a factor linked to childhood mortality.

C. Sleep and Sleep Problems

1. Sleep patterns change in early childhood. Two- and three-year-olds sleep 12–13 hours daily, but four- to six-year-olds only 10–11 hours.

2. Common sleep problems in early childhood include difficulty falling asleep, nighttime waking, and night terrors.

3. Scientists believe that sleep is important because it may help young children learn about their bodies, it allows the brain to recharge, it helps to consolidate memories, and because it is the time when the growth hormone is released.

4. Regular bedtime rituals and routines, consistent sleep schedules, and a quiet time before lights out all help young children sleep better.

D. Stress in Early Childhood

1. When humans are stressed, the level of the hormone **cortisol** in the bloodstream increases. A "spit test" that measures the level of cortisol in the saliva can help researchers discern what situations are stressful to young children.

2. Temperament affects cortisol levels, with higher levels in children who have trouble regulating emotion, who are fearful of unfamiliar situation, and who have difficulty playing with peers.

3. Attachment security also affects cortisol levels, with secure attachments buffering the child from the higher cortisol levels when starting a new childcare arrangement.

4. The quality of the childcare arrangement itself is also related to cortisol levels. Poor quality care is associated with cortisol levels increasing over the day, while high quality care is associated with cortisol levels decreasing over the day.

E. Physical Abuse and Neglect

1. Maltreatment in childhood seems to have effects long after the abuse has stopped. Evidence suggests that this may be because such early patterns become part of one's biological makeup.

2. Abused children are more sensitive to anger cues than non-abused children. Emotional experiences that occur while the brain is still plastic can have

long-lasting effects. In a dangerous environment where adults are unpredictable, being sensitive to anger cues can be adaptive because it gives a child time to hide or strike out. In more stable situations, however, this skill becomes maladaptive and is viewed as "oversensitivity." It is not clear if children can "unlearn" these responses.

3. Neglect involves having few interactions with adults, rather than being exposed to physical harm. Children sent to Romanian orphanages were tragically confined to cribs without much adult or peer interaction, and upon adoption, had difficulty identifying any emotions.

F. Autism Spectrum Disorder

1. **Autism Spectrum Disorders (ASD)** range from mild physical and social awkwardness (Asperger Syndrome) to severe motor and mental disabilities (Childhood Disintegrative Disorder). Children with ASD have problems with social interaction, verbal and nonverbal communication, and repetitive behavior.

2. Children with ASD need consistency in their environment. They tend not to engage in pretend play, and lack a *theory of mind*, which is the understanding that other people have different thoughts and perspectives from one's own.

3. Although ASD diagnoses have increased, researchers argue this is largely because the definition of ASD has been expanded to include more behavior than it used to, and because the public is more aware of the syndrome and thus parents report concerns related to ASD more frequently.

4. Scientists are looking for the origins of ASD, as well as ways to treat it. Some forms of autism can be inherited via Fragile X Syndrome and Rett's Syndrome. No cure exists, but children with ASD do benefit from behavioral therapy.

KEY TERMS

1. **Norms** are standards for what is "typical" at different ages, often used in constructing or interpreting tests. (see Physical Growth and Development)

2. **Normative development** is a pattern of development that is typical, or average. (see Physical Growth and Development)

3. **Individual differences** is the variation among individuals on a characteristic. (see Physical Growth and Development)

4. **Body Mass Index (BMI)** is calculated by dividing weight (measured in kilograms) by height (measured in meters) squared, or wt/ht^2. (see Physical Growth and Development)

5. Being **obese** involves having a body mass index that is at the 90th percentile or higher for one's age. (see Physical Growth and Development)

6. **Neurons** are cells that carry information across the body and brain, as well as back and forth within the brain. (see Brain Development)

7. **Dendrites** are antenna-like extensions of neurons that pick up signals from other neurons. (see Brain Development)

8. **Axons** are the part of the cell that carries signals away from the cell body toward other neurons. (see Brain Development)

9. **Synapses** are junctions between neurons where axons and dendrites are in close proximity. (see Brain Development)

10. **Synaptogenesis** is the creation of new synapses. (see Brain Development)

11. **Synaptic pruning** is the selective elimination of some synapses; also referred to as "competitive elimination." (see Brain Development)

12. **Myelination** is the process through which cell axons become sheathed in myelin. (see Brain Development)

13. **Myelin** is a fatty substance that wraps itself around the axon, providing insulation and improving transmission. (see Brain Development)

14. **Mirror neurons** are a type of brain cell that fires when an action is performed by another. (see Brain Development)

15. **Lateralization** is the fact that each hemisphere of the brain specializes in certain functions. (see Brain Development)

16. The **corpus callosum** is a brain structure which connects and coordinates the brain's left and right hemispheres. (see Brain Development)

17. **Frontal lobes,** sometimes called the "executive" of the brain, are responsible for planning and organizing new actions, problem solving, and regulating emotions, as well as focusing attention. (see Brain Development)

18. **Effortful control** is ability to withhold a first response and choose another. (see Brain Development)

19. **Brain plasticity** is the degree to which the brain can be altered by experience. (see Brain Development)

20. **Sensitive Period** is a time in development during which the organism is especially open to environmental influence. (see Brain Development)

21. **Strabismus** is a condition in which a child's eyes are crossed toward the nose or veer toward the ears. If not corrected by eyeglasses before age five, the child will not develop normal depth perception. (see Brain Development)

22. **Hemispherectomy** is a surgery in which one hemisphere of the brain (half the brain) is removed. (see Brain Development)

23. **Gross motor skills** are abilities required to control the large movements of the arms, legs, and feet, or the whole body, such as running, jumping, climbing, and throwing. (see Motor Development)

24. **Fine motor skills** are abilities required to control smaller movements of the hand and fingers, such as picking up small objects and tying one's shoes. (see Motor Development)

25. **Maturation** is growth that proceeds by a genetic timetable. (see Motor Development)

26. **Kwashiorkor** is a form of malnutrition in which individuals have an adequate intake of calories, but an inadequate intake of protein. (see Physical Health)

27. **Marasmus** is a form of malnutrition in which individuals are not receiving enough protein or enough calories. (see Physical Health)

28. **Cortisol** is a hormone secreted when individuals are exposed to stress. (see Physical Health)

29. **Autism Spectrum Disorder (ASD)** is a disorder that can range from mild to severe, characterized by problems with social interaction, verbal and nonverbal communication, and repetitive behavior. (see Physical Health)

FILL-IN-THE-BLANKS KEY TERMS

This section will help you check your knowledge of the key terms introduced in this chapter. Fill in each blank with the appropriate term from the list of key terms in the previous section.

1.   _____ are responsible for planning and organizing new actions, problem solving, and regulating emotions, as well as focusing attention.

2.   Standards for what is "typical" at different ages, often used in constructing or interpreting tests, are called _____.

3.   _____ is the hormone secreted when individuals are exposed to stress.

4.   _____ are abilities required to control the large movements of the arms, legs, and feet, or the whole body, such as running, jumping, climbing, and throwing.

5.   The degree to which the brain can be altered by experience is referred to as _____.

6.   _____ is growth that proceeds by a genetic timetable.

7.   _____ is calculated by dividing weight (measured in kilograms) by height (measured in meters) squared.

8.   _____ is a disorder that can range from mild to severe, characterized by problems with social interaction, verbal and nonverbal communication, and repetitive behavior.

9.   _____ is the creation of new synapses.

10.   The type of brain cell that fires an action potential when an action is performed by another individual is called a _____.

APPLIED LEARNING AND CRITICAL THINKING

It is one thing to read about physical development in early childhood, and another to actually observe it. Finding situations that allow you to apply the findings you read about also gives you a chance to see if those findings actually bear out in your observations. Indeed, in the behavioral sciences (developmental science included), research findings are often based on the "average" behavior of a group of participants and the probability that any particular participant will behave within a particular range of possibilities. This basis for predicting behavior will often be correct, but there are certainly many individual differences. Finding real-world settings gives you a chance to test the degree to which the findings apply in a particular setting, and to think critically about why they may not if your own observations of preschoolers fail to conform to the predicted pattern.

1.   Parents of small children who have been diagnosed on the autistic spectrum often have difficulty finding suitable childcare to give them much-needed breaks. Autistic children require a great deal of consistency, and parents of such children spend a lot of time implementing behavioral interventions to help them develop better communication skills, social awareness, and social skills. A great opportunity for service-learning is to find parents of children on the autistic spectrum and offer to babysit or help implement some of the behavioral programs they have from the therapists with whom they work. You will learn a lot about the variability in behavior amongst autistic children, be able to assess your ability to work with such children day in and day out, as well as be providing a valuable service.

2. Your text provides you with the range of BMI scores for 4-year-olds in the United States in Figure 7.3. Think about the children you know who are that age, and if you know their parents well enough, ask them for the weight and height of those 4-year-olds. If they provide that information in pounds or inches, you can easily convert these data to metric by multiplying weight in pounds times 2.2 to yield weight in kilograms, and by multiplying their length in inches by .0254 to yield their length in meters. You can then use those conversions to calculate each child's BMI. What sort of percentile score do these children have for their BMI scores? Are any overweight? Underweight? What sort of factors can you think of that would explain BMI scores that are out of the "normal" range?

3. Many occupational, physical, and speech therapists work with children in early childhood. Consider trying to arrange a practicum experience with someone from this profession. If you like working with children, this sort of career is a great way to do so. Shadowing an occupational, physical, or speech therapist who works with preschoolers will give you a very concrete sense of what "working with children" entails. Many people like the idea of working with children, but find the day-to-day frustration of doing so less appealing than they had expected. Additionally, shadowing such a professional over an extended period of time will also allow you to see how therapists help to develop motor skills that facilitate basic life activities in early childhood, like speaking, eating, and walking.

4. Work with your instructor to develop an opportunity to administer the Bayley Scales of Infant Development to a preschooler. Administering tests like this is an important skill in being able to assess children and identify potential developmental delays. Following the testing directions to the letter is really important, and actually quite difficult to do, because many preschoolers don't follow the script! What parts of administering the test were most difficult? What parts went smoothly? How did the testing environment affect the child's performance? Do you think that the test scores are a true reflection of that child's abilities?

MULTIPLE-CHOICE QUESTIONS

Quiz 1

1. Standards of what are typical for different ages are called

    a. norms.
    b. individual differences.
    c. body mass indices.
    d. synapses.

2. At what percentile is a child considered overweight?

    a. The 5th percentile
    b. The 50th percentile
    c. The 85th percentile
    d. The 95th percentile

3. Just as a boat can carry supplies from one side of a river to another, _____ can carry information from one neuron across a space to the next neuron.

    a. axons
    b. dendrites
    c. synapses
    d. neurotransmitters

4.   Three-year-old Molly watches her mom work puzzles. Day after day she watches, until one day Molly seems to spontaneously pick up the puzzle pieces and work a 6-piece jigsaw puzzle on her own. What sorts of neurons are involved in Molly's ability to learn from watching her mother?

    a.   Corpus callosum neurons
    b.   Mirror neurons
    c.   Myelin neurons
    d.   Gross motor neurons

5.   Three-year-old Henry is playing *Simon Says* with his teacher and school friends. He seems to be having a really hard time getting the game. His teacher will give a string of commands preceded by "Simon Says," and then sneaks in a command that is NOT preceded by that phrase. Simon almost always messes up and performs the command, even though the teacher didn't say "Simon Says." Simon lacks

    a.   frontal lobes.
    b.   lateralization.
    c.   effortful control.
    d.   All of these

6.   What is the sensitive period for strabismus correction?

    a.   Up to age 2 or 3 years
    b.   Up to age 4 or 5 years
    c.   Up to age 7 or 8 years
    d.   Up to adolescence

7.   Which of the following skills is a fine motor skill?

    a.   Running
    b.   Swimming
    c.   Jumping
    d.   Drawing

8.   The view that the emergence of new skills is determined by a genetic timetable is called

    a.   maturation.
    b.   learning theory.
    c.   synaptic pruning.
    d.   synaptogenesis.

9.   Which of the following statements is true about the scores on the Bayley Scale?

    a.   Scores that are high indicate a propensity for extreme athleticism as a child grows.
    b.   The scores don't relate at all to one's future physical abilities.
    c.   Low scores warn that a child might have a developmental problem.
    d.   The scores predict future physical achievements in a linear fashion.

10. At what age do children begin to attempt to draw recognizable objects?

    a.   18 months to 2 years
    b.   Around 3 years of age
    c.   Around 4 years of age
    d.   5 to 6 years of age

11. Which type of accident is most likely to result in the death of a toddler?

    a.   Drowning
    b.   Automobile accident
    c.   Burns
    d.   Airway obstruction

12. Failure to receive enough protein and enough calories is called

    a.   kwashiorkor.

    b.   marasmus.

    c.   cortisol.

    d.   ASD.

13. Which of the following strategies will NOT help a child learn to fall to sleep on their own?

    a.   Bath, book, and snuggle before going to bed

    b.   Quiet time before lights out

    c.   Consistent bedtime

    d.   Rocking the child to sleep

14. Jana is in a day care with lots of turnover in staff throughout the day. The staff is minimally trained and tends to interact very little with the children, and there are a lot of kids in her class. Jana's cortisol level is likely to

    a.   decrease over the course of the day.

    b.   increase over the course of the day.

    c.   peak in the middle of the day and then decline.

    d.   rise and fall unpredictably throughout the day.

15. Children with mild physical and social awkwardness likely merit a diagnosis of

    a.   Asperger Syndrome.

    b.   ASD.

    c.   Childhood Disintegrative Disorder.

    d.   Fragile X Syndrome.

Quiz 2

Use this quiz to reassess your learning after taking Quiz 1 and reviewing the chapter.

1. Differences in psychological functioning that are seen among individuals of roughly the same chronological age are called

    a.   norms.

    b.   individual differences.

    c.   sensitive periods.

    d.   maturation.

2. Which of the following strategies will NOT help minimize a child's risk for overweight and obesity?

    a.   Pressuring the child to eat the healthy food that's available

    b.   Providing healthy food at meal and snack times

    c.   Not using food as a bribe

    d.   Encouraging active play

3. The junction between axons and dendrites in close proximity is called a

    a.   neurotransmitter.

    b.   synapse.

    c.   myelin.

    d.   mirror neuron.

4. At what age does synaptic pruning peak?

    a.   Infancy

    b.   Early childhood

    c.   Adolescence

    d.   Adulthood

5.   Which of the following is a sign of brain lateralization?

    a.   The fact that language acquisition seems easier during early childhood than other times

    b.   The fact that the window for correcting strabismus tends to close around age 5

    c.   The development of handedness

    d.   None of these

6.   Little Jason has developed severe seizures that have been uncontrolled by medication. His pediatrician has suggested a surgery that might help. The surgery is probably a(n)

    a.   synaptogenesis.

    b.   myelination.

    c.   laser treatment.

    d.   hemispherectomy.

7.   Which of the following is a gross motor skill?

    a.   Drawing

    b.   Eating

    c.   Tying shoes

    d.   Jumping rope

8.   Ali believes that child development is determined totally by the type of environment and experiences the child has. Ali probably ascribes to

    a.   the notion of maturation.

    b.   learning theory.

    c.   the Bayley Scales.

    d.   the idea of brain plasticity.

9.   The context in which motor development occurs is

    a.   influential on what skills are acquired at a particular juncture.

    b.   immaterial to when skills develop.

    c.   solely responsible for when and what skills develop.

    d.   Both b and c

10.   At what age does a child begin to pay attention to the printed word on a page?

    a.   1 year

    b.   2 years

    c.   3 years

    d.   4 years

11.   Immunizations in the United States

    a.   are given to all children on time.

    b.   are easily affordable.

    c.   are rare and not very helpful in reducing childhood mortality.

    d.   have nearly eliminated diseases such as polio.

12.   Protein deficiency without caloric deficiency is called

    a.   marasmus.

    b.   kwashiorkor.

    c.   strabismus.

    d.   BMI.

13.   Waking in a state of fright with no memory of why, is a condition known as

    a.   night terrors.

    b.   nightmares.

    c.   transitional object difficulty.

    d.   Fragile X Syndrome.

14. Which of the following is true of abused children's ability to identify emotions?
    a. They are more sensitive to all emotional cues.
    b. They are more sensitive to emotional cues related to happiness.
    c. They are more sensitive to emotional cues related to sadness.
    d. They are more sensitive to emotional cues related to anger.
15. Kristopher is waving to a neighbor walking by. The neighbor is across the street, not looking at him, and all the windows in the house are shut. Kristopher doesn't understand why the neighbor isn't waving back. This lack of awareness for the *neighbor's* perspective illustrates Kristopher's lack of
    a. a theory of mind.
    b. a Fragile X.
    c. cortisol.
    d. frontal lobes.

ANSWERS TO FILL-IN-THE-BLANKS KEY TERMS

1. Frontal lobes (see Brain Development)

2. norms (see Physical Growth and Development)

3. Cortisol (see Physical Health)

4. Gross motor skills (see Motor Skills)

5. brain plasticity (see Brain Development)

6. Maturation (see Motor Development)

7. Body Mass Index (BMI) (see Physical Growth and Development)

8. Autism Spectrum Disorder (ASD) (see Physical Health)

9. Synaptogenesis (see Brain Development)

10. mirror neuron (see Brain Development)

ANSWERS TO MULTIPLE-CHOICE QUESTIONS

Circle the question numbers you answered incorrectly.

Quiz 1

1. *a is the answer.*   Norms are standards for what is typical at different ages. The degree to which individuals vary from these average scores is referred to as individual differences. (see Physical Growth and Development)

2. *c is the answer.*   A child is considered overweight once they reach the 85th percentile up to the 94th percentile. At the 95th percentile, a child is considered obese. (see Physical Growth and Development)

3. *d is the answer.*   Neurotransmitters can carry messages from the axon of one neuron across the space of the synapse to the dendrite of the next neuron. (see Brain Development)

4. *b is the answer.*   Mirror neurons fire when a child observes another having an experience or performing an activity. As such, they allow a child to learn by watching rather than by having to always do an activity themselves. (see Brain Development)

5.   *c is the answer.*   Effortful control is the ability to suppress an initial response (e.g., perform the command the teacher says) in favor of a second response (realizing she didn't say Simon Says and so I should do nothing). The development of the frontal lobes allows a child to increase effortful control, but Henry always has frontal lobes even when they are not well developed yet.   (see Brain Development)

6.   *b is the answer.*   If strabismus is not corrected by age 4 or 5, normal three-dimensional vision does not develop. The sensitive period for correction of strabismus, thus, is up to age 4 or 5. (see Brain Development)

7.   *d is the answer.*   Drawing is a fine motor skill that relies on the smaller movements of the hands and fingers. Running, swimming, and jumping all involve the larger movements of the whole body, and are considered gross motor skills. (see Motor Development)

8.   *a is the answer.*   Maturation is the notion that new skills emerge according to a genetic timetable. (see Motor Development)

9.   *c is the answer.*   Scores that are significantly below age norms indicate that a child may have developmental problems and further testing is called for. Other than that, the scores do not significantly predict future physical achievements. (see Motor Development)

10. *b is the answer.*   Around 3 years of age, children begin to try to draw recognizable objects. Prior to that, they tend to engage in scribbling. (see Motor Development)

11. *a is the answer.*   Drowning leads the list of unintended injury deaths among children aged 1 to 4. (see Physical Health)

12. *b is the answer.*   Marasmus is failure to receive sufficient protein and sufficient calories. (see Physical Health)

13. *d is the answer.*   Rocking the child to sleep will not help him or her learn to fall asleep on their own. It is better to snuggle and then lay them down *before* they fall asleep. (see Physical Health)

14. *b is the answer.*   Jana is in a low-quality day-care situation, and cortisol levels tend to increase across the day in children in such settings. (see Physical Health)

15. *a is the answer.*   Asperger Syndrome involves mild physical and social awkwardness. (see Physical Health)

Now turn to the quiz analysis table at the end of this chapter to find which areas you know well and which areas you need to work on. Circle the numbers in the table for items on Quiz 1 that you answered correctly.

Quiz 2

1.   *b is the answer.*   Individual differences refer to differences in psychological functioning that are seen among individuals of roughly the same chronological age. (see Physical Growth and Development)

2.   *a is the answer.*   Actually, pressuring the child to eat increases the risk of the child for overweight or obesity. (see Physical Growth and Development)

3.   *b is the answer.*   The synapse is the gap between the axon of one neuron and nearby dendrite of another neuron. (see Brain Development)

4.   *b is the answer.*   Synaptic pruning, or selective elimination of some synapses, begins in the early years and continues into young adulthood, peaking during early childhood. (see Brain Development)

5.   *c is the answer.*   Handedness is a sign of brain lateralization. For most right-handed individuals, the left hemisphere of the brain is used to process language information. For left-handed individuals, right hemisphere dominance is more frequent. (see Brain Development)

6.   *d is the answer.*   Hemispherectomy is a surgery in which one hemisphere of the brain is removed, usually performed when continuous seizures have been unable to be controlled with medication. (see Brain Development)

7.   *d is the answer.*   Jumping rope is the only activity on this list which involves movement of the whole body, which is what a gross motor skill is. (see Motor Development)

8.   *b is the answer.*   Learning theory is the idea that all development is shaped by experience in a particular environment, which is exactly what Ali is stated to believe in this question. (see Motor Development)

9.   *a is the answer.*   Context has a measurable impact on when and what motor skills develop, although genetic influences do as well. (see Motor Development)

10.   *d is the answer.*   Around age 4, children begin to attend to the printed word on the page. (see Motor Development)

11.   *d is the answer.*   Although immunizations have been quite successful at eliminating diseases like polio, they are not always affordable to families, and increasingly are not given on time. However, they are hardly rare. (see Physical Health)

12.   *b is the answer.*   Kwashiorkor is inadequate protein intake with adequate caloric intake. (see Physical Health)

13.   *a is the answer.*   Night terrors involve waking in a state of fright with no memory of why. (see Physical Health)

14.   *d is the answer.*   Abused children are more sensitive to anger cues, as such awareness was adaptive during the abusive situation. (see Physical Health)

15.   *a is the answer.*   Theory of mind is the ability to understand what other people perceive and know. Children on the autism spectrum show little progress in developing this skill, which normally emerges during early childhood. (see Physical Health)

Now turn to the quiz analysis table at the end of this chapter to find which areas you know well and which areas you need to work on. Circle the numbers in the table for items on Quiz 2 that you answered correctly.

For each question you answered correctly, circle its number. (Quiz 1 numbers are not shaded; Quiz 2 numbers are shaded.) Are there patterns in the types of questions or the topics you got wrong that could direct your further study? Did you improve from Quiz 1 to Quiz 2?

QUIZ REVIEW

Topic	Type of Question		
	Definition	**Comprehension**	**Application**
Physical Growth and Development	1	2	
	1	2	
Brain Development		3, 6	4, 5
	3	4, 5	6
Motor Development	8	9, 10	7
		9, 10	7, 8
Physical Health	12, 15	11, 13	14
	12, 13	11, 14	15

Total correct by quiz:

Quiz 1:	
Quiz 2:	

CHAPTER 8

Cognitive Development in Early Childhood

LEARNING OBJECTIVES

1. Describe the characteristic thinking processes and limitations of children in Jean Piaget's preoperational period.

2. Explain Piaget's perspective on how cognitive growth occurs in children.

3. Describe current psychological views challenging Piaget's ideas about cognitive development in early childhood.

4. Define "theory of mind" and explain how children develop a theory of mind.

5. Describe how children learn about symbols and representation.

6. Show how Lev Vygotsky's Zone of Proximal Development explains children's cognitive development.

7. Compare and contrast Piaget's and Vygotsky's views on the role of language in the cognitive development of children.

8. Show how children's improving ability to focus their attention contributes to their cognitive development.

9. Describe the three steps in memory processing (sensory memory, short-term memory, and long-term memory) suggested by the information processing model of cognitive development.

10. Describe the three basic types of long-term memory, and the factors that influence their accuracy and longevity.

11. Explain how both innate abilities and experience may contribute to children's development of language.

12. List the stages of language development in children.

13. Define syntax, semantics, and pragmatics.

14. Describe the development of literacy in children, and explain how adults can encourage this process.

15. Describe the four basic mathematical concepts that preschoolers generally master.

16. Describe the three most common child-care arrangements.

17. Describe the factors that make up quality child care, and explain how they are measured.

18. Describe the short-term and long-term effects of early childhood education programs.

OUTLINE

I. Piaget's Theory: The Preoperational Period

Piaget saw the **preoperational period** as the second stage of cognitive development. He viewed children's thinking during this period from age 2 to about age 7 as qualitatively different from cognition in older and younger children.

A.   Accomplishments of the Preoperational Period
   1.   During the preoperational period, children gain the ability to hold symbolic representations of objects and events that are not in the "here and now." One notable consequence of this ability is language acquisition, with words functioning as **symbols**.
   2.   **Pretend play** is another example of symbolic representation, with a block standing for a telephone or truck, for example. **Deferred imitation** of actions another has produced also illustrates the child's acquisition of symbolic representational skills.

B.   Gaps in Preoperational Thinking
   1.   In spite of gains in symbolic representation, children in the preoperational period continue to struggle with logical operations such as **reversibility** (understanding that an item that has been changed can return to its original state by reversing the process) and **classification** (understanding that items can be grouped along multiple dimensions at the same time).
   2.   Additionally, children in the preoperational period are unable to grasp **conservation**, the notion that some characteristics of an object do not change in spite of changes in form or appearance. Children struggle with this in a variety of forms, including *conservation of volume*, *conservation of mass*, and *conservation of number*. They struggle with these tasks for several reasons, including that they focus solely on appearance, and think about the object in terms of one dimension, which Piaget called *centration*. Finally, lack of a sense of reversibility hinders the child's ability to understand conservation, as well.
   3.   Children in the preoperational period do not take into account other points of view and perspectives, a characteristic Piaget called **egocentrism**. Piaget used the *three mountain task* to illustrate egocentrism.
   4.   Preoperational children fail to discriminate between human and non-human perspectives, ascribing thoughts, motives, feelings and so forth to inanimate objects. Piaget called this **animism**.

C.   Can Parents and Teachers Accelerate Logical Thinking in Preschoolers?
   1.   Piaget felt that parents and teachers could not accelerate logical thinking in preschoolers, and that to attempt to do so would only encourage rote memorization without understanding.
   2.   In contrast, Piaget argued that peers might accelerate logical thinking in preschoolers, as in disagreements they push each other to make accommodations in thinking.

II.   Beyond Piaget
A.   Contemporary Challenges to Piaget's Thinking
   1.   Contemporary scientists see cognitive development more as a series of overlapping waves than discrete shifts in categories.
   2.   Careful research has revealed that children understand more than Piaget gave them credit for. The situation in which the test occurs, the familiarity of the child with the task, who asks the questions and how they ask them all influence the child's ability to correctly respond.
B.   Theory of Mind

1. **Theory of mind** refers to one's awareness of other people's thought processes and mental states. Age four is considered a watershed in the development of theory of mind, classically demonstrated in the *false belief task*.

2. Both cognitive and language abilities facilitate the development of theory of mind, but so do interactions with adults and especially siblings. Children smiling at their mother as they disobey show an awareness of what might provoke their mother, indicating an awareness of her mental processing.

3. Teasing siblings also illustrates an emerging theory of mind, as a child has to understand what will "set off" a sibling to effectively tease them.

C. Symbol-Referent Relations

1. DeLoache has conducted recent work on symbol-referent relations. Her research invites a child to a room in which there is a doll that the researcher and the child hide together under some furniture. Then, the researcher shows the child a model of the room and says the model doll is hidden in the same spot as the big room. Two-and-a-half year olds tend to be unable to find the doll, while three-year-olds generally can, indicating an ability to connect the model (symbol) to the referent (the actual room).

2. This ability to connect the symbol to the referent depends on the similarity of the model to the actual room, and on the degree to which the researcher pointed out the similarities to the child. Even two-and-a-half year olds can do this task if it is adequately supported, and three-year-olds can't if the support is insufficient. This suggests the development of symbolic representations is gradually acquired, not a qualitative shift as Piaget proposed.

III. Vygotsky's Sociocultural Theory

Vygotsky saw cognitive development as a collaboration embedded in a sociocultural setting. He focused on the child taking increasingly important social roles and responsibilities, not just on the use of logic on an individual basis. Vygotsky saw cognitive development as continuous, in contrast to Piaget's discrete categorical approach.

A. Zone of Proximal Development

1. Vygotsky felt that the **zone of proximal development (ZPD)**—the area between what a child can do alone versus with assistance—is the space in which cognitive development occurs. Parents and others provide a **scaffolding** to assist the child, and as the skills are acquired, gradually withdraw the scaffold.

2. When parents read to children and ask questions about the book, they begin with simple queries asking the child to label a known object on the page, and then eventually ask more and more sophisticated questions. The parent's questions help the child learn to do the reading on her own, and serve as the scaffold.

3. Pretend play is another zone of proximal development, allowing a child to try on roles.

B. Guided Participation

1. Vygotsky described the various ways in which children learn societal values through participation in family and community activities as **guided participation**.

2. Guided participation is seen across cultures, although the content of what is guided varies culturally.

3. In addition to content variability, the rules for participating in guided participation vary across cultures. For example, Inuit people expect children to learn by listening and not speaking, which is a very different set of rules from Euro-American standards.

C. Language and Thought

1. Vygotsky saw language and thought as developing together, as opposed to Piaget's view that thought preceded the development of language. Vygotsky argued that children's initial efforts to speak serve to establish a social connection placing them in the zone of proximal development. This **social speech** serves, then, an important function.

2. Around age 3–4, Vygotsky saw children as beginning to use language to organize their thought and activity. To do so, they talk out loud to themselves, which eventually becomes silenced as **inner speech**.

IV. Information Processing in Early Childhood

The information processing approach likens the brain to a computer. The brain acquires and selects information (perception and attention), stores information (memory), and uses information to plan for the future (problem-solving). Here we focus on attention and memory, both essential to learning.

A. Attention

1. **Attention** consists of focusing on some information and ignoring other information. The **Continuous Performance Task** (CPT) is the classic way to measure attention. The task requires a child to watch a TV screen and push a button whenever a targeted object (e.g., a chair) appears on screen. Attention is measured by how often the child hits the button when the object is present. **Impulsivity**, or lack of **inhibitory control**, is measured by how often the child hits the button when the object is *not* on screen.

2. On this task, three-year-olds and most four-year-olds perform poorly, some four-year-olds and most five-year-olds do a little better, and six-year-olds make few mistakes. Thus, attention and inhibitory control appear to improve over early childhood.

3. Improvements in attention are likely linked to prefrontal cortex and basal ganglia development, but environment is also a contributing factor. Children from stimulating homes with warm, responsive parents do better on the CPT than children from lower-quality environments.

B. Memory

1. **Sensory memory** is the gateway to memory, picking up sensory information and generating impressions that are fleeting and determining what will be stored in **working memory**, which contains conscious, short-term representations of what a person is actually thinking about at a given time. Working memory, as measured by the digit span task, improves over early childhood. The development of working memory is based on brain development and environment quality.

2. Working memory is relatively brief, but **long-term memory** has a potentially unlimited capacity and duration. It involves both recall and recognition, the latter of which is easier for children and adults alike. Preschoolers are capable of using memory strategies in familiar situations.

3. There are several types of long-term memory. **Generic memory** involves the development of scripts for familiar sequences of action. **Episodic memory** is recall for events at a specific time and place. **Autobiographical memory** is recall for episodes that are personally meaningful in one's life, and it begins at around age 4. Such memories become part of the child's developing self-concept.

4. Early memories are more likely to last if they are of highly unique events, if they involved the child's active participation, and if the child talked about the events with his or her parents.

5. The development of memory is partly a social process guided by interaction with parents and others. Parents with a *highly elaborative style* introduce new information in conversation, using conventions like leading questions. Parents with a *repetitive style* tend to ask the same question repeatedly, leading to less collaborative conversations.

6. The development of memory and language work hand in hand, with remembering words facilitating the acquisition of language, while at the same time being able to put a memory into words supports the ability of the child to manipulate that memory.

7. Children may *construct* memories out of what caught their attention rather than what actually happened.

V. Language Literacy and Mathematics in Early Childhood

A. Language Development in Young Children

Linguistic nativists argue that all humans possess basic linguistic competencies in the form of a universal grammar, and that these innate capacities help children acquire language. Usage-based linguists, in contrast, focus on the role of experience in language acquisition—which particular language a child learns, what social rules govern the language, the grammatical rules particular to that language, and so forth.

1. Vocabulary
   a) Around age 2, children's vocabularies expand rapidly. By age 3, they know 900–1000 words, and by age 6, they know 8,000–14,000 words.
   b) **Fast-mapping**, the ability to guess at the approximate meaning of a word after only hearing it two or so times in conversation, helps promote vocabulary growth. Additionally, the more language a child hears, the larger his or her vocabulary is likely to be.

2. Morphology and Syntax
   a) Between 18 and 36 months, children begin to put together **telegraphic sentences**, simple (usually) two-word utterances. By age 2 ½ to 3, they usually advance to a three-word sentence.
   b) Noteworthy in these short utterances is the child's tendency to apply the basic grammatical rules in the short sentences they compose. **Overregulation**, the tendency to apply rules of grammar even when such rules do not actually apply (e.g., Mommy *goed* to work), also illustrates that the child's acquisition of basic grammatical rules.

3. Semantics
   a) **Semantics** refers to the meaning of words, or the content of speech. In learning the meaning of words, children learn how their culture uses *concepts* to organize their perceptions of the world.
   b) Children build their concepts using cues from authority figures. Mastering the concepts involves understanding how they relate to each other. In general, young children learn the mid-level concepts first (e.g., flower), but struggle with relationships between categories (e.g., flowers are plants, which differ from animals).
   c) Current research indicates children's concepts are more advanced than Piaget believed, involving both concrete and some abstract material. Specialized knowledge, acquired from someone with expertise, accelerates the development of concepts in that area.

4. Pragmatics

a) **Pragmatics** refers to the social uses and conventions of language. Understanding of these conventions helps a child communicate more effectively.

b) Children begin to learn pragmatics during infancy, but it is in early childhood that they learn the finer points. They begin to understand that not all language is literal. Storytelling is one means of learning pragmatics.

B. Emergent Literacy

1. The foundations of literacy emerge during early childhood, although the expectations for what a child should know at specific times have changed over the years. Researchers agree that exposure to books and language is extremely valuable to the emergence of literacy.

2. Hart and Risley (1995) studied parent-child interaction from birth to age 3 each month and found notable differences between children of well-off versus welfare families at age 3. Well-off children knew about 1,000 words to welfare children's 500, and these differences persisted in the form of later IQ scores. Reasons for these differences lay in the frequency and content of communication to the children by the parents. Well-off parents spoke more often to their children each hour, and provided more affirmations and fewer disapprovals than the welfare parents did.

C. Mathematical Thinking

1. During early childhood, children master concepts of *magnitude*, *numbers*, *counting*, and *addition and subtraction*. In mastering counting, 3-year-olds understand the *one-to-one principle*, the *stable order principle*, the *cardinality principle*, the *abstraction principle*, and the *order-irrelevance principle*.

2. Some scientists believe the early mathematical competence has a biological basis, citing early emergence of mathematical thinking and universality of many everyday mathematical concepts as support. But experience also matters in mathematical thinking's emergence.

3. At the beginning of kindergarten, children's mathematical skills vary widely, in part based on child care or preschool quality.

VI. Child Care and Early Education Programs

A. Child Care in the United States

1. As the number of working women increases, the number of children in child care has increased as well.

2. **In-home care** occurs in the child's own home. **Child-care homes** involve a caregiver taking one to six children into her home. **Child-care centers** involve dividing children into same-age groups and planning developmentally appropriate activities. Staff members at child-care centers tend to have more education and training.

B. Child-Care Quality Matters

1. Research on child-care quality looks at two aspects of quality.

a) **Structural quality** refers to the characteristics of the child-care setting, such as group size, child/adult ratio, and level of training for the caregivers.

b) **Process quality** refers to the child's experiences with the caregiver, peers and materials.

2. The two types of quality are related. Higher structural quality tends to support higher process quality.

3. Children who attended higher quality care tend to have higher scores on cognitive development tests, with this advantage persisting into elementary school.

4.   High-quality child care is difficult to find in the United States, with only 10% of settings qualifying as "excellent."
C.   Effects of Different Types of Care Settings
Children who attended child-care centers tend to score higher on standardized tests of memory, and preacademic skills at age 2, 3, and 4 ½ than children in in-home or child-care homes.

D.   Early Education Programs
1.   Several studies indicate that economically disadvantaged children can start school on more equal footing with peers based on early education programs. Both the Perry Preschool Project in Michigan and the Abecedarian Project in North Carolina found that high quality early education can have a lasting impact, but the programs were small. The study of the Chicago Parent-Child Centers found that such an impact could be implemented on a broader scale.
2.   **Project Head Start** was an attempt to implement such a program on a national scale. It is a comprehensive program, designed to involve low-income community members in children's education; to provide children with medical and dental care, as well as nutritious meals; and to help families and children to cope with social and emotional problems. The project does appear to have substantially lowered the achievement gap, as well as reduced behavioral problems.
3.   Pre-kindergarten programs have documented short-term positive effects, as well, that are currently being investigated to determine if the positive effects will persist.

KEY TERMS

1.   The **preoperational period** is the second stage in Piaget's theory of cognitive development, from about age 2 to age 7, during which a child is able to think about objects and events that are not present but cannot yet reason logically. (see Piaget's Theory: The Preoperational Period)

2.   A **symbol** is any entity that stands for something other than itself. (see Piaget's Theory: The Preoperational Period)

3.   **Pretend play** is make-believe play in which common objects are often used to symbolize other objects. (see Piaget's Theory: The Preoperational Period)

4.   **Deferred imitation** occurs when a child reproduces actions that s/he has seen produced by others. (see Piaget's Theory: The Preoperational Period)

5.   **Reversibility** is the understanding that an item that has been changed can be returned to its original state by reversing the process. (see Piaget's Theory: The Preoperational Period)

6.   **Classification** is the ability to group items along multiple dimensions at the same time. (see Piaget's Theory: The Preoperational Period)

7.   **Conservation** is the understanding that some characteristics of objects (including volume, mass, and number) do not change despite changes in form or appearance. (see Piaget's Theory: The Preoperational Period)

8.   **Egocentrism,** in Piaget's theory of cognitive development, refers to a child's inability to see other people's view point. (see Piaget's Theory: The Preoperational Period)

9.   **Animism** is the assumption that inanimate objects have thoughts, feelings, and motives like humans. (see Piaget's Theory: The Preoperational Period)

10. **Theory of mind** is the awareness of one's own and other people's thought processes and mental states. (see Beyond Piaget)

11. The **zone of proximal development (ZPD)** is the gap between what a child can do alone and what a child can do with assistance. (see Vygotsky's Sociocultural Theory)

12. **Scaffolding** is providing learning opportunities, materials, hints, and clues when a child has difficulty with a task. (see Vygotsky's Sociocultural Theory)

13. **Guided participation** refers to the varied ways children learn their society's values and practices through participation in family and community activities. (see Vygotsky's Sociocultural Theory)

14. **Social speech** is verbal speech that elicits and maintains social interaction. (see Vygotsky's Sociocultural Theory)

15. **Inner speech** refers to silent, self-directed talk. (see Vygotsky's Sociocultural Theory)

16. **Attention** is the process of focusing on some information while ignoring other information. (see Information Processing in Early Childhood)

17. The **Continuous Performance Task** is a laboratory task designed to assess a child's attentiveness, in which a child is asked to push a button when a specific object appears on the computer screen. (see Information Processing in Early Childhood)

18. **Impulsivity** is the inability to control one's attention or behavior. (see Information Processing in Early Childhood)

19. **Inhibitory control** is the ability to control one's own attention or behavior. (see Information Processing in Early Childhood)

20. **Sensory memory** is a subconscious process of picking up sensory information—sights, sounds, smells, touch—from the environment. (see Information Processing in Early Childhood)

21. **Working memory** contains the conscious, short-term representations of what a person is actively thinking about at a given time; also known as "short-term memory." (see Information Processing in Early Childhood)

22. **Long-term memory** contains the collection of information that is mentally encoded and stored; it is believed to have potentially unlimited capacity and no time limits. (see Information Processing in Early Childhood)

23. **Generic memory** is a script or general outline of how familiar activities occur based on experience. (see Information Processing in Early Childhood)

24. **Episodic memory** is recall of a particular incident that took place at a specific time and place. (see Information Processing in Early Childhood)

25. **Autobiographical memory** is recall of individual episodes that are personally meaningful, which begins at about age 4 and may last for decades. (see Information Processing in Early Childhood)

26. **Fast mapping** is a child's ability to guess a word's approximate meaning after hearing it just once or twice in conversation. (see Language Literacy and Mathematics in Early Childhood)

27. **Telegraphic speech** refers to the simple, meaningful two-word utterances spoken by young children. (see Language Literacy and Mathematics in Early Childhood)

28. **Overregulation** refers to the same, regular grammatical mistakes that children often make with irregular plurals. (see Language Literacy and Mathematics in Early Childhood)

29. **Semantics** refers to the meaning of words and sentences, or the content of speech. (see Language Literacy and Mathematics in Early Childhood)

30. **Pragmatics** refers to the social uses and conventions of language. (see Language Literacy and Mathematics in Early Childhood)

31. **In-home care** is child care that occurs in the child's own home with a relative, nanny, or babysitter. (see Child Care and Early Education Programs)

32. **Child-care homes** are child care settings in which a caregiver takes from one to six children into his/her home. (see Child Care and Early Education Programs)

33. **Child-care centers** are child-care settings generally run by trained staff in which children are divided into classes or groups of same-age children, and activities are designed for their particular level of development. (see Child Care and Early Education Programs)

34. **Structural quality** refers to characteristics of child-care settings, such as group size, child-adult ratios, and caregiver education and training. (see Child Care and Early Education Programs)

35. **Process quality** refers to an assessment of children's interactions and experiences in the child-care settings. Higher process-quality is characterized by more sensitive and caring interactions with adults, rich conversations, and stimulating materials and activities. (see Child Care and Early Education Programs)

36. **Project Head Start** is a comprehensive pre-school program designed to involve low-income community members in children's education, to provide children with medical/dental care and meals, and to help families and children to cope with social and emotional problems. (see Child Care and Early Education Programs)

FILL-IN-THE-BLANKS KEY TERMS

This section will help you check your knowledge of the key terms introduced in this chapter. Fill in each blank with the appropriate term from the list of key terms in the previous section.

1. _____ is the ability to group items along multiple dimensions at the same time.

2. The social uses and conventions of language are called _____.

3. _____ is providing learning opportunities, materials, hints, and clues when a child has difficulty with a task.

4. _____ are child-care settings in which a caregiver takes from one to six children into his/her home.

5. When a child reproduces actions that s/he has seen produced by others, we call it _____.

6. _____ is a child's ability to guess a word's approximate meaning after hearing it just once or twice in conversation.

7. The _____ is the gap between what a child can do alone and what a child can do with assistance.

8. The _____ is a laboratory task designed to assess a child's attentiveness, in which a child is asked to push a button when a specific object appears on the computer screen.

9.   _____ refers to the same, regular grammatical mistakes that children often make with irregular plurals.

10.   The awareness of one's own and other people's thought processes and mental states is called _____.

APPLIED LEARNING AND CRITICAL THINKING

Watching cognitive development unfold during early childhood is truly a staggering experience. By finding ways to interact with small children at this period of development, you will have an opportunity to informally test drive some of the ideas you read about in this chapter. Seeing ideas in action will allow you to assess the scope and generalizability of those ideas.

1.   In the previous chapter, providing babysitting for a family of an autistic child was mentioned as a good way to get a closer look at physical development, and in particular the unique challenges that present to autistic youngsters. That same service will also allow you to gain a richer understanding of the cognitive skills one might expect in autistic children, as well as some of their social communication deficits. Depending on the severity of the diagnosis of the child, you will see that the communication may range from nearly non-existent to highly verbal with inattention to paraverbal and nonverbal elements of communication. Talk to the parents about the strategies they use to communicate with their child and teach better social skills. How do their strategies fit with your instincts and the research you've read in the text.

2.   If your university has a study away (or study abroad) program, consider visiting the historical sites associated with Piaget's research. He attended University of Neuchâtel, where he earned a Ph.D. He then spent a semester at University of Zurich, where he found an interest in psychoanalysis, and then moved to France to work at a school that had been founded by the famous Alfred Binet. He had many appointments in Switzerland and France throughout his career. If you are studying abroad in Europe, your proximity to some of these sights will allow you to walk the same paths Piaget did as he developed his theory of cognitive development. You can read more about Piaget on the Jean Piaget Society website at www.piaget.org, and find information there to plan a trip around the sequence of his career.

3.   Using observation as your tool, design a research study to compare the kinds of scaffolding that preschoolers tend to receive from their parents, caregivers, and teachers. Comparing these different adults in the lives of a preschooler for variance in their scaffolding might help you formulate ideas about why children behave in different ways for different people. Is one of these adults more apt to provide a "sturdier" scaffold than the others? Who is quickest to "pull" the scaffolding away? Be sure to work with your instructor to gain IRB approval for the study, as well as to procure informed consent from any participants. Your instructor will also be invaluable as you develop an observational coding system to help you answer questions like the ones above.

4.   If you are interested in working with preschool-aged children, consider doing an internship or getting a part-time job with a child-care center, or providing in-home care, if you can schedule it. If possible, interview at a number of different places for this sort of work, and compare them all in terms of the structural and process quality. As you do this comparison, consider why it is that high-quality care is so difficult to find in the United States. Are the wages in child care not competitive enough to attract high-quality employees? What other factors can you think of that contribute to the dearth of quality child care? Once you are working at a facility, you will have a new perspective on how to answer these questions, as compared to how you might at the interview process.

MULTIPLE-CHOICE QUESTIONS

Quiz 1

1. Little Carter picks up a calculator and puts it to his ear to "talk" on it, as if it were a telephone. Carter is engaged in
    a. deferred imitation.
    b. pretend play.
    c. egocentrism.
    d. scaffolding.

2. Which of the following is NOT a gap in preoperational thinking?
    a. Reversibility
    b. Classification
    c. Conservation
    d. Deferred imitation

3. Three-year-old Sadie stubbed her toe on the wall, and cries out, "Mommy! The wall kicked me!!!" Sadie's remark illustrates
    a. egocentrism.
    b. theory of mind.
    c. animism.
    d. inner speech.

4. Theory of mind is a challenge to which feature of Piaget's ideas about preoperational children's cognitive abilities?
    a. Egocentrism
    b. Scaffolding
    c. Classification
    d. Reversibility

5. The gap between what a child can do alone and what he or she can do with assistance is called
    a. the scaffolding.
    b. the zone of proximal development.
    c. the continuous performance task. d. fast mapping.

6. Shara is telling her dad about her day. "First, we went to the craft area, and then we had a story." "What happened next?" her dad asked. "Well, then we had a snack," she replies. "And then….?" Her dad queried. "And then we all went home," Shara ended. Shara's dad's prompting is teaching her about the narrative form used in all storytelling. Shara is engaged in
    a. deferred imitation.
    b. guided participation.
    c. inner speech.
    d. the continuous performance task.

7. Rex has a series of thoughts running through his mind: "First I separate the edges from the middle pieces. Then I assemble the edge of the puzzle. I end by putting the middle pieces together in the middle." Rex's thoughts illustrate
    a. inner speech.
    b. social speech.
    c. overregulation.
    d. fast mapping.

8.   The part of memory responsible for whatever someone is actively thinking about is known as

   a.   sensory memory.
   b.   working memory.
   c.   long-term memory.
   d.   autobiographical memory.

9.   Which of the following is a key to the rapid vocabulary growth seen in early childhood?

   a.   Pretend play
   b.   Autobiographical memory
   c.   Telegraphic speech
   d.   Fast mapping

10. Joshua ran up to his mom and said, "Our teacher has mouses for our class pets!!!" Joshua's references to "mouses" instead of "mice" illustrates

   a.   pragmatics.
   b.   scaffolding.
   c.   overregulation.
   d.   impulsivity.

11. A child's ability to distinguish "a lot" from "a little" illustrates the mathematical concept of

   a.   magnitude.
   b.   one-to-one correspondence.
   c.   cardinality.
   d.   order irrelevance.

12. Stacy has hired a nanny to watch her preschool daughter, Ella, while she works. Which type of care is Stacy using?

   a.   In-home care
   b.   A child-care home
   c.   A child-care center
   d.   Both A and B

13. High process-quality in child care is characterized by

   a.   highly educated caregivers.
   b.   warm and sensitive interactions with adults.
   c.   small class sizes.
   d.   Both A and C

14. On average, which type of day care has the best outcomes for children in terms of cognitive ability on standardized tests?

   a.   In-home care
   b.   A child-care home
   c.   A child-care center
   d.   All forms of child care are equal in these outcomes.

15. Which Early Education Program was implemented on a national scale?

   a.   The Perry Preschool Project
   b.   The Abecedarian Project
   c.   Project Head Start
   d.   Chicago Parent-Child Centers

Quiz 2

Use this quiz to reassess your learning after taking Quiz 1 and reviewing the chapter.

1. Carlin's parents are visiting with friends in the living room, when Carlin charges in pushing her plastic lawn mower. The little preschooler announces to the group that she is mowing. Carlin has seen her dad mow the yard the past few weeks, but this is the first time she has done this. Carlin's behavior illustrates

    a. deferred imitation.
    b. reversibility.
    c. animism.
    d. scaffolding.

2. The ability to group items along multiple dimensions at the same time is called

    a. conservation.
    b. classification.
    c. reversibility.
    d. egocentrism.

3. Terrelle doesn't seem to show much awareness of what other people are thinking. He waves to his neighbors from inside his house with the windows shut, and doesn't understand why they don't wave back. His mom tries to explain that they can't see him, but Terrelle just can't comprehend that. Terrelle

    a. has a well-developed theory of mind.
    b. appears to lack a theory of mind.
    c. has a well-developed zone of proximal development.
    d. appears to lack a zone of proximal development.

4. Which of the following statements best describes the results of DeLoache's work on symbol referent relations using "Big Terry"?

    a. Most children aged 2½ or older could find Little Terry in the model.
    b. Two-year-olds could find Little Terry in the model about 50% of the time, while 3-year-olds could 100% of the time.
    c. Two-year-olds could find Little Terry in the model about 20% of the time, while 3-year-olds could about 75% of the time.
    d. Very few children under the age of 5 could find Little Terry in the model.

5. The support that a parent supplies to a child in the zone of proximal development is called

    a. enabling.
    b. symbol-referent.
    c. reversibility.
    d. scaffolding.

6. Using words to gain someone's attention and support interaction is called

    a. inner speech.
    b. autobiographical speech.
    c. social speech.
    d. process quality.

7. The Continuous Performance Task (CPT) is used to measure

    a. attention.
    b. memory.
    c. processing speed.
    d. overregulation.

8.   Generic memory tends to start around age_____, and autobiographical memory tends to
     start around age_____ .
     a.   2; 2
     b.   2; 4
     c.   4; 2
     d.   4; 4

9.   Two-year-old Marlon tells his mom, "Go store. Need cookies." Marlon's speech is
     a.   telegraphic.
     b.   overregulated.
     c.   semantically correct.
     d.   Both B and C

10. Which statement about concepts is a preschooler most likely to master?
     a.   A pug is a dog.
     b.   An ostrich is a bird.
     c.   A dog is a kind of animal.
     d.   A bird is a kind of animal.

11. Mrs. Fitzmorris is teaching her preschool class to count. She tells them to touch each object
     that they count. Having a student gently touch each object as she calls out "one, two,
     three…" helps the child master which mathematical principle?
     a.   Magnitude
     b.   Cardinality
     c.   Stable order
     d.   One-to-one

12. Which form of day care is most preferred by parents of 3–5 year olds?
     a.   In-home care
     b.   Child-care homes
     c.   Child-care centers
     d.   Both B and C

13. Which day care has the best overall quality?
     a.   The day care in which all the staff have bachelor's degrees.
     b.   The day care in which all the staff have associate's degrees in early childhood.
     c.   The day care in which the staff largely didn't graduate high school, but love kids.
     d.   The day care with staff possessing associates degrees who like to engage the children.

14. According to your text, can early childhood preschool programs help disadvantaged
     children catch up and start kindergarten on level with their peers?
     a.   No, never.
     b.   Yes, but only on a local scale.
     c.   Yes, but only in children of particular ethnic backgrounds.
     d.   Yes, nationally.

15. Project Head Start's goals are to
     a.   involve low income community member's in children's education.
     b.   provide medical and dental care to children.
     c.   foster learning and good classroom behavior.
     d.   All of these

ANSWERS TO FILL-IN-THE-BLANKS KEY TERMS

1.   Classification (see Piaget's Theory: The Preoperational Mind)

2.   pragmatics (see Language, Literacy, and Mathematics in Early Childhood)

3.   Scaffolding (see Vygotsky's Sociocultural Theory)

4.   Child-care homes (see Child Care and Early Education Programs)

5.   deferred imitation (see Piaget's Theory: The Preoperational Mind)

6.   Fast mapping (see Language, Literacy, and Mathematics in Early Childhood)

7.   zone of proximal development (see Vygotsky's Sociocultural Theory)

8.   Continuous Performance Task (see Information Processing in Early Childhood)

9.   Overregulation (see Language, Literacy, and Mathematics in Early Childhood)

10.   theory of mind (see Beyond Piaget)

ANSWERS TO MULTIPLE-CHOICE QUESTIONS

Circle the question numbers you answered incorrectly.

Quiz 1

1.   *b is the answer.*   Pretend play occurs when a child uses a common object (e.g., a calculator) to represent something else (e.g., a phone). (see Piaget's Theory: The Preoperational Period)

2.   *d is the answer.*   Deferred imitation occurs when someone imitates an action he or she has seen another produce. Children in the preoperational period are able to do this. However, they generally struggle to reverse operations, conserve matter, and classify things along multiple dimensions at the same time. (see Piaget's Theory: The Preoperational Period)

3.   *c is the answer.*   Sadie's remark indicates a belief that the wall had an intention to harm her. The belief that inanimate objects, like walls, can hold intents, wishes, and so forth, is called animism. (see Piaget's Theory: The Preoperational Period)

4.   *a is the answer.*   Egocentrism is the idea that preoperational children are locked into their own points of view and perspectives. Yet research on theory of mind, along with common place observances of children altering their speech to engage babies in "baby talk," illustrates an awareness that others (i.e., the baby) do not share the same perspective and abilities. The emergence of theory of mind during the preoperational period undermines the notion of egocentrism. (see Beyond Piaget)

5.   *b is the answer.*   The zone of proximal development is the gap between what a child can do on his or her own versus what he or she can do with assistance. (see Vygotsky's Sociocultural Theory)

6.   *b is the answer.*   Shara's dad is *guiding* Shara in how the narrative form is used to tell a story. This guided participation will help Shara understand a common practice—storytelling—in her world. (see Vygotsky's Sociocultural Theory)

7.   *a is the answer.*   Rex's series of thoughts illustrates inner speech as he runs through the solution to putting a puzzle together in his head rather than out loud. (see Vygotsky's Sociocultural Theory)

8.   *b is the answer.*   Working memory is the conscious, short-term representation of whatever a person is actively thinking about. (see Information Processing in Early Childhood)

9.   *d is the answer.*   Fast mapping is the ability to infer the meaning of a word after only hearing it once or twice in conversation. This ability is essential to vocabulary growth in early childhood. (see Language, Literacy, and Mathematics in Early Childhood)

10.   *c is the answer.*   Overregulation refers to the same, regular grammatical mistakes that children often make with irregular plurals. The plural of "mouse" is irregular, as it doesn't follow the rule of "add an *s*" to the end. (see Language, Literacy, and Mathematics in Early Childhood)

11.   *a is the answer.*   Magnitude refers to the amount of a substance. A lot is more than a little, referring to amounts as well. (see Language, Literacy, and Mathematics in Early Childhood)

12.   *a is the answer.*   Stacy is using in-home care, which is defined as care in which an individual, such as a nanny, grandmother, or other person, comes to the home to watch the child in his or her own environment. (see Child Care and Early Education Programs)

13.   *b is the answer.*   Process quality is related to the kinds of experiences the child has with the people and materials in a child care setting. Only the description of interactions as sensitive and warm fits this definition, as both A and C illustrate structural quality. (see Child Care and Early Education Programs)

14.   *c is the answer.*   Children in child-care centers tend to score better on tests of memory and pre-academic skills than their counterparts. (see Child Care and Early Education Programs)

15.   *c is the answer.*   Only Project Head Start was implemented nationally. The Perry Preschool Project was in Michigan, the Abecedarian Project in North Carolina, and the Chicago project, of course, in Chicago. (see Child Care and Early Education Programs)

Now turn to the quiz analysis table at the end of this chapter to find which areas you know well and which areas you need to work on. Circle the numbers in the table for items on Quiz 1 that you answered correctly.

Quiz 2

1.   *a is the answer.*   Carlin is imitating her dad, but not right as he mows the lawn. Instead, she waits, or defers, her imitation until she is inside and spies her plastic lawn mower days and weeks after she actually saw her dad mowing. (see Piaget's Theory: The Preoperational Period)

2.   *b is the answer.*   The definition of "classification" is the ability to group items along multiple dimensions at the same time. (see Piaget's Theory: The Preoperational Period)

3.   *b is the answer.*   Theory of mind refers to one's awareness of other people's thought processes and mental states. Terrelle's inability to grasp that his neighbor is not aware of him waving shows a lack of awareness of his neighbors thought processes; thus, Terrelle lacks a theory of mind. (see Beyond Piaget)

4.   *c is the answer.*   In DeLoache's study, 2½-year-olds found Little Terry in the model less than 20% of the time, while 3-year-olds found him over 75% of the time. (see Beyond Piaget)

5. *d is the answer.* Scaffolding is the support provided by parents in the form of learning opportunities, materials, hints and so forth while the child is in a zone of proximal development. (see Vygotsky's Sociocultural Theory)

6. *c is the answer.* Social speech is used to elicit and maintain social interaction. (see Vygotsky's Sociocultural Theory)

7. *a is the answer.* The Continuous Performance Task is a classic measure of attention. (see Information Processing in Early Childhood)

8. *b is the answer.* Generic memory (memory for scripts) begins around age 2, while autobiographical memory tend to appear closer to age 4. (see Information Processing in Early Childhood)

9. *a is the answer.* Telegraphic speech refers to the two-word utterances that children begin putting together around age 18–36 months. (see Language, Literacy, and Mathematics in Early Childhood)

10. *a is the answer.* A preschooler will probably first understand that a pug is a dog. The concept that an ostrich is a bird is harder because an ostrich is an atypical bird. The latter two statements are also difficult for preschoolers because they involve relationships between concepts, not just the classification itself. (see Language, Literacy, and Mathematics in Early Childhood)

11. *d is the answer.* Teaching preschoolers to touch each object they count helps to reinforce the notion of one-to-one correspondence, as the child can associate each saying of the number with each object. (see Language, Literacy, and Mathematics in Early Childhood)

12. *c is the answer.* The majority of parents of 3- to 5-year-olds prefer child-care centers. (see Child Care and Early Education Programs)

13. *d is the answer.* This day care has both structural quality (staff trained in early childhood) and process quality (they like to engage the kids). All the other options focus on either structure or process quality alone, not both together. (see Child Care and Early Education Programs)

14. *d is the answer.* Although initial evidence focused on local implementations of early childhood programs, more recent evidence has focused on a national study. Early data supports the local data, indicating that the preschool is helpful in "catching up" children. (see Child Care and Early Education Programs)

15. *d is the answer.* Project Head Start holds all three of these goals. (see Child Care and Early Education Programs)

Now turn to the quiz analysis table at the end of this chapter to find which areas you know well and which areas you need to work on. Circle the numbers in the table for items on Quiz 2 that you answered correctly.

For each question you answered correctly, circle its number. (Quiz 1 numbers are not shaded; Quiz 2 numbers are shaded.) Are there patterns in the types of questions or the topics you got wrong that could direct your further study? Did you improve from Quiz 1 to Quiz 2?

QUIZ REVIEW

Topic	Type of Question		
	Definition	**Comprehension**	**Application**
Piaget's Theory: The Preoperational Period		2	1, 3
	2		1
Beyond Piaget		4	
		4	3
Vygotsky's Sociocultural Theory	5		6, 7
	5, 6		
Information Processing in Early Childhood	8		
		7, 8	
Language, Literacy, and Mathematics in Early Childhood	11	9	10
		10	9, 11
Child Care and Early Education Programs		13, 14, 15	12
		12, 14, 15	13

Total correct by quiz:

Quiz 1:	
Quiz 2:	

CHAPTER 9

Socioemotional Development in Early Childhood

LEARNING OBJECTIVES

1. Describe the self-concept and self-esteem level of the average preschooler.

2. Explain how the resolution of Erikson's normative crisis of initiative vs. guilt contributes to the development of a child's self concept.

3. Explain how a preschooler's internal working model of the self is affected by her or his parents' behavior, the type of attachment between child and parents, and their family stories.

4. Describe children's evolving concept of gender identity and their changing gender-specific behaviors.

5. Explain how children develop gender schemas based on biological and social influences.

6. Describe the development of primary and secondary emotions in early childhood.

7. Define emotional intelligence and explain how children develop it.

8. Describe how the development of effortful control helps children regulate their emotions, and show why this is important.

9. Discuss the ways in which culture influences a child's ideas about emotional displays and the acceptability of particular emotions.

10. Describe the development of the conscience in young children, and explain how it affects the development of prosocial behavior.

11. Describe the three different types of aggression and the three reasons why children might become aggressive.

12. Describe the changes in the forms of aggression through early childhood.

13. List the factors that influence the development of aggression in early childhood.

14. Describe the four parenting styles suggested by Diana Baumrind and Eleanor Maccoby, and explain how each affects children's personalities and behaviors.

15. Explain how relationships with siblings help children develop their social and communication skills.

16. Explain how relationships with peers help children develop their social and communication skills.

17. Describe the factors that influence the quality of peer relationships in early childhood.

OUTLINE

Socialization, the process of teaching children cultural values and rules for behavior, becomes more explicit during early childhood. How children respond to these new demands is influenced by a variety of factors.

I.   Development of the Self
     The development of a sense of **self** begins in early childhood. The **self** is a cognitive and social construction that reflects the child's interactions and experiences with other people, especially parents.

     A.   Self-Concepts and Self-Esteem
          1.   **Self-conceptions** are evaluative statements about specific areas of competence, while **self-esteem** reflects a global assessment of self-worth.
          2.   Young children's self-concepts are usually focused on concrete, observable characteristics. They tend to be unrealistically positive, in part because they have limited cognitive conservation skills.
          3.   Young children's self-esteem levels have behavioral consequences in terms of confidence, curiosity, and independence. Children with high self-esteem tend to try new things eagerly, persist in the face of frustration, and cope better with teasing or criticism than those with low self-esteem. Yet self-esteem at this age is not necessarily linked to competence in a particular area, suggesting that the origins of confidence are not necessarily linked to abilities.
     B.   Initiative versus Guilt
          1.   Another aspect of the developing sense of self is that of **initiative versus guilt**, the third stage of Erikson's theory of psychosocial development. During this period, the mastery of new skills becomes increasingly important.
          2.   Parental acceptance and encouragement of such efforts without too much interference supports the development of initiative. Parental criticism, restrictions, or ridicule supports the development of a sense of failure and guilt.
          3.   Children at this age do not engage in much social comparison, but rather learn to judge themselves through interactions with the important adults in their life.
     C.   Internal Working Models
          1.   Attachment researchers focus on children's **internal working models** of the self. These models are derived from the nature of the parent-child attachment. Parents who are supportive and warm nurture secure attachments, which results in an internal working model of the self as someone worthy of love.
          2.   Such models are considered working models, indicating that they are revised based on ongoing experiences.
          3.   Abused and/or neglected children have problematic internal working models, characterized by fragmentation and lack of self-awareness.
     D.   Family Stories
          1.   As family stories are told about children, the children use these stories to anchor the development of the self.
          2.   Family stories provide a way for children to learn about what their culture values.
II. Gender Development
     A.   Gender Awareness, Identity, and Constancy
          1.   Gender awareness develops quite early (before children even walk or talk), but **gender identity** (the awareness of one's self as male or female) emerges during early childhood.

2. Gender identity is perceived as changeable initially. **Gender constancy**, the understanding that gender is permanent and immutable, develops around the age of 6 or 7, as conservation abilities emerge.

3. Some children experience Gender Identity Disorders of Childhood, expressing a desire to be the other sex. How to respond to such children is controversial, with recommendations ranging from allowing them to be themselves, to discouraging such behavior.

B. Behavioral Differences

1. Behavioral differences along gender lines emerge around the age of three, with children beginning to prefer to play with members from their own sex.

2. Boys play tends to be more physically active and focused on establishing dominance. They tend to prefer transportation toys, Lego sets, and action figures.

3. Girls tend to play more cooperatively and prefer quieter activities in comparison to boys of this age. Girls often prefer dolls, kitchen sets, and dress up.

C. Sources of Gender Differences in Early Childhood

1. Gender differences during early childhood are in part determined by biological factors, especially **androgens**, and the particular androgen called **testosterone**. These hormones influence biological differences in males and females, but also behavior as well. For example, girls who were exposed to high androgen levels prenatally tend to prefer male toys and male play styles.

2. Another biological difference that may underlie gender differences is the density of the connections in the **corpus callosum**. Girls tend to have denser connectivity between the two brain hemispheres. These brain areas have been linked to preferences for physical activity, self-regulation, and effortful control.

3. Social factors also influence gender differences. Parents and teachers give boys and girls different messages, encouraging boys to be more independent than girls, but talking more to girls, particularly about emotions. This **gender socialization** process occurs through everyday interactions with peers as well as adults, though. For example, boys' initial preference for **rough-and-tumble play** is magnified across a school year as boys interact with each other over time.

4. Cognitive factors also influence gender differences emergent in early childhood. **Gender schemas** are mental networks of beliefs and expectations about males and females. As children develop a sense of gender identity, they begin to classify things as "male" or "female." The cognitive ability to classify objects corresponds to the emergence of gender identity between the ages of 3 and 5.

III. Emotional Development

A. Understanding Emotions

1. Awareness of one's own and other's emotions increases throughout early childhood. As part of this, children become increasingly capable of understanding the causes and consequences of emotions.

2. **Self-conscious emotions**, which require a sense of the self as distinct from others, knowledge of behavioral standards, the ability to evaluate one's own performance in terms of these standards, and a sense of responsibility for success or failure, are particularly noteworthy for emergence in early childhood.

3. Embarrassment, a type of self-conscious emotion, has two forms: when a child is the object of positive attention for an accomplishment or when a child is the object of negative attention for a failure. Only the latter form results in a stress reaction.

B. Individual Difference in Emotional Understanding

1. **Emotional intelligence**, the ability to monitor one's own and other's feelings and to use that information as a guide to future action, varies widely amongst children. Children who demonstrate emotional intelligence are more popular with their peers than those who do not.

2. Girls' skills in decoding emotions in general are stronger than boys'.

3. Parental conversations about how a child will feel or did feel provide the scaffolding for children to develop deeper emotional understanding. Without these warm, supportive relationships, emotional development is impaired. Children who have been abused are prone to interpret neutral behavior as hostile, and children who have been neglected have difficulty discriminating emotions. Children of depressed mothers tend to experience too much empathy and too great a sense of responsibility.

C. Regulating Emotions

1. **Emotional regulation** refers to the ability to inhibit, enhance, maintain, and modulate emotional arousal to accomplish a goal. These skills improve greatly during early childhood.

2. **Effortful control** contributes to a child's ability to emotionally regulate oneself. The inability to control oneself and suppress dominant responses can lead to externalizing behaviors.

3. Although effortful control skills are rooted in temperament, they are modulated by parenting style. Intrusive or hostile parents tend to blunt a child's ability to engage in emotional regulation and effortful control, while positive parenting promotes these skills.

D. Emotions in a Cultural Context

1. What is considered "good" emotional regulation depends on culture. In *individualistic* cultures, self-development is emphasized, making pride a "good" emotion and "shame" a bad one. In contrast, *collectivist* cultures emphasize social harmony, making pride the "bad" emotion and "shame" the good one.

2. As a rule, European-American mothers tend to promote emotional self-expression, while Asian mothers tend to see emotional displays as disruptive and needing to be controlled.

IV. Prosocial Behaviors, Conscience, and Aggression
One goal of socialization in early childhood is to morally develop the child. Two approaches to studying moral development exist. Some researchers focus on changes in moral reasoning as cognitive skills advance. Alternately, others focus on the development of prosocial behavior in young children. Great strides are made in exhibition of prosocial behavior in early childhood.

A. Development of Conscience

1. **Prosocial behaviors** are voluntary actions intended to benefit another person. Such behaviors may be motivated by self-interest, or by **conscience**, an internal sense of right and wrong.

2. Researchers have developed special experimental tasks to study feeling of guilt, empathy, and compliance and internalization, features critical to the development of a conscience. They found evidence of these feelings in children as young as 33 months, and a big increase in empathy and internalization of standards at 45 months. High scores on these tasks at a young age tend to correspond to measures of conscience longitudinally.

B. Factors Associated with the Development of Conscience

1. Effortful control is related to conscience during early childhood. Emotional regulation is related to prosocial behavior during this time, too.

2. Although prosocial behavior is somewhat intrinsically motivated (e.g., children just wanting to "be nice"), it is also influenced by parenting. Children with secure attachments to parents are more capable of sympathy than those with insecure attachments.

3. The quality of childcare can also influence the development of prosocial behavior. Mothers of children at childcare situations with a low child/adult ratio and small classes report more prosocial behavior in their children than mothers of children in less quality childcare contexts. The emotional warmth of the caregiver can also facilitate prosocial behavior in young children.

4. Prosocial behavior also depends on cultural norms, as well. Collectivist cultures may be somewhat more likely to promote prosocial behavior than individualist cultures.

C. Aggression

1. **Aggression** is any action intended to harm another. The key element of the definition is *intentionality*. Aggression can take many forms: **physical aggression, verbal aggression,** and **relational aggression**.

2. Types of aggression can also be distinguished based on the underlying reason for it. **Reactive aggression** is defensive, **instrumental aggression** is goal-directed, and **hostile aggression** has harm as its intent. Behavior that unintentionally harms is called **agonism**.

3. Though infants are incapable of aggression (but very capable of agonism!), toddlers are very capable of aggression, and certainly agonism. About half of toddler's interactions involve aggression or agonism, but these aren't necessarily the opposite of prosocial behavior. Those same children can be very prosocial. The amount of aggression and prosocial behavior are based on how sociable the child is.

4. Between ages 2 and 4, physical aggression decreases and verbal aggression increases. The reasons underlying aggression change, as well, from arguments over resources to differences of opinion. By the time a child is 4 or 5, they have developed several strategies for dealing with such conflicts.

5. To determine if early aggression predicts later aggression, a study of **developmental trajectories** was conducted. This study found that only 3% of the population studied was high in aggression for the entire 7 years of the study. These children were at risk for later problems, both **internalizing** and **externalizing problems**.

D. Influences on Aggression

1. Aggression levels in early childhood are influenced by temperament (poor effortful control and emotional regulation increase risk of aggression), gender (boys are more aggressive), socialization (punitive parenting practices increase aggressive behavior), and child care (large group settings and longer hours are associated with aggression).

2. Large group childcare may be linked to aggression because those settings increase cortisol levels in children.

V. Social Relationships in Early Childhood

A. Parenting

1. Baumrind identified three parenting styles based on the dimensions of warmth/acceptance and control.
   a) **Authoritative parents** are high on both dimensions.
   b) **Authoritarian parents** are high on control but low on warmth.
   c) **Permissive parents** are low on control but high on warmth.

2.   Maccoby later identified a fourth style, **disengaged parents**, who are low on both warmth and control.

3.   Baumrind linked parenting styles to socioemotional development. She felt that the best social outcomes were achieved with authoritative parenting, which provided a balance of warmth and control.

4.   Criticisms of Baumrind.
   a)   Baumrind has been criticized for not considering the possibility that children elicit the parenting style.
   b)   Baumrind also failed to study multiple cultures, although later work has replicated her initial approach, which emphasized the importance of values in parenting. Latino parents, for example, tend to emphasize *la familia*, *respecto* and *educacion*. Chinese parents, however, emphasize *chia-shun* (training) and *guan* (parental involvement and investment in children). Chinese emphases are associated with academic achievement.
   c)   Some argue that the values of the Chinese parents, which seem somewhat authoritarian, indicate that the authoritative approach is not necessarily the best in all cultures.

B.   Siblings
   1.   Siblings are significant relationships in early childhood. Indeed, in some cultures, four-year-old children become caregivers for younger siblings!
   2.   During early childhood, dyadic sibling interaction provides a vehicle in which children learn how to be friends with others outside the family. Siblings can provide a buffer for socially isolated children.

C.   Peers
   1.   Peer relationships also blossom during early childhood, increasing in frequency and complexity.
   2.   Pretend play is an important way that peer relationships develop. Beginning with **simple pretend play**, children simply watch and mimic one another. During the stage of **associative pretend play**, children create a script with a meaningful sequence, but it involves both children playing the same sort of role. During **cooperative pretend play**, the children actually take on reciprocal roles.
   3.   During early childhood, children usually develop one or more reciprocal friendships. Play with friends is more complex than play with non-friends. Friends have more conflicts, but they are resolved more effectively than non-friend conflicts. Friends provide social support that can buffer the transition into kindergarten.
   4.   Peer groups in early childhood tend to have a stable dominance structure which persists over time. These results suggest peer acceptance/rejection begins quite early.
   5.   Peer relationships are influenced by the quality of the parent-child attachment (securely attached children are more socially competent) and by **homophily,** or preference for similar others.
   6.   Parent-child interactions provide a way to practice social competencies, but in addition to that, parents can influence peer relations simply by offering advice about play strategies.

KEY TERMS

1.   **Socialization** is the process of teaching children cultural values and rules for behavior. (see introductory section)

2. · The **self** is a cognitive construction that reflects the child's level of mental development and a social construction that reflects the child's interactions and experiences with other people. (see Development of the Self)

3. **Self-conceptions** are evaluative judgments of oneself in a specific domain. (see Development of the Self)

4. **Self-esteem** is a global assessment of self-worth. (see Development of the Self)

5. **Initiative versus guilt** is the third stage in Erikson's theory of psychosocial development during which mastery of new skills becomes a primary goal. (see Development of the Self)

6. An **internal working model** is a child's evaluation of his or her self-worth as a person, often derived from the parent-child relationship. (see Development of the Self)

7. **Gender identity** is a person's sense of self as male or female. (see Gender Development)

8. **Gender constancy** is the concept that gender is permanent and immutable. (see Gender Development)

9. **Androgens** are hormones that control the development of masculine characteristics, generally found in higher levels in males than females. (see Gender Development)

10. **Testosterone** is an androgen secreted by the testicles or ovaries. (see Gender Development)

11. The **corpus callosum** is a brain structure which connects and coordinates the brain's left and right hemispheres. (see Gender Development)

12. **Gender socialization** refers to social norms conveyed to children that concern characteristics associated with being male or female. (see Gender Development)

13. **Rough-and-tumble play** is physical play with other children. (see Gender Development)

14. **Gender schemas** are mental networks of beliefs and expectations about males versus females. (see Gender Development)

15. **Self-conscious emotions** are emotions that involve evaluation of oneself, such as embarrassment or pride. (see Emotional Development)

16. **Emotional intelligence** is the ability to monitor one's own and others' feelings and to use that information to guide thinking and action. (see Emotional Development)

17. **Emotional regulation** is the ability to inhibit, enhance, maintain, and modulate emotional arousal to accomplish a goal. (see Emotional Development)

18. **Effortful control** is the ability to withhold a dominant response in order to make a nondominant response, to engage in planning, and to regulate reactive tendencies. (see Emotional Development)

19. **Prosocial behaviors** are voluntary actions intended to benefit another person. (see Prosocial Behaviors, Conscience, and Aggression)

20. **Conscience** is an inner sense of right and wrong that invokes good feelings about doing the right thing and bad feelings about doing something wrong. (see Prosocial Behaviors, Conscience, and Aggression)

21. **Empathy** refers to understanding and sharing another person's feelings. (see Prosocial Behaviors, Conscience, and Aggression)

22. **Aggression** is behavior that is intended to harm or injure another person. (see Prosocial Behaviors, Conscience, and Aggression)

23. **Physical aggression** is aggressive behavior that is physical. (see Prosocial Behaviors, Conscience, and Aggression)

24. **Verbal aggression** refers to aggressive behavior such as threats. (see Prosocial Behaviors, Conscience, and Aggression)

25. **Relational aggression** is aggressive behavior designed to lower another child's self-esteem, social standing, or both. (see Prosocial Behaviors, Conscience, and Aggression)

26. **Reactive aggression** is aggressive behavior that is a defensive response to provocation. (see Prosocial Behaviors, Conscience, and Aggression)

27. **Instrumental aggression** is aggressive behavior designed to achieve a goal for oneself. (see Prosocial Behaviors, Conscience, and Aggression)

28. **Hostile aggression** is aggressive behavior that is aimed at a specific person intending to cause harm. (see Prosocial Behaviors, Conscience, and Aggression)

29. **Agonism** is behavior that inflicts unintentional harm to another person. (see Prosocial Behaviors, Conscience, and Aggression)

30. A **developmental trajectory** is a pattern that describes changes in an individual over a relatively long period. (see Prosocial Behaviors, Conscience, and Aggression)

31. **Externalizing problems** are psychosocial problems that are manifested in outward symptoms, such as aggression or noncompliance. (see Prosocial Behaviors, Conscience, and Aggression)

32. **Internalizing problems** are psychosocial problems that are manifested in inward symptoms, such as depression and anxiety. (see Prosocial Behaviors, Conscience, and Aggression)

33. **Authoritative parents** use a parenting style characterized by high warmth and high control. (see Social Relationships in Early Childhood)

34. **Authoritarian parents** use a parenting style characterized by low warmth and high control. (see Social Relationships in Early Childhood)

35. **Permissive parents** use a parenting style characterized by high warmth and low control; also known as "indulgent" parenting. (see Social Relationships in Early Childhood)

36. **Disengaged parents** use a parenting style where parents focus on their own needs, not the child's, characterized by low warmth and low control. (see Social Relationships in Early Childhood)

37. **Simple pretend play** is play behavior where children watch or mimic each other but do not collaborate in any organized way. (see Social Relationships in Early Childhood

38. **Associative pretend play** refers to play behavior where children create a story or script with a series of actions in a meaningful sequence. (see Social Relationships in Early Childhood)

39. **Cooperative pretend play** is play behavior where children develop a script and play reciprocal roles. (see Social Relationships in Early Childhood)

40. **Homophily** is the tendency of individuals to associate and bond with others who are similar or "like" themselves. (see Social Relationships in Early Childhood)

FILL-IN-THE-BLANKS KEY TERMS

This section will help you check your knowledge of the key terms introduced in this chapter. Fill in each blank with the appropriate term from the list of key terms in the previous section.

1. _____ are emotions that involve evaluation of oneself, such as embarrassment or pride.

2. Behavior that inflicts unintentional harm to another person is called _____.

3. _____ is the process of teaching children cultural values and rules for behavior.

4. A(n) _____ is a child's evaluation of his or her self-worth as a person, often derived from the parent-child relationship.

5. When children develop a script and play reciprocal roles, we say they are engaged in _____.

6. _____ is the concept that gender is permanent and immutable.

7. _____ are hormones that control the development of masculine characteristics, generally found in higher levels in males than females.

8. _____ is the ability to monitor one's own and others' feelings and to use that information to guide thinking and action

9. _____ are evaluative judgments of oneself in specific domain.

10. Understanding and sharing another person's feelings is called _____.

APPLIED LEARNING AND CRITICAL THINKING

Social and emotional development during early childhood is such a fun process to explore. Finding real-world situations in which to interact with kids as they are developing socioemotional skills can help you develop you own skills in working with children, too.

1. Gender development in early childhood is highly influenced by the culture in which the development takes place. If you have the opportunity to study abroad, you might consider doing a detailed observation of the ways in which gender schema differ from that of your home culture. Are the behavioral differences between young boys and girls in your home culture similar to those that you observe in the culture you are visiting? Are there any differences you can observe? To guide your observations, you could use a chart similar to the one below. Feel free to add additional behavioral categories, and once you've completed the chart, see if you can draw any conclusions about broader cultural differences based on what you observed about gender socialization.

Behavioral Category	Boys	Girls	Similar or Different from Home Culture
Aggression			
Verbal interaction			
Toy preferences			
Preferred play group size			

2. Work with your professor to see if you could do a service-learning project that connects young children with the parents and grandparents in their lives. Develop an interview to elicit family stories from the parents and grandparents about the young child in the family, and about their own childhoods, as well. Then, based on what you've learned about cognitive development in early childhood, pick one or two stories to develop into a children's book, customized for that child, based on a special family story. What stories do you think will be most helpful to young children in developing their cognitive and emotional skills? Think carefully about what sort of text and artwork would be best understood by young children as you develop the story. If you aren't good at artwork, you can collaborate with a student from the art department on your campus to develop pictures to accompany the text. You can then do a "reading" of the book with the family.

3. Work with a faculty member at your university to develop a research partnership with a local juvenile office. A really interesting study would be to explore predictors from early childhood amongst the population of juvenile offenders. Do they collect that sort of data? What sort of archival information might you have to "dig up" to address that research question? Could predictors from early childhood be related to how well the offenders respond to different forms of punishment (e.g., detention, community service, and so forth)?

4. Emotional intelligence has been recognized as an increasingly important construct both in research and in practice. Explore some of the websites devoted to emotional intelligence (http://www.eiconsortium.org is an excellent example, although there are many others). How much information on these sites is devoted to emotional intelligence as a stable trait, as opposed to emotional intelligence as a something that can be taught? To the extent that it is treated as a teachable skill, what sorts of activities do you think could facilitate the development of emotional intelligence in early childhood? In the other sorts of observations you've done of childcare situations throughout the semester, have you seen any evidence of these sorts of activities? Write a short "lesson plan" that you think encapsulates an activity that would develop emotional intelligence in young children. If you enjoy doing this sort of work, you might consider moving beyond a single lesson plan to thinking in terms of an "emotional intelligence curriculum" for early childhood, which might be something that you could develop a full business plan around.

MULTIPLE-CHOICE QUESTIONS

Quiz 1

1. The process of teaching children cultural values and rules for behavior is called
    a. effortful control.
    b. homophily.
    c. agonism.
    d. socialization.

2. Little Marquis tells his mom, "I am the best drawer in my class at school!" Marquis's remark illustrates his
    a. self-concept.
    b. self-esteem.
    c. gender schema.
    d. internal working model.

3. As children become more independent during early childhood, which parenting behaviors will promote the development of initiative rather than guilt?

   a. Eagerly assisting the child with tasks
   b. Critiquing the child's performance
   c. Encouraging the child's efforts without interfering
   d. Pushing the child to aim for total independence

4. Tiffany loves when her mom tells the story of how she crawled in the fireplace as a baby and played with the ashes. Even though she knows the behavior is "bad," as she listens to her mom convey the story, she learns that her mom also really values Tiffany's interest in exploring her environment because she tells the story with a smile on her face and pride in her voice at her daughter's "initiative" to explore a new part of the house. This particular family story has helped Tiffany learn

   a. you don't play in the fireplace.
   b. the cultural value of independent exploration.
   c. obedience.
   d. that her mom was really annoyed with her.

5. Being able to discriminate between males and females is

   a. gender awareness.
   b. gender identity.
   c. gender schema..
   d. gender constancy.

6. Which of the following is evidence that peers contribute to gender socialization in early childhood?

   a. Gender differences in behavior decrease across a school year.
   b. Gender differences in behavior increase across a school year.
   c. Gender differences in behavior remain stable across a school year.
   d. Gender constancy decreases across a school year.

7. Which of the following is NOT a self-conscious emotion?

   a. Embarrassment
   b. Pride
   c. Shame
   d. Happiness.

8. Annaliese's mommy told her that Nana would take her to the park, but when she gets to Nana's house, Nana tells her that it is too hot to go to the park. Annaliese gets furious, but with help is able to calm herself down and get focused on a game rather than her disappointment. Annaliese's ability to calm down and re-focus illustrates

   a. empathy.
   b. emotional intelligence.
   c. emotional regulation.
   d. conscience.

9. Voluntary actions that benefit another are

   a. empathy.
   b. aggression.
   c. prosocial behaviors.
   d. conscience.

10. Apple is eating lunch with a group of friends at day care. She leans over to the girl next to her and says, "Let's play in the tent after lunch, and we won't let Sarah in!" Apple's remark illustrates _____ aggression.

    a. physical
    b. relational
    c. verbal
    d. reactive

11. Which of the following does not involve the element of intent?

    a. Reactive aggression
    b. Instrumental aggression
    c. Agonism
    d. Hostile aggression

12. Research supports which of the following explanations for why children in larger group childcare settings tend to be more aggressive?

    a. The cortisol levels of children in such situations are higher.
    b. There aren't enough caregivers to control the situation in such settings.
    c. More children in such situations model aggressive behavior.
    d. The testosterone levels of children in such situations are higher.

13. Parents who are highly controlling and not very warm are using which parenting style?

    a. Authoritative
    b. Authoritarian
    c. Permissive
    d. Disengaged

14. In which culture might authoritarian parenting yield the best outcomes?

    a. China
    b. Israel
    c. England
    d. United States.

15. Emily is playing with her friend Lilly. "Let's be princesses and run away from the bad witch," she says. Jonathon and Max are playing, and Jonathon says, "Let's play Batman, and I'll be Batman and you be the Joker." Pearl and Emma are playing beside each other, and Pearl sees Emma spin around in a circle and starts to do the same. Which of these is engaged in cooperative play?

    a. Emily and Lilly
    b. Jonathon and Max
    c. Pearl and Emma
    d. Both A and B

Quiz 2

Use this quiz to reassess your learning after taking Quiz 1 and reviewing the chapter.

1. The _____ is a cognitive construction that reflects the child's level of mental development and a social construction that reflects the child's interactions and experiences with other people.

    a. self
    b. conscience
    c. internal working model
    d. gender schema

2. "I'm a bad girl," cried Abby. "I can't do anything." Abby's remarks reflect her

    a. self-conception.
    b. self-esteem.
    c. gender awareness.
    d. gender identity.

3. Which of the following constructs is explicitly tied to attachment?

    a. Initiative versus guilt
    b. Gender socialization
    c. Internal working model
    d. Emotional intelligence

4. Marina told her mom, "When I grow up, I am going to be a boy and play football!" Marina has not yet developed

    a. gender awareness.
    b. gender identity.
    c. gender constancy.
    d. homophily.

5. Which of the following is a hormonal influence on gender differences in early childhood?

    a. The corpus callosum
    b. Agonism
    c. Family stories
    d. Androgens

6. Little Joe is coughing in his friend's face. It is really upsetting his friend, but Joe thinks it is funny. In fact, Joe is so into what he sees as hilarious, that he doesn't even notice he has upset his friend a great deal. Consequently, Joe doesn't stop coughing in his pal's face when he really should. Joe lacks

    a. emotional regulation.
    b. emotional intelligence.
    c. effortful control.
    d. externalizing behaviors.

7. In which culture would pride be most likely to be considered a relatively positive emotion?

    a. United States
    b. China
    c. Mexico
    d. India

8. Thérèse got into her mom's china cabinet even though she knows her mom has told her not to do it. Her mom never caught her in the cabinet, but Thérèse feels guilty anyway because of her

    a. empathy.
    b. conscience.
    c. agonism.
    d. homophily.

9. Which of the following are related to the development of a conscience?

    a. Effortful control
    b. Emotional regulation
    c. Secure attachments
    d. All of these

10. Which type of aggression has "doing harm" as its main goal?

    a. Hostile
    b. Reactive
    c. Instrumental.
    d. Physical

11. Delaney just began kindergarten and seems to be withdrawing. When her mom asks her what happened at school each day, Delaney merely mutters "I don't know." She seems really sad, and doesn't enjoy things that used to bring her pleasure. Delaney has

    a. an externalizing problem.
    b. an internalizing problem.
    c. low emotional intelligence.
    d. All of these

12. Which parenting style is most likely to be associated with aggressive behavior in early childhood?

    a. Authoritative
    b. Authoritarian
    c. Permissive
    d. Disengaged

13. Trey really wants to stay up late and watch a television special, but his bedtime is 8 p.m. and the show doesn't start until 9 p.m. Which of the following parental responses is consistent with an authoritative parenting style?

    a. "Absolutely not! Bedtime is 8 p.m. sharp, young man!"
    b. "Sure, sweetie, whatever you want."
    c. "Tell me why its important to you, honey, and maybe we can tape it for you to watch tomorrow after school."
    d. "Whatever, kid."

14. Wei-shin and Megumi like to play together. They both pretend to drink from the teacups in the play kitchen. They are engaged in

    a. simple pretend play.
    b. associative pretend play.
    c. cooperative pretend play.
    d. rough-and-tumble play.

15. The process of similar others being attracted to each other is called

    a. empathy.
    b. rough-and-tumble.
    c. developmental trajectory.
    d. homophily.

ANSWERS TO FILL-IN-THE-BLANKS KEY TERMS

1. Self-conscious emotions (see Emotional Development)

2. agonism (see Prosocial Behaviors, Conscience, and Aggression)

3. Socialization (see introductory section)

4. internal working model (see Development of the Self)

5. cooperative pretend play (see Social Relationships in Early Childhood)

6. Gender constancy (see Gender Development)

7. Androgens (see Gender Development)

8.   Emotional intelligence (see Emotional Development)

9.   Self-conceptions (see Development of the Self)

10. empathy (see Prosocial Behaviors, Conscience, and Aggression)

ANSWERS TO MULTIPLE-CHOICE QUESTIONS

Circle the question numbers you answered incorrectly.

Quiz 1

1.   *d is the answer.*   Socialization is the process of conveying to children cultural values and rules for behavior. (see introductory section)

2.   *a is the answer.*   The self-concept refers to evaluative judgments about specific areas, like drawing ability. Marquis's remark is about his ability in that specific area, not a more global assessment of his own worth, which would be self-esteem. (see Development of the Self)

3.   *c is the answer.*   Parents who accept and encourage their child's efforts, without interfering or pushing, tend to see their children develop a sense of capability that translates into initiative. In contrast, parents who ridicule, critique, or restrict such efforts at independence see the child develop a sense of themselves as failures, accompanied by guilt. (see The Development of the Self)

4.   *b is the answer.*   Family stories help convey cultural values. In this case, Tiffany has learned through her mom's nonverbal cues (e.g., pride in her voice) that the supposedly "naughty" behavior of playing in the ashes is a form of "independent exploration" that her mom and culture value. (see The Development of the Self)

5.   *a is the answer.*   Gender awareness emerges as children begin to discriminate between males and females, including knowing which category they fit into themselves. (see Gender Development)

6.   *b is the answer.*   When gender differences increase across a school year, it may be due to the fact that there is greater peer exposure during the school year than the summer. It would be particularly compelling if the differences increased more quickly during the school year and remained stable or decreased during the summer time. (see Gender Development)

7.   *d is the answer.*   Self-conscious emotions involve awareness of the self as distinct, awareness of standards for behavior and how one's own performance ranks against those standards, and a sense of responsibility for success or failure. Happiness does not involve all of these features and evaluations. Embarrassment, pride, and shame do. (see Emotional Development)

8.   *c is the answer.*   Emotional regulation is the ability to inhibit, enhance, maintain, and modulate emotional arousal to accomplish a goal. Annaliese's original goal in going to the park was to have fun. Even though her initial reaction to disappointment was fury, she is able to modulate that and inhibit the tantrum to focus on the game, which allows her to have fun in a different way than she had planned. (see Emotional Development)

9.   *c is the answer.*   Prosocial behaviors are voluntary actions that benefit another. (see Prosocial Behaviors, Conscience, and Aggression)

10.   *b is the answer.*   Relational aggression involves attempts to lower a child's social standing or relations with others. By barring Sarah from the play in the tent, Apple has diminished Sarah's relationship with the other child in the tent. (see Prosocial Behaviors, Conscience, and Aggression)

11.   *c is the answer.*   Reactive, instrumental, and hostile aggression all involve intent to harm for different reasons (defense, goals, and harm, respectively). Agonism, in contrast, is harm done accidentally, without the element of intent. (see Prosocial Behaviors, Conscience, and Aggression)

12.   *a is the answer.*   Cortisol levels tend to be higher in large group childcare settings, indicating a stress response to the situation. These high levels are seen most in children with difficulty regulating negative emotions and behavior. (see Prosocial Behaviors, Conscience, and Aggression)

13.   *b is the answer.*   Authoritarian parents are high on control but low on warmth. (see Social Relationships in Early Childhood)

14.   *a is the answer.*   Chinese parents often use a more authoritarian style than parents from Western nations. It is focused on *chia-shun* (training) and *guan* (parental investment and involvement), which are often controlling and low on warmth. This emphasis is associated with higher academic achievement in China, and some argue better outcomes more generally. In Western cultures, though, authoritative parenting is associated with better outcomes. (see Social Relationships in Early Childhood)

15.   *b is the answer.*   Only Jonathon and Max are engaged in cooperative play because they are taking on reciprocal roles (one is the "good guy" and one is the "bad guy"). Emily and Lilly are both being princesses (associative play), and Pearl and Emma are not collaborating on play at all, other than mimicking (simple pretend play) each other. (see Social Relationships in Early Childhood)

Now turn to the quiz analysis table at the end of this chapter to find which areas you know well and which areas you need to work on. Circle the numbers in the table for items on Quiz 1 that you answered correctly.

Quiz 2

1.   *a is the answer.*   The self is defined as both a cognitive construction that reflects the child's level of mental development and a social construction that reflects the child's interactions and experiences with other people. (see Development of the Self)

2.   *b is the answer.*   Self-esteem refers to global assessment of self-worth. Abby's remarks are global in nature, rather than directed at a specific area of performance. (see Development of the Self)

3.   *c is the answer.*   Attachment researchers see the internal working model as growing out of attachment relationships, with sensitive and warm parenting promoting secure attachment and the working model of the self as a person of value. (see Development of the Self)

4.   *c is the answer.*   Gender constancy is the understanding that one's gender is permanent and immutable. Marina's remark suggests that she still sees gender as changeable. (see Gender Development)

5.   *d is the answer.*   Androgens are hormones that control the development of masculine characteristics. (see Gender Development)

6.   *b is the answer.*   Emotional intelligence is the ability to monitor one's own and other's emotions, and to use that information to guide future action. Joe is not able to monitor his friend's emotions effectively, which means he can't use his friend's emotional experience as a guide to stop his annoying behavior. (see Emotional Development)

7.   *a is the answer.*   Pride is considered a positive emotion in individualistic cultures, a signal of individual accomplishment. The United States is the most individualistic culture on this list. (see Emotional Development)

8.   *b is the answer.*   The conscience is the internal standard of right and wrong that causes a child to feel guilt and shame even when no one observed a wrong behavior directly. (see Prosocial Behaviors, Conscience, and Aggression)

9.   *d is the answer.*   Effortful control is associated with greater empathy and greater guilt and shame on conscience assessments. Emotional regulation is associated with being sympathetic and helpful, and a willingness to share with and comfort others. Secure attachments are associated the ability to experience sympathy, providing a pathway to the development of conscience, as well. (see Prosocial Behaviors, Conscience, and Aggression)

10.   *a is the answer.*   Hostile aggression intends harm as its primary goal. (see Prosocial Behaviors, Conscience, and Aggression)

11.   *b is the answer.*   Delaney's behavior is depressed, which is a form of an internalizing problem. (see Prosocial Behaviors, Conscience, and Aggression)

12.   *b is the answer.*   Punitive, coercive, and harsh parental discipline are associated with aggression problems in early childhood and beyond. These behaviors are consistent with the high control/low warmth characteristics of authoritarian parenting. (see Prosocial Behaviors, Conscience, and Aggression)

13.   *c is the answer.*   Only this response reveals warmth with limits (i.e., control), the hallmarks of authoritative parenting. The "a" response is high on control, but low on warmth, which is authoritarian. The "b" response is high on warmth, but low on control, characteristic of permissive parenting. The "d" response is low on both warmth and control, indicating a disengaged parent. (see Social Relationships in Early Childhood)

14.   *a is the answer.*   Wei-shin and Megumi are not creating a story to act out (associative play) or using reciprocal roles (cooperative play). Rather, they are pretending alongside each other without collaborating in any way, which is simple pretend play. (see Social Relationships in Early Childhood)

15.   *d is the answer.*   Homophily is the process of associating or bonding with those that are like or similar to ourselves. (see Social Relationships in Early Childhood)

Now turn to the quiz analysis table at the end of this chapter to find which areas you know well and which areas you need to work on. Circle the numbers in the table for items on Quiz 2 that you answered correctly.

For each question you answered correctly, circle its number. (Quiz 1 numbers are not shaded; Quiz 2 numbers are shaded.) Are there patterns in the types of questions or the topics you got wrong that could direct your further study? Did you improve from Quiz 1 to Quiz 2?

QUIZ REVIEW

Topic	Type of Question		
	Definition	Comprehension	Application
Development of the Self	1	3	2, 4
	1	3	2
Gender Development	5	6	
		5	4
Emotional Development		7	8
		7	6
Prosocial Behaviors, Conscience, and Aggression	9	11, 12	10
	10	9, 12	8, 11
Social Relationships in Early Childhood	13	14	15
	15		13, 14

Total correct by quiz:

Quiz 1:	
Quiz 2:	

CHAPTER 10

Physical Development in Middle Childhood

LEARNING OBJECTIVES

1. Describe the changes that take place in the brain during middle childhood.

2. Explain how differences in brain development seem to affect the development of an individual's intelligence.

3. Describe the possible consequences of a traumatic brain injury during middle childhood.

4. Define Attention Deficit Hyperactivity Disorder (ADHD) and explain how some structural and functional differences in the brain may contribute to this condition.

5. Explain how the brain reacts to stress, and describe some of the long-term effects of stress on children's brains.

6. Describe the effects of Post-traumatic Stress Disorder (PTSD) on children's brains.

7. Describe the changes in gross motor skills during middle childhood, and explain how they are influenced by a child's level of physical activity.

8. Explain the effects of daily physical activity on a child's cognitive development.

9. Describe both the positive and negative consequences of organized children's sports.

10. Explain how the development of fine motor skills in middle childhood both influences and is influenced by brain development.

11. Describe the physical changes children experience during middle childhood.

12. List the factors that contribute to childhood obesity.

13. Explain the physical and psychological consequences of childhood obesity.

14. Describe some successful programs used to counteract childhood obesity.

15. Describe the amount of sleep required in middle childhood and explain how sleep contributes to a child's mental and physical capabilities.

16. List the most common types of accidental injuries experienced by children aged 2–11 years old.

17. Describe the most common acute illnesses and chronic medical conditions found in children aged 2–11 years old, and show how these conditions may affect the children's development, and how they are treated.

OUTLINE

Middle childhood spans age 5 to 12, sometimes called the "school years."

I. Physical Growth and Development
    A. **Normative Development**
        1. During middle childhood, children gain 2–3 inches in height and several pounds each year. For girls, this is the beginning of their adolescent growth spurt, and

signals the onset of **puberty**. Growth spurts occur, and body proportions change, making school age children appear leggy.

2. Baby teeth are lost and most permanent teeth are in by the end of middle childhood. Near-sightedness often develops during this time, too.

3. The hormonal changes that become physically apparent in puberty have their beginnings in early childhood. Hormones signal the **hypothalamus** and **pituitary gland**, which in turn send hormonal signals to the **gonads**. The earliest signs of sexual maturation occur in girls with the development of breast buds between ages 7–13, followed by **menarche** (between ages 9–15). The age of menarche has dropped over time, a pattern called a **secular trend**.

4. Children are growing faster and bigger during middle childhood, often having a higher **body mass index (BMI)**. This pattern—also a secular trend—is based on the better nutrition that is available today than to previous generations.

B. Obesity
Childhood obesity is on the rise, with nearly 40% of children being overweight or at risk for being overweight. Many factors influence this trend.

1. Families today increasingly rely on fast food—either from restaurants or supermarket prepared food—which is higher in calories and lower in nutrition than home-cooked meals.

2. Two-thirds of advertisements on television during children's prime viewing hours are either for food (usually convenience food) or for passive entertainment other shows, games, etc.). This combination may affect children's propensity for overweight.

3. School lunches, though they must meet minimal nutritional requirements, have to be food that children will eat because if sales drop federal subsidies are reduced. Consequently, many of the lunches mirror the fast food industry. Additionally, healthier items are more expensive to include in these lunches, and many schools have vending machines where children can buy high-calorie/low-nutrition snacks and drinks.

4. Neighborhoods used to be designed to promote walking and biking, but the modern suburban neighborhoods tend to support driving over these physical activities. Children tend to be driven to school, have less play time outside after school, and are often in neighborhoods without easy access to parks and outdoor recreation areas.

5. Physical inactivity is clearly linked to overweight. Children who tend to be inactive have homes with fewer toys and adult-structured activities, and tend to spend more time watching television, which promotes sitting and snacking.

C. Physical and Mental Consequences of Being Overweight

1. Overweight and obesity carry serious health consequences. Children who are overweight or obese are at risk for being diagnosed with diabetes, **asthma**, or sleep apnea. Children do not tend to outgrow overweight; rather, these problems are magnified over time.

2. Overweight and obesity also carry social and emotional consequences, including risk of rejection, lower sense of self-worth, less confidence in athletic ability, and risk for internalizing problems in general.

D. Promising Interventions

1. Many interventions have not been effective, but a few have. One program taught by a school nurse focused on reducing soft drink consumption, and produced a reduced percentage of overweight children as compared to controls.

2. Another program focused on reducing time spent watching television by having children first monitor their watching, then asking them to go through a "turn off" period, and finally have them develop a "budget" to promote more selective use of media. Children in this program had slower increases in BMI and were more active than controls.

3. After school programs can also help limit risk for overweight, as these programs tend to result in reduced time in front of the television and lower snack/soft drink consumption.

II. Brain Development

A. Normative Changes

1. Many of the processes begun in early childhood brain development continue into middle childhood, with **axons** and **dendrites** continuing to establish new **synapses**, and the speed of neurotransmission increasing with the growth of **myelin.** Synapses that are not frequently used are removed via **competitive elimination** and **synaptic pruning**. This increases **lateralization**, and the **corpus callosum** thickens to support cross-hemisphere communication.

2. Brain development usually occurs in a cyclical pattern around the **cortex**, moving from longest connections in one hemisphere to the shortest connections, and then to the other hemisphere in reverse order. **Magnetic resonance imaging (MRI)** supports this view of brain development, showing growth spurts in different parts of the brain at different times. Across all parts of the cortex, **gray matter** follows a pattern of growth beginning with proliferation of neurons and their connections that reach a peak, and then decline via competitive elimination, not **apoptosis.**

3. During middle childhood, a growth spurt occurs in the **frontal lobes** between ages 6–8, with gray matter in the **prefrontal cortex** increasing slowly to age 8, and rapidly thereafter to age 14. The **temporal** and **parietal lobes** also experience a great deal of change.

4. Unlike gray matter, **white matter** (i.e., myelin) follows a linear increase throughout middle childhood. As a result, much improvement in coordination between brain regions occurs.

B. Differences in Brain Development

1. Patterns of change in gray and white matter vary depending on the gender of the child. During middle childhood, girls experience rapid growth in synaptic networks devoted to spatial-visual discrimination and gross motor development, while boys experience synaptic growth related to language and fine motor skills.

2. Boys' brains tend to be larger than girls' at this age, but this difference is unrelated to intelligence. The thickness of the **cerebral cortex**, however, is. Superior intelligence tends to be correlated with a pattern of brain development described by proliferation of gray matter during middle childhood, but pruning of that during adolescence.

3. **Traumatic brain injury (TBI)** is a sudden injury to the brain either via a blow to the head or a penetrating wound. Over a million children in the U. S. receive a TBI each year, often resulting in lifelong disabilities that may be physical, cognitive, social or emotional in nature. Symptoms often lead to children being misdiagnosed as having a learning disability, emotional problem, or mental retardation.

4. **Attention deficit hyperactivity disorder (ADHD)** is also linked to brain development. There are three types: predominantly inattention, predominantly hyperactive, or a combination of these two. About 6% of school age children have this diagnosis, with twice as many boys receiving the diagnosis as girls.

Differences in the **cerebellum** and abnormalities in **neurotransmitters** may underlie this condition. ADHD children's gray matter peaks about three years later than non-ADHD children's.

C.   Brain Reactions to Stress

1.   As in adults, stress exposure for children results in a release of **cortisol**, which stimulates a flow of energy to muscles and brain. Prolonged exposure to cortisol is toxic, destroying neurons in the **hippocampus**, a brain structure that supports memory, learning, and emotion. Prolonged exposure can result in **post-traumatic stress disorder (PTSD).** Although normally associated with combat, children who have been abused can merit this diagnosis.

2.   Children with the most severe PTSD symptoms tend to have the highest cortisol levels and the most reduction in size to the hippocampus.

3.   Children of parents with volatile relationships, however, tend to have lower levels of cortisol, as if a thermostat "shut off" the cortisol to try to maintain more normal levels. The low levels of cortisol in these children were later associated with externalizing problems, as if the children were less capable of attending to social cues.

D.   Coping with Stress

1.   **Behavioral coping** is effortful or purposeful response to challenging situations. It begins with regulating emotional arousal, followed by assessment of the situation, and then implementing a solution that will address the parts of the situation under one's own control. This third step, often called **problem-focused coping**, occurs when a child is able to identify the difficulty and do something constructive about it.

2.   Individual children vary in their strategies, but four broad categories have been identified.

a)   Active coping

b)   Aggressive coping

c)   Denial coping

d)   Ruminative coping

3.   The effectiveness of these strategies varies, with active coping being in general associated with the most favorable outcomes. Ruminative and aggressive coping tend to associate with internalizing problems. The effectiveness of denial coping is somewhat more mixed. Child temperament can affect which strategy a child is most prone to use.

III.   Motor Development

A.   Gross Motor Skills

1.   **Gross motor skills** become smoother and more coordinated in middle childhood. This allows increased physical activity, and the child uses the muscles in new ways which may result in some "growing pains."

2.   Although boys used to be better at motions such as throwing and running, and girls better at flexibility and balance, it is not clear if this is a true difference or a result of the difference in motor experiences that school-age boys and girls have. A recent study suggests that the difference is likely grounded in experience.

3.   Middle childhood is in some ways a sensitive period for motor development, as learning to ride a bike or swim is much easier at this age than it will be in adulthood. While some children may struggle with motor development— particularly obese children—research suggests that high quality physical education can help remediate these problems.

B. Physical Activity
   1. Physical activity is essential to growth and development, and pediatricians recommend 60 minutes daily of activity for school-age children.
   2. Exercise may be associated with brain development, and research indicates a correlation between physical fitness and scores on standardized tests.
   3. School-age children get about half the recommended amount of physical activity during the school week, often because P.E. programs are no longer offered daily at their schools. Weekends and youth sport participation may help offset this deficit.
C. Youth Sports
   1. Many children participate in youth sports. Conventional wisdom suggests such activity teaches character, leadership, as well as fitness, but youth sports can create a lot of anxiety in school-age children.
   2. The Coach Effectiveness Training (CET) program teaches coaches to emphasize fun and effort over winning, and to provide support in the face of failure. Children with trained coaches generally like their coaches, teammates, and the sport itself better than children who have untrained coaches. They also show bigger gains in self-esteem.
   3. Parents can be the biggest challenge for coaches in youth sports. Parents who are enthusiastic and supportive, as opposed to interfering and overly focused on winning, tend to reduce performance anxiety in their little athletes.
D. Fine Motor Skills
   1. **Fine motor skills** involve small muscle movements of the hand and fingers, often coordinated with the eyes. During middle childhood, children make great strides in this area—writing in cursive, playing an instrument, typing on a keyboard, and so forth. Brain development allows children to practice these skills, and the practice in turn promotes brain development.
   2. Children with significant difficulty with gross and fine motor skills have **Developmental Coordination Disorder**.

IV. Sleep
   A. Amount of Sleep that Children Need
      1. An **actigraph** is a motion detector that measures sleep onset, morning awakening, and nighttime awakenings. Using these measures, researchers can determine a child's *sleep period* (onset of sleep to morning awakening) and *true sleep times* (sleep period minus nighttime awakenings). Parents tend to overestimate the amount of sleep their child gets.
      2. True sleep times are about 30–44 minutes less than sleep periods. Many children are poor sleepers, and nearly all get an hour or more *less* than the recommended ten to eleven hours of sleep.
      3. One sleep disruption the actigraph does not measure is **apnea**, which affects one to three percent of children.
   B. The Sleep Context
      1. Family circumstances can affect the quality of a child's sleep. Children from more affluent families tend to get better quality sleep than those from poorer families. Children from families under stress tend to sleep less well than families who are not stressed.
      2. Children today are exposed to a number of influences that can "steal" sleep, ranging from caffeine to exposure to electronic media.
   C. Sleep and Cognitive Functioning
      1. Sleep helps consolidate the days learning, and clears the mind for focused attention and learning the following day.

2.   Fragmented sleep adversely impacts children's performance on a number of cognitive tests. Lack of adequate sleep does much the same.

3.   Going to sleep at the same time each night is positively associated with verbal ability. During middle childhood, a preference for a particular **circadian rhythm** emerges.

V.   Physical Health

A.   Unintentional Injuries

1.   Motor vehicles are the leading cause of death during middle childhood. Many of these deaths could have been prevented by having the child sit in the back and wear a safety belt.

2.   Drowning is the second leading cause of death during middle childhood. Drowning is more likely for African-American or Native Americans than for whites, as learning to swim is not a routine part of childhood in these cultures.

B.   Illnesses

1.   After injury deaths, cancer is the leading cause of death in middle childhood. White children are at greater risk for cancer than minorities. Although the incidence of cancer diagnoses has increased, the survivability of the illness reached 79% during the 1990s based on improved treatments.

2.   Vaccines have greatly reduced the number of childhood deaths due to illness, and previous exposures from early childhood strengthen the immune system during middle childhood to support this pattern as well.

3.   No vaccination exists for HIV, but new antiretroviral medications can significantly delay the development of full-blown AIDS. In the U. S., only a few children a year develop HIV/AIDS, and most of these acquire the disease from their mothers. Mothers who are aware they have HIV/AIDS can take medication during pregnancy and choose not to breastfeed their baby, which reduces the likelihood of the baby having the illness to one percent. In theory, children with HIV/AIDs can live a "normal" life, but in practice such children tend to experience significant developmental delays.

C.   Chronic Medical Conditions

1.   Nearly 10% of children age 5–11 suffer from asthma, a sharp increase from previous estimates. The reason for this spike is unknown. Asthma is more likely for non-white children, for boys, and for poorer children.

2.   Allergies are common in middle childhood. Both asthma and allergies can impact a child's quality of life by negatively affecting the quality of sleep the child has, the ability of the child to participate in some sports or attend field trips, and so forth.

3.   Diabetes is a third common chronic condition in middle childhood. There are two types of diabetes. In **Type 1 diabetes**, the immune system destroys the cells in the pancreas that produce insulin. It tends to have a sudden onset in children and young adults and requires daily injections of insulin throughout life. **Type 2 diabetes** is associated with being overweight, and involves the body not being able to use insulin efficiently. As more children are overweight and inactive, the incidence of Type 2 diabetes is on the rise. It can be delayed or prevented through diet and exercise. Children often do not believe diabetes is as serious as it is, and it can be difficult to get them to take their treatment seriously.

KEY TERMS

1. **Normative development** refers to typical changes in body size and shape and motor skills.

2. **Puberty** refers to physical changes, including sexual maturation, that occur from childhood into adulthood. (see Physical Growth and Development)

3. The **hypothalamus** is a small cone-like structure of the brain that is involved in hormonal signals that result in sexual maturation. (see Physical Growth and Development)

4. The **pituitary gland** is one of the chief glands responsible for regulating levels of hormones in the body.

5. The **gonads** are the primary reproductive organs (ovaries for females and testes for males). (see Physical Growth and Development)

6. **Menarche** is the time of first menstruation, one of the important changes to occur among females during puberty. (see Physical Growth and Development)

7. A **secular trend** refers to changes over generations. (see Physical Growth and Development)

8. **Body mass index** is calculated by dividing weight (measured in kilograms) by height (measured in meters) squared, or wt/ht^2. (see Physical Growth and Development)

9. **Dendrites** are branched extensions of a neuron that picks up signals from other neurons. (see Brain Development)

10. **Axons** are the part of the cell that carries signals away from the cell body toward other neurons. (see Brain Development)

11. **Synapses** are the connection between one neuron's axon and another neuron's dendrite. (see Brain Development)

12. **Myelin** is a white fatty substance that encases cell axons. It provides insulation and improves the transmission of signals. (see Brain Development)

13. **Competitive elimination** refers to a process that strengthens synapses that are used regularly, and prunes unused synapses to eliminate clutter. It accelerates the speed with which children can process information. (see Brain Development)

14. **Synaptic pruning** is elimination of unused and unnecessary synapses. (see Brain Development)

15. **Lateralization** refers to the localization of function in one of the hemispheres of the brain.

16. The **corpus callosum** is the connection between the two halves or hemispheres of the brain. (see Brain Development)

17. The **cortex** refers to the thin layers of outer tissue that covers the brain. (see Brain Development)

18. **Gray matter** refers to the cortex of the brain which contains nerve cell bodies (neurons, axons, and dendrites). The gray matter is in contrast to the white matter, the part of the brain that contains myelinated nerve fibers. (see Brain Development)

19. **Apoptosis** is programmed cell death in the brain. (see Brain Development)

20. The **frontal lobes** are part of the brain located in front of the parietal lobes and above the temporal lobes that is involved in recognizing future consequences, overriding unacceptable social responses, and remembering emotional experiences.

21. The **prefrontal cortex** is the part of the brain involved in higher-order cognitive skills, such as decision making and planning. It is located in front of the brain, right behind the forehead. (see Brain Development)

22. The **temporal lobes** are the part of the brain that is involved in speech, memory, and hearing. They are located at the side of the brain. (see Brain Development)

23. The **parietal lobes** are part of the brain associated with movement, orientation, recognition, perception of stimuli. (see Brain Development)

24. **White matter** refers to the part of the brain that is made up of myelinated nerve fibers. (see Brain Development)

25. The **cerebral cortex** is the extensive outer layer of gray matter of the brain, largely responsible for higher brain functions, including sensation, voluntary muscle movement, thought, reasoning, and memory. (see Brain Development)

26. A **traumatic brain injury (TBI)** is a sudden injury to the brain, and can be caused by a blow to the head or a penetrating wound. (see Brain Development)

27. **Attention deficit hyperactivity disorder (ADHD)** is a condition in which children have difficulty getting organized, focusing on a task, or thinking before acting. (see Brain Development)

28. The **cerebellum** is the part of the brain associated with balance and control of body movements. (see Brain Development)

29. **Neurotransmitters** are chemical substances in the brain that carry electrical impulses across synapses. (see Brain Development)

30. **Cortisol** is a hormone produced when we are exposed to stress. (see Brain Development)

31. The **hippocampus** is part of the limbic region of the brain involved in memory, learning, and emotion. (see Brain Development)

32. **Post-traumatic stress disorder** is caused by chronic and prolonged stress. Symptoms include intrusive thoughts and flashbacks, nightmares and sleep disorders, withdrawal, and problems with emotional control. (see Brain Development)

33. **Behavioral coping** refers to the effortful or purposeful response to challenging situations. (see Brain Development)

34. **Problem-focused coping** occurs when children are able to identify what the difficulty is and then do something about it. (see Brain Development)

35. **Gross motor skills** are large movements of the arms, legs, and feet, or the whole body, such as running, jumping, climbing, and throwing. (see Motor Development)

36. **Fine motor skills** refer to small movements of the hand and fingers, such as picking up small objects and tying one's shoes. (see Motor Development)

37. **Developmental Coordination Disorder (DCD)** is characterized by a marked impairment in motor coordination given what would be expected for the child's chronological age and intelligence. (see Motor Development)

38. An **actigraph** is a motion detector that measures sleep onset and awakenings. (see Sleep)

39. **Apnea** refers to a sleep disruption in which there are temporary pauses in breathing, ranging from a few seconds to a minute. (see Sleep)

40. A **circadian rhythm** is a daily, rhythmic activity cycle, based on 24-hour intervals. (see Sleep)

41. **Asthma** is a chronic respiratory condition that causes sudden attacks of wheezing, coughing, and shortness of breath.

42. **Type 1 diabetes** refers to a type of diabetes where the immune system destroys the beta cells in the pancreas so that pancreas produces little or no insulin. People with type 1 diabetes often need daily injections of insulin throughout their lives. (see Physical Health)

43. **Type 2 diabetes** is a type of diabetes in which the body does not use insulin efficiently. Type 2 diabetes is brought on by a combination of genes, overweight, and inactivity. (see Physical Health)

FILL-IN-THE-BLANKS KEY TERMS

This section will help you check your knowledge of the key terms introduced in this chapter. Fill in each blank with the appropriate term from the list of key terms in the previous section.

1. A(n) _____ is a motion detector that measures sleep onset and awakenings.

2. The time of first menstruation, one of the important changes to occur among females during puberty, is called _____.

3. A(n) _____ is a daily, rhythmic activity cycle, based on 24-hour intervals.

4. _____ occurs when the body does not use insulin efficiently and is brought on by a combination of genes and overweight .

5. The process that strengthens synapses that are used regularly and prunes unused synapses to eliminate clutter is called_____.

6. _____ refers to changes that occur over generations.

7. _____ is programmed cell death in the brain.

8. _____ is characterized by marked impairment in motor coordination given what would be expected for a child's chronological age and intelligence.

9. _____ is a sudden injury to the brain, caused by a blow to the head or penetrating wound.

10. The effortful or purposeful response to challenging situations is called _____.

APPLIED LEARNING AND CRITICAL THINKING

Middle childhood showcases enormous changes in physical development. Finding ways to observe these changes in real-world contexts through service, internships, travel, and research can help you explore them in more detail.

1. As discussed in previous chapter's versions of this column, many school districts have mentoring program in which you can volunteer. One way to explore the brain-body connection in middle childhood might be to volunteer in an elementary school with the school counselor serving as your point of contact. Increasingly, school counselors develop and implement many programs to help school-aged children cope more effectively with stress so that they can learn more effectively at school. See if a school counselor might be willing to work with you to take some of what you have learned in this chapter and use it to develop a program to help school-aged children manage their stress. Doing so will give you

a good idea of what a school counselor's job entails, and some of the challenges involved in engaging children of this age in group-oriented programs.

2.   Many city programs offer internships or summer jobs that involve working with school-aged children. For example, summer programming for youth sports requires people to work as coaches. Consider seeking a position doing this one summer as a part-time job. If your career plans involve working with children, this opportunity (while not the best paying) will give you volumes of experience in working with school-aged children. Additionally, you will get to see first-hand some of the issues related to how parents approach youth sports, and develop some skills in managing parents who are overly involved in their young athlete's experience.

3.   If your university experience will involve travel abroad, take that opportunity to make some observations about the childhood obesity epidemic here in the United States as opposed to in the countries you visit. Your text outlines how changes in a child's physical context over the past few generations (e.g., neighborhood layouts, media exposure, etc.). See if those changes are as present in other countries, and if childhood obesity is as prevalent there. Do children walk to school there? Are television and video games as easily available? Do the neighborhoods promote walking to run errands, or do families have to drive? How available is inexpensive fast food? What do school lunches seem to be like?

4.   Your text reports that many school-aged children do not get the recommended 10–11 hours of sleep each night. Work with one of your professors to conduct a survey of parents of school-aged children in your area to see what local parents report for the amount and quality of sleep their children get nightly. You could then parse that data according to demographics, such as average home price in the neighborhood, to see if you can replicate the findings reported in your text that children from more well-to-do families tend to have better sleep habits.

MULTIPLE-CHOICE QUESTIONS

Quiz 1

1.   Which of the following are gonads?

    a.   Hypothalamus
    b.   Ovaries
    c.   Testes
    d.   Both B and C

2.   The average age of menarche decreasing over time is an example of

    a.   normative development.
    b.   a secular trend.
    c.   competitive elimination.
    d.   a circadian rhythm.

3.   Which child is LEAST at risk for being overweight or obese based on the risk factors discussed in your text?

    a.   Sarah, who lives in an urban setting, is on free/reduced lunch at public school, and watches a lot of television
    b.   Joel, who has two working parents who pick up fast food frequently
    c.   Abby, who lives in a suburban neighborhood several miles from the stores
    d.   Luke, who walks to school and has a mom who packs his lunch for school

4.   Reductions in neurons during middle childhood are largely due to

   a.   apoptosis.
   b.   magnetic resonance imaging.
   c.   competitive elimination.
   d.   myelinization.

5.   Changes during middle childhood in the ability to think critically and solve problems are most related to development of which part of the brain?

   a.   Frontal lobes
   b.   Parietal lobes
   c.   Temporal lobes
   d.   The hippocampus

6.   Connor has a laid-back personality, but he seems unable to listen when his teacher is talking to the class as a whole, or when a peer is trying to get his attention. He isn't disruptive to the class, though. He has recently had a diagnosis. Based on this information only, what diagnosis might Connor most likely merit?

   a.   TBI
   b.   ADHD: IA
   c.   ADHD: HI
   d.   ADHD: C

7.   Intrusive thoughts, difficulty sleeping, withdrawal, and problems with emotional control are part of

   a.   ADHD.
   b.   TBI.
   c.   PTSD.
   d.   apnea.

8.   Amelia is upset that some kids are teasing her on the school playground. She tells herself, "It doesn't matter what they think!" Amelia is engaged in _____ coping.

   a.   active
   b.   aggressive
   c.   denial
   d.   ruminative

9.   Which of the following is NOT a gross motor action?

   a.   Running
   b.   Hopping.
   c.   Skipping
   d.   Writing

10. Impairment in motor coordination given what would be expected for a child's age and intelligence is called

   a.   menarche.
   b.   developmental coordination disorder.
   c.   apnea.
   d.   apoptosis.

11. An actigraph directly measures

   a.   sleep onset, morning awakenings, and nighttime wakenings.
   b.   sleep periods.
   c.   true sleep times.
   d.   body mass index.

12. What percent of children are affected by apnea?

    a. 1–3%
    b. 7–10%
    c. 12–15%
    d. 20–22%

13. During middle childhood, preferences for being a "night owl" or an "early bird" become more noticeable because of emerging

    a. myelinization.
    b. circadian rhythms.
    c. obesity.
    d. secular trends.

14. What is the leading cause of death for school-aged children?

    a. Cancer
    b. HIV/AIDS
    c. Vehicle accidents
    d. Drowning

15. Who is most likely to be plagued by asthma?

    a. Joan, who is Mexican
    b. Claire, who is white
    c. Michael, who is black
    d. James, who is white

Quiz 2

Use this quiz to reassess your learning after taking Quiz 1 and reviewing the chapter.

1. The onset of menstruation in girls is called

    a. the larche.
    b. menarche.
    c. puberty.
    d. the secular trend.

2. Which of the following statements about childhood obesity is true?

    a. The kids tend to lose their baby fat by adulthood.
    b. The weight that kids are as children is proportionally similar to their adult weight.
    c. The risk for overweight and obesity increase with age.
    d. Both B and C

3. Which of the following statements about brain development in middle childhood is true?

    a. Dendrites and axons quit building synapses.
    b. Dendrites and axons continue to build new synapses.
    c. Synaptic pruning occurs.
    d. Both B and C

4. MRI research indicates that significant brain growth during middle childhood occurs

    a. in the front part of the brain.
    b. in the back part of the brain.
    c. rarely.
    d. sporadically.

5. Who is most likely to experience the most rapid improvement in their fine motor skills during middle childhood, based on patterns of brain development?

   a. Jack
   b. Jackie
   c. Linda
   d. Mariah

6. Which of the following patterns of brain development is associated with superior intelligence in middle childhood?

   a. Proliferation of gray matter
   b. Rapid pruning of gray matter
   c. Proliferation of gray matter without pruning
   d. Both A and B

7. What percentage of school-age children have been diagnosed with ADHD?

   a. 1%
   b. 10%
   c. 6%
   d. 25%

8. What is likely to be high in a child diagnosed with PTSD?

   a. BMI
   b. Cortisol level
   c. Myelin level
   d. All of these

9. Augie's parents constantly argue. It really stresses him out. They just never seem to resolve their differences. They argue and yell at dinner time so often that Augie just tunes them out. Augie may well have

   a. hypercortisolism.
   b. hypocortisolism.
   c. TBI.
   d. apnea.

10. Trey is being bullied by Donaldo on the playground. Trey thinks it is wrong and he doesn't like it, so he decides to visit the school counselor and see if she can help him find a way to make Donaldo stop it. Trey is engaged in

    a. problem-focused coping.
    b. denial coping.
    c. aggressive coping.
    d. ruminative coping.

11. Growing pains in the calf and thigh and behind the knee are caused by

    a. the growth itself.
    b. increased physical activity.
    c. using the muscles there in new ways.
    d. Both B and C

12. Which of the following is NOT one of the principles of the Coach Effectiveness Training program?

    a. Failure is not the same thing as losing.
    b. Success is not equivalent to winning.
    c. Winning is everything—and the only thing.
    d. Success is found in striving for victory.

13. Which of the following is NOT a fine motor skill likely to be mastered in middle childhood?
    a.   Cursive writing
    b.   Cutting with scissors
    c.   Jumping rope
    d.   Typing on a keyboard

14. Research has shown that extending a child's sleep by_____ can increase their performance on tests of memory and reaction time.
    a.   two hours
    b.   one hour
    c.   30 minutes
    d.   10 minutes

15. _____ appears most often in children, adolescents, and young adults and involves the immune system destroying the beta cells in the pancreas that produce insulin.
    a.   Type 1 diabetes
    b.   Type 2 diabetes
    c.   Asthma
    d.   The flu

ANSWERS TO FILL-IN-THE-BLANKS KEY TERMS

1.   actigraph (see Sleep)

2.   menarche (see Physical Growth and Development)

3.   circadian rhythm (see Sleep)

4.   Type 2 diabetes (see Physical Health)

5.   competitive elimination (see Brain Development)

6.   Secular trend (see Physical Growth and Development)

7.   Apoptosis (see Brain Development)

8.   Developmental Coordination Disorder (see Motor Development)

9.   Traumatic Brain Injury (TBI) (see Brain Development)

10. behavioral coping (see Brain Development)

ANSWERS TO MULTIPLE-CHOICE QUESTIONS

Circle the question numbers you answered incorrectly.

Quiz 1

1.   *d is the answer.*   Gonads are the primary reproductive organs. In girls they are ovaries, in males they are testes. (see Physical Growth and Development)

2.   *b is the answer.*   A secular trend is a change over generations. The average age of menarche decreasing over time is a generational change.   (see Physical Growth and Development)

3.   *d is the answer.*   Luke is least at risk for overweight or obesity. The other children all have some of the risk factors mentioned. Sarah is exposed to lots of advertising (which promotes sugary snacks) via television (which promotes sitting). Joel has a lot of fast food, which is high in calorie. Abby's neighborhood situation limits her

exercise somewhat. Luke seems able to exercise by walking to school and his mom is less likely to put in high-calorie/low nutrition food which might be in some of the school lunches. (see Physical Growth and Development)

4.   *c is the answer.*   Competitive elimination accounts for the loss of neurons during middle childhood. Apoptosis, or programmed cell death, is more likely during prenatal development and early infancy. (see Brain Development)

5.   *a is the answer.*   The frontal lobes are most related to critical thinking and problems solving. The parietal and temporal lobes are more related to memory and information processing, and the hippocampus helps in the formation in new memories. (see Brain Development)

6.   *b is the answer.*   Connor may well have a diagnosis of ADHD that is predominantly inattentive (IA). The description does not mention any hyperactivity or impulsivity (HI) particularly, so it isn't likely to be either that or the combination (C) of those two types of ADHD. Nothing suggests that he has had a traumatic brain injury (TBI), either.   (see Brain Development)

7.   *c is the answer.*   Post-traumatic stress disorder (PTSD) is characterized by intrusive thoughts, sleep disturbance, withdrawal, and problems with emotional regulation. (see Brain Development)

8.   *c is the answer.*   Telling yourself that something doesn't matter is denying the event—denial coping. (see Brain Development)

9.   *d is the answer.*   Gross motor activity refers to movements of the large muscles that support running, hopping and so forth. Writing is a smaller movement, and rests more on fine motor skills. (see Motor Development)

10.   *b is the answer.*   Developmental coordination disorder (DCD) refers to marked impairment in motor skills for one's age and intelligence. (see Motor Development)

11.   *a is the answer.*   The actigraph *directly* measures sleep onset, morning awakening, and nighttime awakening. These measures are then used to *compute* measures of sleep periods and true sleep times. (see Sleep)

12.   *a is the answer.*   Apnea affects 1–3% of children, often in association with asthma, allergies, and obesity. (see Sleep)

13.   *b is the answer.*   Preference for circadian rhythms tends to emerge in middle childhood, leading some children to prefer staying up late and others to become early risers. (see Sleep)

14.   *c is the answer.*   Vehicle accidents are the leading cause of death amongst school-age children, followed by drowning and then cancer. (see Physical Health)

15.   *c is the answer.*   Asthma is more likely for boys than girls, and for black children and Puerto Rican children than white children. The boys are more likely to have asthma in this case, and the black boy is more likely than the white boy. (see Physical Health)

Now turn to the quiz analysis table at the end of this chapter to find which areas you know well and which areas you need to work on. Circle the numbers in the table for items on Quiz 1 that you answered correctly.

Quiz 2

1.   *b is the answer.*   Menarche is the onset of menstruation in girls. The larche is the development of breast buds in girls, and puberty refers more generally to all the physical changes encompassing growth from childhood to adulthood in preparation for the ability to reproduce. (see Physical Growth and Development)

2.   *d is the answer.*   Overweight and obese children tend to remain overweight or obese into adolescence and adulthood. They do NOT outgrow their pudginess. Additionally, the risk for overweight and obesity increases with age. (see Physical Growth and Development)

3.   *d is the answer.*   Dendrites and axons continue to branch and build new synapses in response to new experiences throughout middle childhood. Complementing this process, synaptic pruning eliminates synapses that aren't used, and strengthens those that are frequently used. (see Brain Development)

4.   *b is the answer.*   Growth in the front part of the brain occurs significantly in early childhood, while growth further back in the brain is more significant during middle childhood. (see Brain Development)

5.   *a is the answer.*   Boys tend to see a spurt of synaptic growth in areas of the brain related to fine motor skills and language development during middle childhood. Girls tend to see the spurt more associated with gross motor movements and visual-spatial discrimination. This is a reverse of the patterns of brain development seen in early childhood. (see Brain Development)

6.   *d is the answer.*   During middle childhood, both greater than average proliferation of gray matter combined with rapid pruning of unused synapses are associated with superior intelligence. (see Brain Development)

7.   *c is the answer.*   Six percent of school-age children have an ADHD diagnosis. (see Brain Development)

8.   *b is the answer.*   Cortisol level is significantly higher amongst children with PTSD. (see Brain Development)

9.   *b is the answer.*   Hypocortisolism tends to occur when children are exposed to volatile parental relationships and unresolved conflicts. (see Brain Development)

10. *a is the answer.*   Trey is identifying the problem (he is being bullied), and looking for a solution (ask the counselor for help). This is problem-focused coping. (see Brain Development)

11. *d is the answer.*   During middle childhood, children engage in new and more complex physical activities. These activities and the increased frequency with which they occur tend to result in "growing pains." (see Motor Development)

12. *c is the answer.* The idea that winning is everything is the opposite of what the CET program teaches. (see Motor Development)

13. *c is the answer.*   Jumping rope is not a fine motor skill, but a gross motor skill. (see Motor Development)

14. *c is the answer.*   Thirty minutes of extra sleep can increase test performance on measures of memory and reaction time. (see Sleep)

15. *a is the answer.* Type 1 diabetes tends to appear in children, adolescents, and young adults, and involves the immune system destroying the beta cells in the pancreas that produce insulin. (see Physical Health)

Now turn to the quiz analysis table at the end of this chapter to find which areas you know well and which areas you need to work on. Circle the numbers in the table for items on Quiz 2 that you answered correctly.

For each question you answered correctly, circle its number. (Quiz 1 numbers are not shaded; Quiz 2 numbers are shaded.) Are there patterns in the types of questions or the topics you got wrong that could direct your further study? Did you improve from Quiz 1 to Quiz 2?

QUIZ REVIEW

Topic	Type of Question		
	Definition	**Comprehension**	**Application**
Physical Growth and Development		1, 2	3
	1	2	
Brain Development	7	4, 5	6, 8
		3, 4, 6, 7, 8	5, 9, 10
Motor Development	10		9
		11, 12	13
Sleep	11	12, 13	
		14	
Physical Health		14	15
	15		

Total correct by quiz:

Quiz 1:	
Quiz 2:	

CHAPTER 11

Cognitive Development in Middle Childhood

LEARNING OBJECTIVES

1. Describe the cognitive capabilities and limitations of children in the concrete operational period.

2. Define micro-genetic analysis, and explain how researchers use it to understand cognitive development in children.

3. Describe the changes in processing speed that happen in middle childhood.

4. Explain how researchers measure working memory and describe how the developing ability to chunk information helps children increase the capacity of their working memory.

5. Describe the types of long-term memory (declarative, procedural, verbatim, and gist), and explain the different strategies children use to improve their long-term memory.

6. Explain how children might develop false memories, and describe the possible consequences of having false memories.

7. Describe the development of the psychometric approach to understanding intelligence.

8. Explain the different views on whether there is one type of intelligence or many different kinds, and describe some of the problems encountered in measuring intelligence.

9. Describe some environmental and genetic influences on IQ.

10. List the common attributes of intellectually "gifted" children.

11. Describe some possible causes of mental retardation.

12. Describe the evolution of language use as children move through middle childhood.

13. Explain the phonics and whole language approaches used to teach children to read.

14. Describe some difficulties children may encounter when learning to read.

15. Discuss the challenges facing children who learn English as a second language.

16. Describe the factors that contribute to a child's facility with mathematics during middle childhood.

17. Describe typical classrooms in first, third, and fifth grades in terms of class size, class structure, the amount of time on task, the amount of teacher support, and the level of instruction.

18. List some of the suggestions for improving educational success in middle childhood.

19. Describe the positive and negative aspects of having computers in children's classrooms and homes.

OUTLINE

I. Piaget and Beyond

A. The Concrete Operational Period
1. Between ages 5 and 12, children's mental activities, or operations, become more logical with respect to what actually is—that is, the concrete world. This is called the period of **concrete operations**.
2. Although preschool children are unable to perform **conservation** tasks, school-age children are aware that some characteristics such as mass or volume do not change even though their form does.
3. Piaget argued that this marked a qualitative shift in thinking, in comparison to early childhood.

B. Hallmarks of Concrete Operations
1. **Classification** is the ability to divide or sort objects into different sets or subsets, and to consider their inter-relations.
2. **Class inclusion** is a logical operation that recognizes that a class (or group) can be part of a larger group. Primary grade math classrooms use "attribute blocks" to help children develop an understanding of classification and class inclusion. These blocks vary in size, shape, and color and allow the children to sort on different dimensions. Children of this age enjoy collections and organization of them, which also is related to developing these logical skills.
3. **Seriation** is the ability to arrange items in a sequenced order according to particular properties.
4. **Transitive inference** builds on an understanding of seriation. It requires that two relations are combined to derive a third relation.
5. **Reversibility** is the understanding that relations can be returned to their original state by reversing operations.
6. As children acquire the above skills, they do not do so in an instantaneous fashion. They acquire the ability, for example, to conserve matter usually before they can conserve numbers. This is called **horizontal decalage**.

C. Experiences that Foster Advances in Concrete Operations
Piaget felt that concrete operational skills unfolded naturally, but research suggests some experiences promote their development.

1. Asking a child to explain their reasoning for conservation tasks helps foster advancement of those skills.
2. Formal schooling in mathematics can promote ability to engage in seriation and transitive inference, and schooling in language arts promotes understanding of classification and class inclusion.

D. Learning and the Development of Strategic Thinking
1. One way to document the development of strategic thinking is through **micro-genetic analysis**. This involves the close study (micro) of development (genetic). This has been used to study and document children's movement from use of computational strategies to more heuristic strategies in mathematics, as well as to study other areas of development.
2. Research based on micro-genetic analysis indicates that Piaget's original idea that once a child shifts into concrete operations he or she is capable of operating on that level constantly is unlikely to be true. Rather, child behavior is highly variable in terms of strategy selection, particularly during periods of rapid learning.
3. After school programs can also help limit risk for overweight, as these programs tend to result in reduced time in front of the television and lower snack/soft drink consumption.

II.   Information Processing
       The information processing approach focuses on how children's attention and memory determine what information can be gathered, and how information is then used to solve problems.

    A.   Processing Speed
        1.   Two strategies have been used to study children's processing speed.
            a)   The Visual Matching procedure involves task cards with 60 rows of 6 digits each. Children are asked to find the two matching rows. Number of cards completed in a set amount of time is the child's processing time.
            b)   The Cross Out procedure involves task cards with a target shape on the left, and 19 similar geometric figures to the right, five of which are identical. The child is asked to cross out the five identical figures. Number of cards completed is the processing time measures.
        2.   Processing speed tends to show the greatest improvements in middle childhood.

    B.   Working Memory
        1.   **Working memory** is conscious, short-term representations of what a person is actually thinking about. It is measured using the **digit span task**, in which people are asked to repeat in order a series of rapidly presented items.
        2.   Five-year-olds can remember about four items on the digit span tasks, 7-year-olds can remember about five items, and 9-year-olds about six items. Chunking information allows this working memory capacity to be functionally much larger.

    C.   Long-term Memory
        1.   **Long-term memory** refers to information encoded and stored, potentially with no time limits. It can be in the form of **declarative memory**, **procedural memory**, **verbatim memory**, and **gist memory**.
        2.   The longer a child focuses his or her attention on a piece of information, the more likely it is stored in long-term memory.
        3.   The sharpest increase in memory skills of this sort occurred during middle childhood, with slower increases to follow throughout adolescence.
        4.   Memory strategies are mental or behavioral activities that improve recall and recognition of material. These include rehearsal and repetition, writing something down, explicitly relating new information to prior knowledge, and organizing material.
        5.   Children in middle childhood can be trained in these strategies and show some related improvements. Development of these strategies is not slow and steady, but discontinuous, jumping from chance performance to near perfect implementation of strategies most of the time.

    D.   False Memory
        1.   **False memories** are memories that distort an actual experience, or that actually are confabulations of events that never occurred. One way to demonstrate the construction of such memories is through the **Deese-Roediger-McDermott (DRM) procedure**.
        2.   The DRM procedure involves presenting a list of words to a person, and then asking them to identify the number of words recalled PLUS any additional "new" words recalled (a recognition task). The "new" words that adults tend to remember on this task tend to be related to the meaning of the words on the list, while five-year-olds "new" memories tend to be based on how the words sounded.

3.   The **misinformation paradigm** is used to demonstrate that memories can be changed when misleading information is presented after the fact. Children in all age groups (3, 5, 8, and 10) were susceptible to false memories in this procedure, with gist memories being more prone to distortion than verbatim memories.

E.   Children's Testimony
Children often testify in custody and delinquency hearings, as well as (more rarely) sexual abuse cases. The accuracy of their testimony can be influenced by misinformation and other things.

1.   False memories are affected by the amount of time between the event and the interview, by the number of times a child is interviewed, and by how biased the interviewer is.

2.   To minimize distortions, a specially trained interviewer has a one-on-one conversation in a child-friendly room with video and audio capability. Observers behind a one-way glass or television pose questions via a small microphone in the interviewer's ear. The interviewer starts with free recall and, if necessary, moves to neutral prompts, then cued recall, on up to paired recall. The interviewer must never add information in the question that the child did not already provide.

III.   Intelligence
A.   A Brief History of Efforts to Measure Intelligence
1.   Although Galton's original approach to measuring intelligence focused on narrow measures like reaction time, Binet and Simon focused on a broader understanding of intelligence. Those ideas arrived at Stanford University with Terman, who developed the Stanford-Binet Intelligence Test. The test has separate parts measuring different abilities, and an average score on it is 100.

2.   Another commonly used test is the Weschler Intelligence Scale for Children III (WISC-III). It has two main scales: verbal and performance.

3.   The quality of an intelligence test is measured by its **reliability** and its **validity**.

B.   Are There Multiple Intelligences?
1.   Spearman argued that intelligence was captured by the notion of *g* for general cognitive abilities, but Thurstone argued that there are specific intelligences. Thurstone based his argument on data from factor analyses.

2.   Gardner developed a theory of **multiple intelligences** with eight different forms of intelligence. He argued that these are relatively independent and related to different modules of the brain.

3.   Sternberg proposed the **Triarchic Theory of Successful Intelligence**, which argues that intelligence is composed of three broad components: analytic, creative, and practical abilities. He argues that an intelligent child (or person) is able to know his or her own strengths and weaknesses, and capitalize on the strengths and compensate for the weaknesses.

C.   Intelligence in Different Social Contexts
1.   Intelligence test scores are affected by the social context in which testing takes place. Indeed, intelligence is always "contextualized" with certain test scores being more predictive in certain situations.

2.   There is some evidence that intelligence tests favor white, middle-class children.

D.   Are IQ Scores Malleable?
1.   IQ scores in infancy are quite unreliable, but stabilize in middle childhood.

2.   Research based on the Romanian and English Adoptees Study indicates that severe deprivation in the first two years of life can have long-term impact on a

child's intelligence. However, early enrichment in one's environment, as in the Abecedarian Project, can have a positive impact on childhood intelligence.

3. Twin studies comparing similarity between **monozygotic (MZ)** and **dizygotic (DZ) twins** helps to determine the genetic influence on intelligence. The correlation between MZ twins' IQ's is on average .86, but between DZ twins it is .60, indicating that intelligence has high **heritability**.

E. Very High and Very Low IQ Scores

1. **Giftedness** has varying definitions, but those based on IQ usually describe it as the top 1% (IQ > 135) or 2% (IQ > 132) of individuals. Other definitions focus on broader creativity within a narrower domain.

2. Terman's longitudinal study of gifted individuals suggests that gifted individuals grow to become well-adjusted, successful adults.

3. The Individual's with Disabilities Act defines mental retardation as sub-average intellectual functioning accompanied by deficits in adaptive behavior that have adverse educational outcomes. Operationally, this has been interpreted as an IQ below 70 or 75.

4. **Down Syndrome** and **Fragile X Syndrome** are the two most common genetic causes of intellectual disabilities, although many other causes do exist. Other causes are environmental.

IV. Language, Literacy, and Mathematics

A. Language Development

1. **Root word** vocabulary continues to increase throughout middle childhood, moving from 5200 words on average in second grade to over 8400 in fifth grade.

2. Use of language becomes more precise and complex, and children become adept at **code** switching.

3. Children's language is heavily influenced by their experiences in the home.

B. Literacy

1. Reading is one of the crowning accomplishments of middle childhood, and it rests on **decoding** (applying letter/sound knowledge to written material) and **comprehension** (understanding what you've read).

2. Professionals have debated whether or not the **phonics approach** or the **whole language approach** is the better way to teach reading. Research supports the importance of both approaches used together to create effective reading programs.

3. Skills in decoding and comprehension begin in early childhood, with some kindergarteners able to isolate beginning and ending **phonemes**. While this is a necessary skill, it is not sufficient, as a complementary focus on comprehension is essential, with the emphasis on comprehension increasing from third grade forward.

C. Difficulties Learning to Read

1. Children from low-income backgrounds often encounter difficulty in reading, possibly because there is less reading material in the home or because the parents have low literacy or learning disabilities. Schools and families can make a difference, though. First grade teachers who spend more time on literacy and language instruction tend to see their pupils show great strides in this area.

2. Addressing reading difficulties early is important, as difficulty reading is associated with poor academic performance as well as aggression in future grade levels.

3. **Dyslexia** is a learning disability characterized by poor word recognition, decoding, and spelling skills. Today, schools usually **mainstream** these children.

D. English Language Learners
    1. The number of **English Language Learners (ELLs)** has dramatically increased in the United States since 1979, with some states even offering bilingual education.
    2. ELLs are at risk for losing their first language, although this is buffered if parents are highly educated. Using the first language at home does not harm the acquisition of English as long as English is also used at home.

E. Mathematics
    1. Math skills in middle childhood have three main components.
       a) Knowing math facts and procedures.
       b) Using those facts and procedures to solve routine problems.
       c) Using those facts and procedures to solve non-routine problems.
    2. Throughout middle childhood they become adept at using strategies to solve problems, but struggle to develop reflective questioning to evaluate their solutions.
    3. Informal mathematics embeds math in real-world, meaningful contexts, such as music (how many half notes make up a whole note?) or cooking (doubling a recipe).
    4. School-age girls tend to earn better grades in math than boys, but boys tend to do better on standardized tests of mathematics than girls. This is likely due to girls' willingness to put forth more effort at school than boys, and to be more compliant to teacher requests. Additionally, testing situations are often competitive, a situation to which boys tend to respond well.

V. Schools and Schooling
A. A Typical Classroom
    1. Children on average spend 90% of their time in whole-class instruction or seat work, and little time in small-group instruction. More time is spent on basic skills than on problem-solving.
    2. Emotional quality of classrooms tends to be moderately positive, while instructional climate (how challenging the teaching was) was low.
    3. How time was spent in the classroom was reflected in student achievement scores.

B. The Nation's Report Card
    1. The National Assessment Educational Progress issues report cards on student knowledge in math, reading, history, and science.
    2. Average reading and math scores have increased since 1971, but there is still a great deal of room for improvement.
    3. NAEP notes a large **achievement gap** between low-income Black and Hispanic students and middle-income White and Asian students.

C. International Comparisons
    1. Children in the U. S. are about average at math and slightly above average in science scores, in international comparisons.
    2. The National Academy of Science suggests that such scores will harm the U.S.'s ability to compete internationally in a knowledge- and technology-based economy.

D. No Child Left Behind
    1. **No Child Left Behind** is a federal law that has sought to hold schools accountable for student performance using standardized achievement tests. Failure to perform adequately on these **high-stakes tests** can result in sanctions and loss of federal funds.

2.   Testing in reading and math begins in third grade. Although ELL's scores are separated out, all other children, including disabled children, minority children, and economically disadvantaged children, are tested and held to the same standard.

3.   Some evidence suggests that NCLB has slowed gains in reading and math achievement, and has halted movement towards reducing the achievement gap because it focuses too much on tests and not enough on instruction.

E.   Strategies to Improve Student Learning and Achievement
1.   Lower class size tends to be associated with higher student achievement.
2.   Teacher quality significantly impacts student achievement. Effective teachers are knowledgeable in the subject matter, believe students can learn, and have a large toolkit of teaching strategies.
3.   The length of the school year historically began when children needed time off in the summer to help their family with planting and harvesting activities. This largely is no longer necessary. Although affluent families tend to find ways to enrich summer activities, lower-income families often cannot afford to do so, and children may spend much time in front of the television. Lengthening the school year may help with this problem.
4.   Lengthening the school day may also help. The shorter school day has a similar historical background (help with chores before daylight ends), and doing away with the truncated day may help student achievement.
5.   Reorganizing the curriculum to focus on higher-order thinking and integration of knowledge may help student achievement.
6.   High quality early childhood education can help students come to kindergarten more prepared to learn.
7.   Greater family involvement in school can help improve student achievement.

F.   Technology and Learning
Media multi-tasking is now quite common, and has had an impact on what goes on in schools.

1.   Although many good computer programs exist to help improve students' academic skills, they may not always be used effectively. To be helpful, they must be embedded in high-quality teaching.
2.   More affluent families have computers in their home than low-income families do, causing a **digital divide**. Computers in the home tend to be associated with math and science skills, though a causal link has not been established.

KEY TERMS

1.   **Concrete operations** are the third stage of cognitive development in Piaget's theory when mental activities become more logical with respect to actual (that is, *concrete*) objects and materials. (see Piaget and Beyond)

2.   **Conservation** refers to the understanding that some characteristics of objects (including volume, mass, and number) do not change despite changes in form or appearance. (see Piaget and Beyond)

3.   **Classification** is the ability to divide or sort objects into different sets and subsets, and to consider their inter-relationships. (see Piaget and Beyond)

4.   **Class inclusion** is a logical operation that recognizes that a class (or group) can be part of a larger group. (see Piaget and Beyond)

5. **Seriation** is the ability to arrange items in a sequenced order according to particular properties.   (see Piaget and Beyond)

6. **Transitive inference** is a logical operation that builds on an understanding of seriation. It requires that two relations are combined to derive a third relation. (see Piaget and Beyond)

7. **Reversibility** is a logical operation that requires an understanding that relations can be returned to their original state by reversing operations—if nothing has been added or taken. (see Piaget and Beyond)

8. **Horizontal decalage** refers to differences in performance on conceptually related Piagetian tasks. For example, children typically understand conservation of mass before they understand conservation of number. (see Piaget and Beyond)

9. **Micro-genetic analysis** is a research strategy that involves frequent, detailed observations of behavior. (see Piaget and Beyond)

10. **Working memory** contains conscious, short-term representations of what a person is actively thinking about at a given time.   (see Information Processing)

11. **Digit span task** refers to a research procedure in which people are asked to repeat in order a series of rapidly presented items. (see Information Processing)

12. **Long-term memory** refers to information that is mentally encoded and stored, potentially with no time limits.   (see Information Processing)

13. **Declarative memory** is memory of facts, such as names of people and places, and phone numbers. (see Information Processing)

14. **Procedural memory** refers to memories of complex motor skills, such as riding a bicycle and typing on a keyboard.   (see Information Processing)

15. **Verbatim memory** refers to detailed memories of specific events. (see Information Processing)

16. **Gist memory** is a generalized, rather than specific, memory of common occurrences. (see Information Processing)

17. **False memory** is a distortion of an actual experience, or a confabulation of an imagined one. (see Information Processing)

18. **Deese-Roediger-McDermott (DRM) procedure** is an experimental task that demonstrates the creation of false memories; participants often recollect or recall words that they have not heard because they make associations based on conceptual commonalities. (see Information Processing)

19. The **misinformation paradigm** is a research procedure that demonstrates that memories can be changed when misleading information is provided after the fact. (see Information Processing)

20. **Reliability** is a way to assess the consistency of a test. A reliable test is one in which individuals receive similar or relatively consistent scores each time they are tested. (see Intelligence)

21. **Validity** is the extent to which a test measures what it was designed to measure. (see Intelligence)

22. *g* is a general intelligence factor believed to govern performance on cognitive tasks, proposed by Charles Spearman. (see Intelligence)

23. **Multiple Intelligence** refers to Gardner's theory that proposes intelligence to have at least eight distinct forms: linguistic, logical-mathematical, spatial, musical, bodily-kinesthetic, interpersonal, intrapersonal, and naturalistic. (see Intelligence)

24. **Triarchic Theory of Successful Intelligence** is Sternberg's theory that intelligence is composed of three broad components: analytical abilities, creative abilities, and practical abilities. (see Intelligence)

25. **Monozygotic (MZ) twins** are also called identical twins. They occur when a single egg is fertilized and then divides into two separate embryos, resulting in two individuals whose genetic makeup is identical. (see Intelligence)

26. **Dizygotic (DZ) twins** are also called fraternal twins. They are twins born when two separate eggs are fertilized, who are therefore no more alike genetically than other brothers and sisters. (see Intelligence)

27. **Heritability** is a term, used in behavioral genetics, to designate the proportion of statistical variance associated with genes. (see Intelligence)

28. **Giftedness** is indicated by extraordinary creativity or performance in music, sports, or art, as well as traditional academic subjects. (see Intelligence)

29. **Down Syndrome** is a syndrome in which children have a third copy of chromosome 21. It is one of the most common genetic causes of mental retardation. (see Intelligence)

30. **Fragile X Syndrome** is a syndrome in which children have a change in a single gene on the X chromosome. It is one of the most common genetic causes of mental retardation. (see Intelligence)

31. **Root words** are vocabulary that must be learned, in contrast to derived and compound words that build on root words. (see Language, Literacy, and Mathematics)

32. **Code switching** refers to changing speech to reflect the audience and situation. (see Language, Literacy, and Mathematics)

33. **Decoding** is applying knowledge of letter-sound relationships to read written words. (see Language, Literacy, and Mathematics)

34. **Comprehension** refers to understanding what is read or said. (see Language, Literacy, and Mathematics)

35. The **phonics approach** emphasizes decoding in which readers match the printed alphabet to spoken sounds. (see Language, Literacy, and Mathematics)

36. The **whole language approach** emphasizes comprehension and context, and inferring what words are from context. (see Language, Literacy, and Mathematics)

37. A **phoneme** is the smallest contrastive sound unit. (see Language, Literacy, and Mathematics)

38. **Dyslexia** is a learning disability characterized by difficulties with word recognition and by poor spelling and decoding skills. (see Language, Literacy, and Mathematics)

39. **Mainstreaming** is inclusion of children with special needs in regular classrooms. (see Language, Literacy, and Mathematics)

40. **English language learners (ELL)** are children who speak languages other than English in their homes or as their first language. (see Language, Literacy, and Mathematics)

41. The **achievement gap** is an observed disparity on educational measures between the performance of groups of students, especially social class and ethnic disparities. (see Schools and Schooling)

42. **No Child Left Behind (NCLB)** is a federal law that holds schools accountable for student performance. NCLB requires that states meet specific goals as measured by standardized achievement tests. (see Schools and Schooling)

43. A **high stakes test** is a test that results in serious sanctions if performance standards are not met. (see Schools and Schooling)

44. **Media multi-tasking** is the simultaneous use of multiple forms of media. (see Schools and Schooling)

45. The **digital divide** is the technology gap that separates children who have ready access to computers and those who do not have access. Low-income and ethnic minority families are less likely to have computers and related materials in their homes. (see Schools and Schooling)

FILL-IN-THE-BLANKS KEY TERMS

This section will help you check your knowledge of the key terms introduced in this chapter. Fill in each blank with the appropriate term from the list of key terms in the previous section.

1. The _____ is an experimental task that demonstrates the creation of false memories by having participants recollect or recall words that they have not heard because they make associations based on conceptual commonalities.

2. The _____ is an observed disparity on educational measures between the performance of groups of students, especially social class and ethnic disparities.

3. Differences in performance on conceptually related Piagetian tasks are called _____.

4. _____ emphasizes comprehension and context in learning reading, and inferring what words are from context.

5. A research procedure in which people are asked to repeat in order a series of rapidly presented items is called the _____.

6. Applying knowledge of letter-sound relationships to read written words is called_____.

7. _____ is a logical operation that recognizes that a class (or group) can be part of a larger group.

8. Sternberg's theory that intelligence is composed of three broad components—analytical abilities, creative abilities, and practical abilities—is called the_____.

9. The _____ is a research procedure that demonstrates that memories can be changed when misleading information is provided after the fact.

10. The simultaneous use of multiple forms of media is called _____.

APPLIED LEARNING AND CRITICAL THINKING

Cognitive changes in middle childhood are best understood in context. Below are some strategies for observing these changes in meaningful situations.

1. Depending on where you live, your public school district may have an ESL program and almost certainly will have a reading program for children who struggling with their reading skills. Talk to someone at the district about volunteering with these children so that you can

see first-hand how phonics and whole language complement each other. What sorts of cues can a child give you to let you know what they are struggling with when they read? What strategies can you think of to help them acquire the skills that are presently deficient?

2. If you will be traveling internationally during your university experience, consider gathering a little information on your travels about how your host country (or countries) structure their school year and school days. What is the duration of the school year and the school day? How many children are in a class? Do they invest heavily in early childhood education? How are their strategies similar to and different from what has been tried in the United States?

3. Oftentimes internships or practica are available in the offices of prosecuting attorneys or related local offices. See if you can gain such a position, and use the opportunity to observe how they prepare witnesses. How are their strategies different when they prepare a child versus an adult? Do they use some of the techniques recommended in your text for avoiding tainting a child's testimony?

4. Survey the literature on micro-genetic analysis and try to get a sense of what it would take to execute this research strategy. Then consider working with a professor in your department to develop a research project that will use this methodology to observe a school-aged child whom you know well. Make sure to get IRB approval and parental consent before collecting any data. How does this research tool differ from the more typical experimental and observational methods?

MULTIPLE-CHOICE QUESTIONS

Quiz 1

1. Janet's little girl is upset that she doesn't have more candy. She has lined her row of gumdrops up and is hollering for more. Janet spreads the gum drops out so that they are more widely spaced, because in the past her little girl has interpreted the wider line to mean more candy. This time, her daughter looks at her like she is an idiot, and says, "That's not more!" Janet's daughter is probably entering which of Piaget's stages of development?

    a. Sensorimotor
    b. Preoperational
    c. Concrete operational
    d. Formal operational

2. Marnie is helping her mom organize the Tupperware cabinet. She puts the biggest bowls in the back of the cabinet, the next smallest in front of those, on down until the smallest items are in the front of the cabinet. Marnie's organizational strategy illustrates which hallmark of the concrete operational period?

    a. Conservation
    b. Class inclusion
    c. Seriation
    d. Reversibility

3. Understanding that relations can be returned to their original state by undoing the operations (assuming nothing has been added or subtracted) is called

    a. transitive inference.
    b. horizontal decalage.
    c. conservation.
    d. reversibility.

4. In which of the following domains has micro-genetic analysis been applied to the study of cognitive development in middle childhood?

    a. Scientific thinking
    b. Memory
    c. Mathematical reasoning
    d. All of these

5. The digit span task is used for what experimental purpose?

    a. Assessing the capacity of working memory
    b. Demonstrating that false memories can occur
    c. Demonstrating that memories can be changed after the fact
    d. Assessing the heritability of memory

6. When children are exposed to the DRM procedure, how do the results differ from the results of adults exposed to the same procedure?

    a. Children have more false memories than adults do.
    b. Children's false memories are based on conceptual similarity to the list while adults' false memories are based on how words sound.
    c. Children do not have false memories when exposed to this task, but adults do.
    d. Children's false memories are based on how words sound, while adults' false memories are based on conceptual similarity to the list.

7. Which of the following is a good example of a task on the performance subscale from the WISC-III?

    a. Arithmetic problems
    b. Questions about understanding of social customs
    c. Arranging a scrambled set of cartoon pictures in order
    d. Identifying similarities amongst items

8. Which of the following children is displaying spatial intelligence, as defined by Gardner's multiple intelligences?

    a. Tara, who is dancing in a recital and doing an excellent job
    b. Zachary, who is efficiently loading the dishwasher to maximize how much stuff fits
    c. David, who is a first-rate trombone player
    d. Trina, who is reading well above her age level

9. Cole and Brandon share 100% of their genes. They are

    a. monozygotic twins.
    b. dizygotic twins.
    c. fraternal twins.
    d. All of these

10. Changing speech to reflect who you are talking to is

    a. root word management.
    b. code-switching.
    c. mainstreaming.
    d. decoding.

11. At what point is it useful to increase the emphasis on whole language instruction and begin to de-emphasize phonics?

    a. Kindergarten
    b. 1st Grade
    c. Preschool
    d. 3rd Grade

12. A learning disability characterized by difficulty with word recognition, poor decoding and poor spelling skills is called
   a. dyslexia.
   b. Down Syndrome.
   c. Fragile X Syndrome.
   d. ELL.

13. Which of the following states has FAILED to pass balloting referenda to reduce access to bilingual education?
   a. California
   b. Colorado
   c. Arizona
   d. Massachusetts

14. Which of the following children's test scores are reported separately when schools compile their scores for NCLB?
   a. Disabled children
   b. English Language Learners
   c. Children who speak English as a second language
   d. Both A and B

15. Karen is watching television and surfing the Internet at the same time. She is illustrating
   a. the digital divide.
   b. the achievement gap.
   c. media multitasking.
   d. code-switching.

Quiz 2

Use this quiz to reassess your learning after taking Quiz 1 and reviewing the chapter.

1. The understanding that some characteristics of an object do not change despite changes in form or appearance is called
   a. reversibility.
   b. conservation.
   c. seriation.
   d. transitive inference.

2. Rick knows that Cathy weights more than Robin, and he knows that Robin weighs more than Brendan. He therefore understands that Cathy weighs more than Brendan, too. This skill illustrates
   a. transitive inference.
   b. class inclusion.
   c. reversibility.
   d. micro-genetic analysis.

3. The fact that children are generally able to solve conservation of matter problems before they are able to solve conservation of number problems illustrates
   a. working memory capacity.
   b. gist memory.
   c. horizontal decalage.
   d. comprehension.

4. Which of the following is true about working memory capacity in middle childhood?

    a. It is about the same as the capacity for adults.
    b. It is much greater in capacity than for adults.
    c. It is much smaller in capacity than for adults.
    d. It is smaller than for adults, but increases over middle childhood.

5. A memory that is a distortion of a real experience or a confabulation of an imagined one is called

    a. a false memory.
    b. a declarative memory.
    c. a verbatim memory.
    d. a procedural memory.

6. Who is most susceptible to misinformation distorting a memory?

    a. A kindergartner
    b. A second grader
    c. A third grader
    d. A fifth grader

7. A significant correlation between an IQ test score and performance in school supports the_____ of the IQ test.

    a. reliability
    b. validity
    c. mainstreaming
    d. heritability

8. Lateef loves to play with Legos. He prefers not to use the patterns given in the box, however. Instead, he makes up new and inventive ways to use the little blocks to build all kinds of interesting things. Lateef's interest in and use of Legos best illustrates which component of Sternberg's Triarchic Theory of Intelligence?

    a. Practical
    b. Creative
    c. Analytical
    d. All of these

9. Which of the following IQ scores would qualify a child as "gifted"?

    a. 135
    b. 125
    c. 140
    d. Both A and C

10. Applying knowledge of letter-sound relationships to read written words is

    a. comprehension.
    b. code-switching.
    c. decoding.
    d. mainstreaming.

11. Which method of teaching reading emphasizes students inferring the meaning of words from context?

    a. Phonics
    b. Whole language
    c. Micro-genetic analysis
    d. Both A and B

12. Enrique has great difficulty reading and has been diagnosed with dyslexia. Yet he spends most of his day with his peers in the "regular" classroom. Enrique has

    a. been mainstreamed.

    b.   crossed the digital divide.

    c.   bridged the achievement gap.

    d.   All of these

13.   An observed disparity between test scores for students of different social classes and ethnicities is called

    a.   the achievement gap.

    b.   the digital divide.

    c.   whole language.

    d.   the misinformation paradigm.

14.   Shawn is a principle at an elementary school that is going through its spring testing cycle. The results of the tests determine what sort of funding his school will receive in the next year. The tests are an example of

    a.   No Child Left Behind.

    b.   high-stakes testing.

    c.   conservation.

    d.   the digit span test.

15.   The digital divide refers to

    a.   the achievement gap.

    b.   the differential access to technology for children from different socioeconomic classes.

    c.   the use of multiple forms of media simultaneously.

    d.   how results from high-stakes testing divide school access to funding.

ANSWERS TO FILL-IN-THE-BLANKS KEY TERMS

1.   Deese-Roediger-McDermott procedure (see Information Processing)

2.   achievement gap (see Schools and Schooling)

3.   horizontal decalage (see Piaget and Beyond)

4.   Whole language (see Language, Literacy, and Mathematics)

5.   digit span task (see Information Processing)

6.   decoding (see Language, Literacy, and Mathematics)

7.   Class inclusion (see Piaget and Beyond)

8.   Triarchic Theory of Successful Intelligence (see Intelligence)

9.   misinformation paradigm (see Information Processing)

10.   media multitasking (see Schools and Schooling)

ANSWERS TO MULTIPLE-CHOICE QUESTIONS

Circle the question numbers you answered incorrectly.

Quiz 1

1.   *c is the answer.*   Janet's daughter is probably entering the concrete operational period. Her response to her mother's "trick" indicates she is newly capable of mastering conservation tasks, which is a hallmark of the concrete operational period. (see Piaget and Beyond)

2.   *b is the answer.*   Marnie's behavior illustrates seriation—she is arranging items (the Tupperware) in a sequenced order according to particular properties (size).

3.   *d is the answer.*   Reversibility is the understanding that relations can be returned to their original state by reversing, or undoing, the operations so long as nothing has been added or subtracted. (see Piaget and Beyond)

4.   *d is the answer.*   Micro-genetic analysis has been used in all three of these domains. (see Piaget and Beyond)

5.   *a is the answer.*   The digit span task assesses the capacity of working memory by measuring the number of objects one can hold in working memory. Demonstration of false memories is accomplished with the DRM procedure, and demonstration of the ability to alter a memory after the fact is done with the misinformation paradigm. (see Information Processing)

6.   *d is the answer.*   Children's falsely remembered words in the DRM procedure tend to be based on how words sound—that is, they tend to "remember" words that rhyme with the other words. Adults, however, tend to "remember" words that are conceptually similar to other words on the list.   (see Information Processing)

7.   *c is the answer.*   The performance scale includes tasks like sequencing a scrambled cartoon and picture completion tasks. The verbal scale would include the other sorts of tasks, as well as vocabulary assessments. (see Intelligence)

8.   *b is the answer.*   Efficiently loading the dishwasher requires an understanding of the space in the dishwasher and how the objects will best fill it. Dancing in a recital shows bodily-kinesthetic intelligence. Playing the trombone requires musical intelligence, and reading well requires linguistic intelligence. (see Intelligence)

9.   *a is the answer.* Monozygotic twins are identical, sharing 100% of their DNA. (see Intelligence)

10. *b is the answer.*   Code switching is changing one's speech to reflect who one is speaking with. (see Language, Literacy, and Mathematics)

11. *d is the answer.*   Around 3rd grade it is important to devote more time to vocabulary and comprehension than phonics. In pre-school, kindergarten, and 1st grade, however, students to varying degrees will benefit from an emphasis on phonics. (see Language, Literacy, and Mathematics)

12. *a is the answer.*   Dyslexia is a learning disorder that involves poor word recognition, poor decoding, and poor spelling. (see Language, Literacy, and Mathematics)

13. *b is the answer.*   Colorado has failed to pass such legislation. The other three states have done so. (see Language, Literacy, and Mathematics)

14. *b is the answer.*   ELL test scores are reported separately for NCLB. All others are tested and held to the same standard. (see Schools and Schooling)

15. *c is the answer.*   Media multitasking involves using multiple media forms simultaneously. Karen is using both television and the Internet at the same time. (see Schools and Schooling)

Now turn to the quiz analysis table at the end of this chapter to find which areas you know well and which areas you need to work on. Circle the numbers in the table for items on Quiz 1 that you answered correctly.

Quiz 2

1. *b is the answer.*   Conservation is the understanding that some characteristics of an object remain the same despite changes in form or appearance. (see Piaget and Beyond)

2. *a is the answer.*   Transitive inference is the ability to combine two relationships to derive, or infer, a third one. (see Piaget and Beyond)

3. *c is the answer.*   Horizontal decalage refers to differences in performance on conceptually related Piagetian tasks. Both problems described in this question are conservation problems, so they are related, but children seem to acquire one type of conservation skill before the other, creating a performance differential. (see Piaget and Beyond)

4. *d is the answer.*   Working memory capacity is about four items for 5-year olds, five items for 6-year-olds, and six items for 7-year-olds. Adult working memory capacity is seven items. Therefore, the capacity of children is somewhat (though not greatly) less than adults, but increases over middle childhood. (see Information Processing)

5. *a is the answer.*   A false memory is a distortion of a real event, or a confabulation. (see Information Processing)

6. *a is the answer.*   Younger children are more susceptible to misinformation than older children. (see Information Processing)

7. *b is the answer.*   Validity refers to the degree to which the test measures what it was intended to measure. IQ tests intend to measure intelligence, which is supposed to be related to school performance (more intelligent children supposedly do better in school). A correlation between the two supports that the IQ test measures what it tried to measure. (see Intelligence)

8. *b is the answer.*   Creative abilities enable children to invent, discover, and imagine. Lateef is using the toys in a creative way, imagining possibilities that are not in the instruction packet. (see Intelligence)

9. *d is the answer.*   Gifted is usually defined as an IQ in the top 1% (135 or higher), so scores of either 135 or 140 would qualify a person as gifted. (see Intelligence)

10. *c is the answer.*   Decoding is applying knowledge of how letters sound to be able to read, or "sound out" a written word. (see Language, Literacy, and Mathematics)

11. *b is the answer.*   Whole language is an approach to teaching reading that emphasizes comprehension and context, and inferring what words are from context. (see Language, Literacy, and Mathematics)

12. *a is the answer.*   Mainstreaming involves inclusion of children with special needs, like dyslexia, in regular classrooms. (see Language, Literacy, and Mathematics)

13. *a is the answer.*   The achievement gap is the disparity in test scores for students from different groups, especially social classes or ethnicities. (see Schools and Schooling)

14. *b is the answer.*   Test that determine significant outcomes, like funding, are considered high-stakes tests. (see Schools and Schooling)

15. *b is the answer.*   The digital divide refers to the technology gap separating children who have ready access to computers from those who don't—usually divided across income or ethnic lines. (see Schools and Schooling)

Now turn to the quiz analysis table at the end of this chapter to find which areas you know well and which areas you need to work on. Circle the numbers in the table for items on Quiz 2 that you answered correctly.

For each question you answered correctly, circle its number. (Quiz 1 numbers are not shaded; Quiz 2 numbers are shaded.) Are there patterns in the types of questions or the topics you got wrong that could direct your further study? Did you improve from Quiz 1 to Quiz 2?

QUIZ REVIEW

Topic	Type of Question		
	Definition	Comprehension	Application
Piaget and Beyond	3	4	1, 2
	1	3	2
Information Processing		5, 6	
	5	4, 6	
Intelligence			7, 8, 9
	9	7	8
Language, Literacy, and Mathematics	10, 12	11, 13	
	10, 11		12
Schools and Schooling		14	15
	13, 15		14

Total correct by quiz:

Quiz 1:	
Quiz 2:	

CHAPTER 12

Socioemotional Development in Middle Childhood

LEARNING OBJECTIVES

1. Describe how an individual's self-concept becomes more complex and specific in middle childhood.

2. Explain how resolving Erikson's normative crisis of industry vs. inferiority contributes to a child's maturing self-concept.

3. Explain how a child's gender consciousness and understanding of gender schemas changes during middle childhood.

4. Explain how Lawrence Kohlberg studied the development of moral reasoning, and describe his preconventional, conventional, and postconventional levels of moral reasoning.

5. Explain the social and cultural factors that influence the development of altruism in children.

6. Explain how the nature of aggressive behavior changes in middle childhood, and describe the psychological and social influences on a child's level of aggression.

7. Define bullying, and describe the three styles of coping with this behavior.

8. Explain the strategies used to cope with stress in middle childhood, and describe their effectiveness.

9. Describe the influences of household structure on socioemotional development in middle childhood.

10. Describe the effects of divorce, the creation of blended families, and adoption on socioemotional development in middle childhood.

11. Explain how the quality of parent-child relationships and the parents' relationships with each other affect socioemotional development in middle childhood.

12. Describe the possible positive and negative effects of sibling relationships in middle childhood.

13. Define the concept of peer group, and describe the methods researchers use to study children's status within peer groups.

14. Describe the attributes of children who are popular, controversial, rejected, or neglected by their peers.

15. Describe how children form cliques and the potential positive and negative consequences of membership in these groups.

16. Describe the changes in the nature of friendship for boys and girls in middle childhood.

17. List the types of organized activities for children outside of school, and describe children's levels of participation in these activities. Show how their participation influences their academic and social skills.

18. Describe the problems associated with inadequate adult supervision of children in middle childhood.

19. Explain the influences of a child's neighborhood on his or her socioemotional development.

20. Describe the influences of media found in the home (such as TVs, computers, game consoles) on children's socioemotional development.

OUTLINE

I. Socioemotional Accomplishments
    A. Conception of Self
        1. The self-concept becomes more nuanced during middle childhood. Rather than seeing themselves as all good or all bad, school-age children see their strengths and weakness in relation to other children.
        2. The view of the self becomes more multi-faceted in middle childhood, building on correspondent cognitive advances.
        3. During middle childhood, one's self-conception comes to include the views of others of oneself (e.g., parent, peers, society).
    B. Industry versus Inferiority
        1. **Industry versus inferiority**, Erikson's fourth stage of psychosocial development, occurs during middle childhood. Children develop a sense of themselves as industrious, or worthy, rather than inferior, when they produce things by themselves or with others.
        2. School provides a major opportunity for a sense of industry to develop. Other arenas that support this development range widely from participation in scouting, to playing online games and striving for the next level at either of those activities.
        3. The social context in which a child grows up determines in large part the number of opportunities he or she will have to work towards a sense of industry.
    C. Gender
        1. Gender serves an organizing function in middle childhood, serving as a guide to selecting friends and activities, expressing emotion, and so forth. By age 8–9, the self-concept contains gender norms.
        2. In mid to late childhood, gender differences in self-esteem occur, with girls generally having lower self-esteem than boys.
        3. Gender linked personality traits emerge during middle childhood, with **expressivity** encouraged more in girls and **instrumentality** in boys.
        4. Gender segregation intensifies for children of this age, with boys engaging in more **rough and tumble play** than girls, who prefer to stay on the sidelines of such play and who engage in more talking. The notion of the *opposite* sex develops.
        5. **Gender schema**—the conceptualization of what it means to be male or female— becomes more complex during this time. Girls tend to be more flexible about gender roles than boys, although by the end of middle childhood both boys and girls tend to prefer "boy" activities.
        6. **Meta-analysis**, a tool for combining the results of multiple studies, reveals that boys tend to be more active, physically aggressive, better at spatial tasks, and possess better motor skills than girls. Girls, however, tend to have superior

verbal skills and are better at reading interpersonal emotion. There is, however, considerable overlap between the sexes on all such tasks.

II. Moral Reasoning, Prosocial Behavior, and Aggression
   A. Moral Reasoning
      1. Kohlberg studied moral reasoning by examining children's responses to hypothetical moral dilemmas. He was more interested in the reasoning behind their responses than the actual moral judgment they made. Kohlberg identified three levels of moral reasoning.
         a) **Preconventional moral reasoning** is predominant throughout most of childhood. It focuses on rewards or punishments for different courses of action.
         b) **Conventional moral reasoning** is more dominant in late childhood and early adolescence. It focuses on how an individual will be judged by others for different courses of action.
         c) **Postconventional moral reasoning** emerges during adolescence and young adult years. It focuses on broad ethical principles in determining the right course of action.
      2. Kohlberg's research has been criticized because he only interviewed white males from middle-class backgrounds. He has also been criticized for focusing on moral reasoning over moral action.
   B. Prosocial Development
      1. **Prosocial behavior** refers to actions intended to benefit another person, and it generally increases throughout middle childhood.
      2. The increase in prosocial behavior is in part due to school-age children's improving ability to read other's emotions and to regulate their own emotional responses.
      3. Additionally, the increase in prosocial behavior in middle childhood may reflect changes in motivation over time. During early childhood, children tend to use **hedonistic reasoning**, but throughout middle childhood shift to become other-oriented and aimed at gaining social approval. **Altruism** emerges toward the end of elementary school.
      4. Societies vary in terms of which prosocial behaviors are expected. Western cultures tend to value spontaneous, heart-felt acts of kindness, while more collectivist cultures value doing one's duty.
      5. Some scientists have also studied individual variation within cultures, finding that children in China who were rated as more prosocial by a teacher in kindergarten, tended to be rated as more prosocial by a *different* teacher six years later. This may reflect biological factors.
   C. Aggression
      1. Aggression can take different forms, including **physical aggression**, **verbal aggression**, and **relational aggression**.
      2. Physical aggression tends to decrease over middle childhood as they acquire strategies for dealing with conflict, including the use of other forms of aggression. Highly aggressive children tend to perceive ambiguous situations as hostile more than children who are less aggressive.
      3. **Social aggression** and relational aggression both increase in middle childhood, with the former peaking in the transition to adolescence. Although stereotypes suggest girls are more likely to practice social aggression than boys, this may be a result of the fact that social or relational aggression's consequences feel more significant to girls than boys.

D.   Bullies and Victims
1.   **Bullying** refers to aggression by an individual that is repeatedly directed towards particular peers. It is characterized by an imbalance of power between the bully and the victim.
2.   Only 8% of victims respond to bullying constructively, while the remainder either responds with anger or submissive avoidance.
3.   Ten percent of children are victims of bulling. Victims come in two broad categories. Some are shy and others are aggressive themselves. Either category has in common that the victim tends to have few friends.
4.   Both boys and girls engage in bullying, although the form it takes tends to vary across gender. Bullying/victim relationships in middle childhood are usually same-sex pairs.

III.   The Family Context
A.   Household Structure
1.   Household structure refers to who lives in the household. **Post-modern families** have a great variety of possible structures—married versus unmarried, two- versus single -parent households, and so forth. Post-modern families are fairly fluid, with many children living in multiple types of households over the course of their growing-up years.
2.   Most children live in a two-parent household, about 25% live in single-mother homes, 5% with a single-father, and 4% live with no parents.
3.   Nearly 4 million households are multigenerational, and these situations are more common in immigrant families.
B.   Two-Parent versus One-Parent Households
1.   Two-parent families have several built-in advantages, particularly higher household income in general along with greater stability. Children from two-parent households tend to fare better, earning on average better grades and having fewer behavior problems.
2.   When parents divorce, they tend to underestimate the intensity of their children's reactions. Meta-analysis reveals that children of divorce tend to score lower on measures of academic achievement, conduct, psychological adjustment, self-concept, and social relations (although there was overlap between groups of children of divorce and children from intact families).
3.   Children of divorce fare best if relations between the parents are amicable. Significant risk factors include dramatic decrease in family income, abandonment or fear of it, diminished parenting, parental conflict, and dislocation.
C.   Other Family Circumstances
1.   Blended families vary in composition. School-age children have a harder time adjusting to blended families than preschoolers, in part because they have a longer history of living with both parents prior to the divorce, and also because they may resent the added authority figure a step-parent brings. The happier the mother and a new partner are, the more negative the parent-child relations tend to be in such families. Children in such families have, on average, lower academic achievement.
2.   More than 1 million children in the U. S. are adopted. Adoptees tend to have higher IQs than biological siblings who remained with their parents, but have lower school performance in comparison to their adoptive siblings. The reason for these findings may have to do with biological parents' genes, prenatal environment, and early post-natal environment.

3. About 5% of Americans are gay or lesbian, and many are parents. Studies of children raised in gay or lesbian households indicate these children are similar to children living with opposite-sex parents in self-concepts, preference for playmates and activities, social competence, and school grades.

D. The Family System

1. During middle childhood, families shift from parental control to *co-regulation*. Parents establish rules, but leave many smaller decisions to the child. Parental warmth, emotional support, and appropriate expectations are linked to child adjustment and achievement. However, parents spend less time supervising children during middle childhood than they did during early childhood years.

2. The quality of the marital relationship has a significant impact on children. Exposure to frequent and hostile marital conflict can interfere with short-term coping and long-term adjustment.

3. There is variability in sibling relationships, which is explained by several factors. The more similar the temperament between two siblings the more friendly the relationship. Gender matters, too, with sisters exhibiting more closeness than brothers or brother-sister pairs. Good sibling relationships are beneficial to school-aged children because they blunt the impact of rejection or social isolation.

IV. The Peer Context

During middle childhood, about 30% of time is spent with peers, and it is less closely supervised than it would have been in early childhood. The impromptu games and conflicts that emerge in these situations are important training grounds for problem-solving skills.

A. Friendship

1. Friendship expectations change over middle childhood. Early in middle childhood, friendships are based on rewards and costs, but by the end they are based on shared values and understandings.

2. Girls' friendships are more intimate, while boys' are based on physical activity. Because girls' friendships are so close, they are also more fragile.

3. **Homophily** tends to govern the selection of friends during middle childhood. Children tend to maintain friendships that are high quality (cooperative, supportive).

B. Peer Group

1. A **peer group** is a group of children that play together and are seen by others and themselves as having a common identity.

2. **Peer group status** is determined by **sociometric nomination**—asking children who they like to play with and who they prefer not to play with. Such analyses reveal five groups of children.

a) *Popular children* receive many nominations and few rejections from their peers. They are good at maintaining positive interactions with their peers.

b) *Rejected children* receive few positive nominations and many negative ones. Peer rejection is associated with school problems and delinquency.

c) *Controversial children* receive many positive and negative nominations. This classification is fairly rare.

d) *Neglected children* are low in both positive and negative nominations.

e) *Average children* receive some positive and negative nominations. They are moderately sociable with adequate cognitive skills.

C. Networks and Cliques

1. **Cliques** are voluntary, peer-based friendship networks.

2. Cliques are based on similarity, and tend to reinforce mini-cultures within the clique boundaries. Cliques sometimes provide **deviancy training** if clique members encourage and reinforce antisocial behavior and aggression.

V. The Broader Social Context
   A. Out-of-School Time
      1. Children spend about half of their waking hours in school, leaving the remainder of time for both organized and unstructured activities.
      2. Most school-age children are in at least one organized activity. Ability to participate in these activities depends on family income because they often require payment of a fee.
      3. Participation in organized activities is associated with academic and social skills growth, as well as improved peer acceptance. Although there has been some concern that children are overscheduled, research shows that this is the exception, not the rule.
   B. Afterschool Programs
      1. Afterschool programs are held four or five days a week until 5 or 6 p.m., and are usually in the schools themselves at present.
      2. When program quality is high, these programs can have a positive impact on social and academic outcomes.
   C. Time Without Adult Supervision
      1. **Self care** refers to children caring for themselves without supervision. Two percent of children in grades K–2 are in self care, while 7% of children in grades 3–5 are. Self care in middle childhood is linked to later social and academic problems.
      2. Hanging out with peers without adult supervision is also associated with problems in middle childhood, including poor grades, misconduct, and so forth.
      3. Care by siblings is another form that time without adult supervision takes. A fourth of children in the U. S. in grades K–8 are cared for by siblings after school. This form of care is also associated with negative outcomes.
   D. Neighborhoods
      1. One way to study the effect of neighborhoods is to examine the *structural* (or demographic) *characteristics.* Disadvantaged neighborhoods are characterized by low income, female-headed households, unemployed men, and high rates of crime and instability. Such characteristics are associated with outcomes in middle childhood, including peer affiliations, externalizing problems, and psychological distress.
      2. Another way to study neighborhoods is to ask residents about their *perceptions*. One study found that mother's perceptions affected their behavior more than the actual structural quality of the neighborhood, with negative perceptions of the neighborhood leading the mothers to place more limits on children's behaviors.
      3. Many studies of neighborhoods are correlational, making it difficult to determine if the neighborhood is the root cause of the outcomes observed or not. Move To Opportunity (MTO) was a field experiment that allowed such inferences, and confirmed many of the correlational findings previously reported.
   E. Electronic Media: Television, Videogames, and Computers
      1. Children have much more access to media now than they used to, and television is by far the most popular form of media for school-age children. There is a negative relationship between hours spent watching TV and academic achievement, but it is diminished when socioeconomic status is controlled for. The content of the shows viewed is important in determining outcomes.
      2. Children who watch more violent media tend to be more aggressive.

3.   Children who watch more TV tend to hold gender stereotypes more strongly than those who watch little TV.
4.   TV watching also influences eating patterns. Children who watch a lot of TV tend to snack and eat more junk food than those who don't.

KEY TERMS

1.   **Industry versus Inferiority** refers to Erikson's fourth stage of psychosocial development in which children develop a view of themselves as industrious (and worthy) versus inferior. Striving for recognition for their accomplishments, children develop skills and perform tasks that their society values. (see Socioemotional Accomplishments)

2.   **Instrumentality** is a gender-linked personality trait that is characterized by a focus on action and accomplishments. (see Socioemotional Accomplishments)

3.   **Expressivity** is a gender-linked personality trait that is marked by a "caring" orientation, a focus on communication, collaboration, and conciliation. (see Socioemotional Accomplishments)

4.   **Rough and tumble play** refers to physically vigorous behaviors, such as chasing, jumping and play fighting, that are accompanied by shared smiles and laughter. (see Socioemotional Accomplishments)

5.   **Gender schema** is a conceptualization of what it means to be male or female. (see Socioemotional Accomplishments)

6.   **Meta-analysis** is a statistical technique that combines the findings of multiple studies, taking into account the number of children in each of the individual studies and the magnitude of the effect reported in each one. (see Socioemotional Accomplishments)

7.   **Pre-conventional moral reasoning** is a stage of moral development. Individuals at this stage focus on the rewards and punishments associated with different courses of action, not societal standards in justifying moral decisions. (see Moral Reasoning, Prosocial Behavior, and Aggression)

8.   **Conventional moral reasoning** focuses on how an individual will be judged by others for behaving in a certain way. The focus is on receiving the approval of others or maintaining the social order. (see Moral Reasoning, Prosocial Behavior, and Aggression)

9.   **Post-conventional moral reasoning** is a level of moral reasoning not seen until adolescence. At this stage, rules and conventions are seen as relative and subjective, rather than absolute and definitive. (see Moral Reasoning, Prosocial Behavior, and Aggression)

10.   **Prosocial behavior** refers to voluntary actions, such as sharing, cooperating, helping, and comforting, that are intended to benefit another person. (see Moral Reasoning, Prosocial Behavior, and Aggression)

11.   **Hedonistic reasoning** is moral reasoning that focuses on one's own wishes and needs. (see Moral Reasoning, Prosocial Behavior, and Aggression)

12.   **Altruism** refers to helping behaviors that are motivated by helping as an end in itself, without expectation of reward or recognition. (see Moral Reasoning, Prosocial Behavior, and Aggression)

13.   **Verbal aggression** is behavior such as threats, name calling, and yelling with an angry voice. (see Moral Reasoning, Prosocial Behavior, and Aggression)

14. **Relational aggression** is any behavior that is intended to harm someone by damaging or manipulating relationships with others. (see Moral Reasoning, Prosocial Behavior, and Aggression)

15. **Physical aggression** refers to acts such as hitting or pushing with intent to harm. (see Moral Reasoning, Prosocial Behavior, and Aggression)

16. **Social aggression** is behavior that is directed towards damaging another's self-esteem, social status, or both. (see Moral Reasoning, Prosocial Behavior, and Aggression)

17. **Bullying** is aggression by an individual that is repeatedly directed toward particular peers (victims). (see Moral Reasoning, Prosocial Behavior, and Aggression)

18. **Postmodern family** is a term that describes the variation in modern-day families—two parents and single parents, married and unmarried couples, and multi-generational households. (see The Family Context)

19. **Homophily** is the tendency of individuals to associate and bond with others who are similar or "like" themselves. (see The Peer Context)

20. **Peer group** is a group of children who interact frequently and who see themselves, and are seen by others, as having a common identity. Peer groups have boundaries that define who is in and who is out of the group, a structure or hierarchy, and norms about what is acceptable or unacceptable among the group members. (see The Peer Context)

21. **Peer group status** is an indication of children's relative standing in the peer group as measured by peer nominations of acceptance and rejection. (see The Peer Context)

22. **Sociometric nomination** is a research method used by developmental scientists to determine a peer-group status. Typically children are asked to nominate or select three classmates who they like and three classmates who they do not like. (see The Peer Context)

23. **Cliques** are voluntary, friendship-based peer networks, generally of the same sex and age. (see The Peer Context)

24. **Deviancy training** is a process in which clique members praise, encourage, model, and reward one another for aggression or antisocial behavior. (see The Peer Context)

25. **Self care** refers to children caring for themselves without adult supervision. (see The Broader Social Context)

FILL-IN-THE-BLANKS KEY TERMS

This section will help you check your knowledge of the key terms introduced in this chapter. Fill in each blank with the appropriate term from the list of key terms in the previous section.

1. The tendency of individuals to associate and bond with others who are similar or "like" themselves is _____.

2. _____ is a gender-linked personality trait that is characterized by a focus on action and accomplishments.

3. A research method used by developmental scientists to determine a peer-group status in which children are asked to nominate or select three classmates who they like and three classmates who they do not like is called _____.

4. _____ is a statistical technique that combines the findings of multiple studies, taking into account the number of children in each of the individual studies and the magnitude of the effect reported in each one.

5. Moral reasoning that focuses on one's own wishes and needs is called _____.

6.   The phenomenon of children caring for themselves without adult supervision is called
      _____.

7.   _____ is a term that describes the variation in modern-day families—two parents and single
      parents, married and unmarried couples, and multi-generational households.

8.   Reasoning about moral dilemmas that focuses on receiving the approval of others or
      maintaining the social order is called_____.

9.   _____ is a process in which clique members praise, encourage, model, and reward one
      another for aggression or antisocial behavior.

10.   Aggression by an individual that is repeatedly directed toward particular victims is called
      _____.

APPLIED LEARNING AND CRITICAL THINKING

Socioemotional development in middle childhood, when studied in context, reveals great
variability in children. Below are some strategies for studying different aspects of socioemotional
development in middle childhood using context-rich learning, including study abroad, research,
employment, and service-learning.

1.   International adoptions have been on the rise as the number of babies available for adoption
      has declined in the United States. Many universities have study abroad programs in nations
      with babies that may likely be adopted by American parents, particularly China, Russia,
      Guatemala, and South Korea. If you will be studying in a country that has such availability,
      see what you can learn about what happens to the children that aren't adopted as infants or
      during early childhood. What happens to children who remain in these orphanages during
      their middle childhood years? Be sure to work with a professor before you take on such an
      exploration on your own, as the political and legal ramifications of such study can vary from
      country to country.

2.   Most schools today have anti-bullying programs. However, many of these programs are
      school system wide and do not necessarily deal with the particular problems of an
      individual bully or a specific school context very well. Find a community partner at a
      school—like a school counselor or social worker—and talk to them about what they see as
      the strengths and weakness of their anti-bullying program. See if you can develop a service-
      learning project that will address the weaknesses they see in their specific program, or
      involve working with specific students who seem prone to bullying, to develop better social
      skills in those children.

3.   Working in an after-school program is a great job for college students who plan to work
      with children for their career. If you are able to procure such a position, take notice of the
      quality of the program as you are on the job. Do you feel that the relationship between the
      staff is warm? That the activities are engaging and interesting? If you notice any areas of
      weakness, do you think you are able to improve those areas as an employee? Or is it a
      broader problem with the way the program is structured?

4.   Work with a professor to do a survey of families in your community that measures aspects
      of the family context. Include in your survey assessments of household structure (two-
      parent, one-parent, no-parent situations, as well as measures of who the two or one parents
      are in such circumstances—biological, step, foster, and so forth). What percent of children
      are being raised in nuclear versus blended families? Or in lesbian or gay households? What
      percent of households have an adopted child? What other measures of family context might
      be of interest? And what sort of social programs do these results suggest might be helpful
      to families in your community?

MULTIPLE-CHOICE QUESTIONS

Quiz 1

1. Hadley is so discouraged about school. Her second-grade teacher sends home loads of homework, and she is really struggling with her reading. The teacher told her mom that she is the worst reader in the class. On top of all this, Hadley has a speech problem, and she just feels completely incompetent at school. Hadley is in the middle of the _____ crisis.
   a. industry versus inferiority
   b. autonomy versus shame and doubt
   c. instrumentality versus expressivity
   d. initiative versus guilt

2. Madeleine loves to play with others and work on cooperative tasks. She is quick to try hard to get along and reconcile differences. Madeline is probably high on the characteristic of
   a. instrumentality.
   b. expressivity.
   c. altruism.
   d. aggression.

3. A statistical technique that combines results across multiple studies is known as
   a. sociometric nomination.
   b. deviancy training.
   c. meta-analysis.
   d. hedonistic reasoning.

4. Emily's sister confides to her that she is failing math at school. Emily decides she had better tell her mom and dad because they will be mad and possibly punish her if she keeps such an important piece of information from them. Emily's reasoning about whether to keep her sister's confidence or not is at the_____ level.
   a. pre-conventional
   b. conventional
   c. post-conventional
   d. unconventional

5. Prosocial behavior increases in middle childhood because
   a. children's ability to regulate their own emotions improves.
   b. children's ability to read the emotional cues of other's improves.
   c. children's reasoning tends to become more other-centered.
   d. All of these

6. Helping behaviors that are motivated by helping as an end in its own right are known as
   a. altruism.
   b. aggression.
   c. self care.
   d. postmodern.

7. Jake and his friend Christopher decide to shut out another little boy from their clique. Jake and Christopher are engaged in_____ aggression.
   a. verbal
   b. relational
   c. physical
   d. homophilic

8. _____ aggression decreases during middle childhood.

    a. Verbal
    b. Relational
    c. Physical
    d. Social

9. Which of the following is an example of the postmodern family?

    a. A nuclear family with a mom and dad and their two biological children
    b. A blended family with a mom and a stepdad and some children from each of their former marriages
    c. A gay couple raising twins
    d. All of these

10. Which of the following is an advantage for children living in a two-parent household?

    a. Mothers are more depressed in two-parent households.
    b. Income level is higher in a two-parent household.
    c. Parenting styles are more authoritarian in a two-parent household.
    d. All of these

11. The tendency of individuals to bond with those who are similar to themselves is called

    a. homophily.
    b. sociometrics.
    c. cliques.
    d. bullying.

12. Peer group status is determined in sociometric nomination by

    a. who is rated as the most popular.
    b. who is rated as most liked.
    c. who is preferred by the teacher.
    d. who has the most self care.

13. Which of the following is an example of a clique?

    a. The school band
    b. The cheerleader
    c. The reading club
    d. A group of girls who calls themselves the "Mod Squad"

14. Which of the following statements is true about children's participation in organized activities outside of school?

    a. It tends to improve peer acceptance scores.
    b. It tends to make them feel hurried and overscheduled.
    c. It tends to undermine ability to complete homework effectively.
    d. Both A and B

15. Which of the following is NOT a structural characteristic of a neighborhood?

    a. The income of residents
    b. The number of female-headed households
    c. The percentage of unemployed men
    d. The residents' perceptions of the neighborhood's safety

Quiz 2

Use this quiz to reassess your learning after taking Quiz 1 and reviewing the chapter.

1. A gender-linked personality trait that focuses on action and accomplishments is known as

    a. expressivity.
    b. instrumentality.

    c.   homophily.

    d.   physical aggression.

2. Ethan and Ian are wrestling and pushing each other, but smiling and laughing as they do. They are engaged in

    a.   rough and tumble play.

    b.   physical aggression.

    c.   hedonism.

    d.   bullying.

3. Which of the following statements about gender schema in middle childhood is true?

    a.   They increase in rigidity.

    b.   Girls are more rigid about them than boys.

    c.   Boys are more rigid about them than girls.

    d.   They become more simplistic.

4. Which form of moral reasoning would most likely NOT be observed in middle childhood?

    a.   Pre-conventional

    b.   Conventional

    c.   Post-conventional

    d.   All of these

5. Moral reasoning that focuses on one's own wishes and needs is called

    a.   hedonistic reasoning.

    b.   bullying.

    c.   post-conventional

    d.   conventional

6. Yang yells at his little sister, calling her gross and threatening to hit her if she doesn't get out of his room. Yang is engaged in_____ aggression.

    a.   social

    b.   relational

    c.   physical

    d.   verbal

7. Which type of aggression involves behavior aimed at damaging another's self-esteem, status, or both?

    a.   Social

    b.   Sociometric

    c.   Verbal

    d.   Physical

8. LaQuisha is in 3rd grade, and she is the class bully. Who is she most likely to bully?

    a.   Jethro, who is also in 3rd grade

    b.   Jed, who is outgoing and popular

    c.   Marta, who is in 3rd grade

    d.   Maxine, who is in 5th grade

9. What percent of children in the U. S. live with a single mother?

    a.   67%

    b.   25%

    c.   5%

    d.   10%

10. Which of the following is NOT an important risk factor for increasing the negative effects of divorce on child development?

    a.   Dislocation

    b.   Increased family income

    c.   Fear of abandonment

    d.   Diminished parenting

11. A group of children who interact frequently and see themselves and are seen by others as having a common identity is a

    a.   peer group.

    b.   clique.

    c.   gender schema.

    d.   postmodern family.

12. In sociometric research, children who receive few positive or negative nominations are considered

    a.   popular.

    b.   rejected.

    c.   neglected.

    d.   average.

13. Fernando's friends encourage him to shoplift and bully. His clique is engaged in

    a.   deviancy training.

    b.   sociometric nomination.

    c.   verbal aggression.

    d.   rough and tumble play.

14. What percent of children aged kindergarten to 2nd grade are in self care regularly?

    a.   2%

    b.   7%

    c.   10%

    d.   15%

15. Which of the following statements about time spent watching television and academic achievement in middle school is true?

    a.   Television watching always hurts academic achievement.

    b.   Television watching can hurt achievement, but some content actually helps.

    c.   Controlling for socioeconomic status eliminates the TV-academic achievement link.

    d.   Both B and C are true.

ANSWERS TO FILL-IN-THE-BLANKS KEY TERMS

1. homophily (see The Peer Context)

2. Instrumentality (see Socioemotional Accomplishments)

3. sociometric nomination (see The Peer Context)

4. Meta-analysis (see Socioemotional Accomplishments)

5. hedonistic reasoning (see Moral Reasoning, Prosocial Behavior, and Aggression)

6. self care (see The Broader Social Context)

7. Post-modern family (see The Family Context)

8. conventional moral reasoning (see Moral Reasoning, Prosocial Behavior, and Aggression)

9. Deviancy training (see The Peer Context)

10. bullying (see Moral Reasoning, Prosocial Behavior, and Aggression)

ANSWERS TO MULTIPLE-CHOICE QUESTIONS

Circle the question numbers you answered incorrectly.

Quiz 1

1.   *a is the answer.*   Hadley is in the middle of the industry versus inferiority crisis. She will achieve a sense of industry, or worth, when she finds success in some arena, or producing things with others. Right now she is struggling with a sense of inferiority. (see Socioemotional Accomplishments)

2.   *b is the answer.*   Madeleine is high on expressivity, which is a gender-linked personality trait involving a caring orientation that is focused on communication, collaboration, and conciliation. It is more encouraged in girls than in boys. (see Socioemotional Accomplishments)

3.   *c is the answer.*   Meta-analysis is a statistical technique that combines results across multiple studies based on the number of children in each study and the magnitude of the effect reported in each study. (see Socioemotional Accomplishments)

4.   *a is the answer.*   Emily's reasoning is at the pre-conventional level. Pre-conventional reasoning is focused on seeking rewards or avoiding punishments. Emily is trying to avoid a punishment. (see Moral Reasoning, Prosocial Behavior, and Aggression)

5.   *d is the answer.*   All three of these factors—ability to read emotions, ability to regulate emotions, and development of other-centered reasoning—help increase the amount of prosocial behavior observed in middle childhood. (see Moral Reasoning, Prosocial Behavior, and Aggression)

6.   *a is the answer.*   Altruism is helping for helping's sake, without desire for reward or recognition. (see Moral Reasoning, Prosocial Behavior, and Aggression)

7.   *b is the answer.*   Jake and Christopher are engaged in relational aggression, which is behavior that intends to harm another by damaging their relationships with others. By excluding another from their clique, Jake and Christopher are damaging that child's relationship with the other clique members. (see Moral Reasoning, Prosocial Behavior, and Aggression)

8.   *c is the answer.*   Physical aggression decreases in middle childhood, whereas social and relational may actually increase during this time. (see Moral Reasoning, Prosocial Behavior, and Aggression)

9.   *d is the answer.*   Postmodern family refers to the variability in modern-day families—all of these forms of families are part of the postmodern, more flexible definition of "family." (see The Family Context)

10. *b is the answer.*   Income level is higher in two-parent households, which is a significant advantage. It is not true that parenting is more authoritarian in two-parent households, and even if it were this would not be advantageous. Nor is it true that mothers in two-parent homes are more depressed, and again, even if it were, this would be a disadvantage, not an advantage. (see The Family Context)

11. *a is the answer.*   Homophily is the tendency to bond with and associate with others who are like oneself. (see The Peer Context)

12. *b is the answer.*   Peer group status is determined by who is rated as most liked (e.g., who would you most like to play with), not by who is rated as most popular. The former is considered "sociometric" popularity, while the latter is prestige popularity. (see The Peer Context)

13. *d is the answer.*   Only the group of girls who has given themselves a name is a completely voluntary friendship group. The band is determined by interest and ability in music,

cheerleading by athletic ability, and reading club by shared interest or requirements. (see The Peer Context)

14. *a is the answer.* Participation in organized activities outside of school provides opportunities to practice social skills and learn norms of interaction. These tend to positively influence peer acceptance. Evidence that children feel overscheduled, thought available in the popular press, suggests that these children are the minority. (see The Broader Social Context)

15. *d is the answer.* Structural characteristics of a neighborhood refer to demographics. The residents' perceptions are not demographics. (see The Broader Social Context)

Now turn to the quiz analysis table at the end of this chapter to find which areas you know well and which areas you need to work on. Circle the numbers in the table for items on Quiz 1 that you answered correctly.

Quiz 2

1. *b is the answer.* Instrumentality is a gender-linked personality trait that emphasizes action and accomplishment. It is encouraged in boys more than it is in girls. (see Socioemotional Accomplishments)

2. *a is the answer.* Rough and tumble play refers to physically vigorous play like chasing or play fighting, that is accompanied by shared smiles and laughter. (see Socioemotional Accomplishments)

3. *c is the answer.* Boys tend to be more rigid about gender roles in middle childhood, while girls are more flexible. (see Socioemotional Accomplishments)

4. *c is the answer.* Post-conventional, or principled, moral reasoning is generally not seen prior to adolescence. (see Moral Reasoning, Prosocial Behavior, and Aggression)

5. *a is the answer.* Hedonistic reasoning is moral reasoning that focuses on one's own wishes and needs. (see Moral Reasoning, Prosocial Behavior, and Aggression)

6. *d is the answer.* Verbal aggression involves yelling and threatening in a loud, angry voice. Yang is yelling and threatening. (see Moral Reasoning, Prosocial Behavior, and Aggression)

7. *a is the answer.* Social aggression involves behavior that aims to hurt another's self-esteem, status, or both. (see Moral Reasoning, Prosocial Behavior, and Aggression)

8. *c is the answer.* Marta is most likely to be bullied by LaQuisha. Bullies generally pick someone of the same sex as themselves, which eliminates the boy potential victims. LaQuisha will probably select someone younger than herself, as the balance of power would be in her favor. (see Moral Reasoning, Prosocial Behavior, and Aggression)

9. *b is the answer.* About a fourth of children live with a single mother. (see The Family Context)

10. *b is the answer.* Family income tends to decrease after a divorce, not increase. (see The Family Context)

11. *a is the answer.* A peer group is a group of children who interact frequently and are seen as having a common identity. A clique is a group that is friendship based. Not all peer groups are based on friendship. (see The Peer Context)

12. *c is the answer.* Neglected children receive few nominations—either positive or negative. (see The Peer Context)

13. *a is the answer.*   Deviancy training refers to a process by which clique members praise, encourage, model, and reward aggression or antisocial behavior. (see The Peer Context)

14. *a is the answer.*   Two percent of children in grades K–2 are in self care regularly. (see The Broader Social Context)

15. *d is the answer.*   While it is true that hours spent watching television is inversely associated with academic achievement, controlling for socioeconomic status erases this relationship. Also, some content (e.g., Sesame Street) can help academic achievement. (see The Broader Social Context)

Now turn to the quiz analysis table at the end of this chapter to find which areas you know well and which areas you need to work on. Circle the numbers in the table for items on Quiz 2 that you answered correctly.

For each question you answered correctly, circle its number. (Quiz 1 numbers are not shaded; Quiz 2 numbers are shaded.) Are there patterns in the types of questions or the topics you got wrong that could direct your further study? Did you improve from Quiz 1 to Quiz 2?

QUIZ REVIEW

Topic	Type of Question		
	Definition	Comprehension	Application
Socioemotional	3		1, 2
Accomplishments	1	3	2
Moral Reasoning, Prosocial	6	5, 8	4, 7
Behavior, and Aggression	5, 7	4	6, 8
The Family Context		9, 10	
		9, 10	
The Peer Context	11	12	13
	11, 12		13
The Broader Social Context		14	15
		14, 15	

Total correct by quiz:

Quiz 1:
Quiz 2:

CHAPTER 13

Physical Development in Adolescence

LEARNING OBJECTIVES

1. List the five chief physical components of puberty. Explain their manifestations in males and females.

2. Explain the HPG feedback loop that triggers puberty. Show how environmental factors can affect the timing of puberty.

3. Identify the possible psychological and social consequences for adolescents who enter puberty much earlier or much later than their friends.

4. Describe puberty's effects on an adolescent's emotions, sleep patterns, and social behavior.

5. List the stages of sexual activity.

6. Define sexual orientation, sex-role behavior, and gender identity.

7. Explain why so few sexually active adolescents use any form of contraception.

8. List the most common sexually transmitted diseases among adolescents. Identify and rate the effectiveness of the methods used by adolescents to protect themselves from these risks.

9. Describe the consequences of teenage pregnancy for the mother and child.

10. Define disordered eating behavior and identify the eating disorder that affects the greatest number of American adolescents.

11. Describe the major physiological changes in the brain during adolescence.

12. Explain how changes in the brain cause adolescents to be more susceptible to peer pressure and more likely to engage in risky behavior.

13. List the substances most widely abused by adolescents. Describe how widespread substance abuse is among adolescents.

14. Explain how the use of drugs during early adolescence can permanently affect the brain.

15. Identify and explain the four risk factors for substance abuse.

16. List the psychological, social, and physical health problems that may result from substance abuse.

17. List the three factors targeted by drug abuse prevention programs. Describe the most successful approach to reducing substance use by adolescents, and explain why it works.

OUTLINE

I. Puberty and Its Consequences
Technically, **puberty** refers to the period when an individual becomes capable of sexually reproducing; however, it has come to include more generally all the physical changes involved in passing from childhood to adulthood. During this time, adolescents experience

rapid growth, develop primary and secondary sex characteristics, and experience changes in body composition, circulatory, and respiratory systems.

A. The Endocrine System
    1. The **endocrine system** produces, circulates and regulate **hormones** by releasing them from **glands**. Glands are organs that stimulate certain parts of the body. Many of the hormones important in puberty transmit their instructions by activating **gonadotropin releasing hormone (GnRH) neurons**. Gonadotropins are hormones that stimulate sexual maturation and regulate reproductive activity.
    2. The endocrine system receives instructions for the amount of a hormone to release from the brain, mainly through the firing of GnRH neurons.
        a) Like a thermostat, when a level of hormone dips below a **set point** for that hormone at that stage of development, the secretion of the hormone increases until it reaches the level of the set point, at which it is temporarily suspended.
        b) This *feedback loop* is increasingly important during puberty. Prenatally, a feedback loop develops linking the **pituitary gland** to the **hypothalamus** and **gonads** (**testes** in males, **ovaries** in females). It is known as the **HPG axis**. The gonads release the sex hormones (**androgens** and **estrogens**), which in turn stimulate sexual maturation and physical growth.
        c) The onset of puberty is controlled by this feedback loop. When sex hormones drop below a certain level, a signal is sent to increase their secretion.
    3. Feelings of sexual attraction may be stimulated by maturation of the adrenal glands, or **adrenarche**. The brain system that regulates the adrenal gland also regulates response to stress. An adverse side effect of adrenarche is also to heighten one's response to stress, which increases release of **cortisol**, a stress hormone that can at high and chronic levels cause brain cells to die. This may explain why adolescence is a time for the onset of many serious mental disorders.
B. What Triggers Puberty?
    1. During middle childhood, both genetic and environmental factors "awaken" the HPG axis. Genetic factors are "programmed."
    2. Environmental factors include the availability of mature mating partners, nutritional support available for a pregnancy, and the physical maturity and health of the specific child. **Leptin**, a protein produced by fat cells, may be part of this trigger.
C. Changes in Height, Weight, and Appearance
    Growth hormones, thyroid hormones, and androgens combine to stimulate the **adolescent growth spurt**. Puberty also brings the development of **secondary sex characteristics** and is divided into five stages, called the **Tanner stages**.

    1. Sexual Maturation in Boys
        a) The first sign of sexual maturation in boys is growth of the testes and scrotum with the appearance of pubic hair. A year later, the growth spurt for height and the penis begins, with pubic hair growing coarser and darker. Boys are able to produce semen before their appearance is adult-like.
        b) The emergence of facial hair and the deepening of the voice in boys is a late development in puberty. Additionally, the skin becomes rougher and sweat glands become more active.
    2. Sexual Maturation in Girls

       a)   The first sign of sexual maturation in girls is usually elevation of the breasts, though in some girls the appearance of pubic hair comes first.

       b)   **Menarche** (the beginning of menstruation) is a later development. Generally, a girl does not become fertile until several years after her first period.

D.   The Psychological and Social Impact of Puberty

The biological changes of puberty can affect behavior and psychological functioning. In some nonindustrialized societies, adolescents undergo a formal **rite of passage**, a ceremony that certifies them as adult members of the community.

   1.   Puberty and the Adolescent's Emotions

       a)   Puberty can wreak havoc on adolescent emotional functioning, but this is largely dependent upon the social context in which this portion of development unfolds. In general, girls (especially white girls) are more adversely affected by the changes of puberty than boys.

       b)   The connection between hormones and mood is not especially strong, but is most likely to be observed early in puberty when hormonal levels are fluctuating more than usual.

   2.   Changes in Patterns of Sleep

       a)   **Delayed phase preference** (preference for staying up late and sleeping in) emerges in adolescence, and is driven by biological changes of puberty. During adolescence, **melatonin**, a hormone related to sleep, changes the time at which it peaks, allowing adolescents to not feel sleepy until later in the night.

       b)   Although adolescents prefer to go to bed later than they did as children, they still need approximately 9 hours of sleep, though most teens probably do not get that much.

E.   Early and Late Maturation

   1.   Genetic and Environmental Influences on Pubertal Timing

       a)   Every individual inherits a predisposition for when puberty should begin, but this is best seen as an upper and lower age limit, not a fixed deadline.

       b)   The two most important environmental influences on pubertal timing are nutrition and health. Because nutrition and health have improved so greatly during the past two centuries, a decline in the average age at menarche has been observed. This is known as the **secular trend**.

   2.   Early versus Late Maturation Among Boys

Boys who mature early as compared to their peers are more popular and feel better about themselves; however, they are also more likely to get involved in antisocial or deviant activities.

   3.   Early versus Late Maturation in Girls

Early maturing girls have more social difficulty than their later maturing peers, particularly in regards to their self-image and weight. However, this does not generally jeopardize their popularity with peers. Like early maturing boys, early maturing girls are more at risk for problem behavior.

II.   Sexual Activity During Adolescence

   A.   Stages of Sexual Activity

      1.   The first stage of sexual activity for adolescents is usually masturbation. About half of boys and one-fourth of girls have masturbated by the time they are 18 years old.

2.   By the time they reach high school, most adolescents have progressed to sexual activity with a partner rather than masturbation.

B.   Sexual Intercourse During Adolescence
1.   Fewer adolescents today are having intercourse as compared to those from the 1990s, but those who do engage in intercourse do so at younger ages than used to be the case.
2.   Ethnic differences in the age of sexual initiation are greater for males than females. For males, African Americans have the earliest age of initiation, while Asian Americans have the oldest. These differences are smaller among females, but the pattern of African Americans having a lower age of sexual initiation persists.
3.   Sexual activity in adolescence is not generally associated with psychological disturbance, though earlier ages of initiation are associated with risky behavior such as drug experimentation and tolerance for deviance.

C.   Homosexuality during Adolescence
1.   Homosexual sex play or attraction in adolescence is reported by about 8 percent of males and 6 percent of females, with about three to four percent of adolescents self-identifying as gay or lesbian.
2.   Homosexuality appears to be influenced by hormonal, genetic, and environmental factors.
3.   **Sexual orientation** is the extent to which someone is oriented toward heterosexual activity, homosexual activity, or both. **Sex-role behavior** is the extent to which an individual behaves in traditionally masculine or feminine ways. **Gender identity** refers to which gender an individual believes he or she is psychologically. There is no relationship between an adolescent's sexual orientation and his or her sex-role behavior.

D.   Contraceptive Use
1.   Many adolescents who engage in sexual intercourse do not use contraception, or use ineffective methods. Of those who do use contraception, condoms are the most popular method.
2.   Failure to use contraception in adolescence occurs for a variety of reasons, including lack of availability, insufficient education about the need for contraception, and unwillingness to use contraception because it suggests one "planned" to be sexually active.

E.   AIDS and Other Sexually Transmitted Diseases
One of the goals of sex education for adolescents is to help them avoid the risks of **sexually transmitted diseases** such as **gonorrhea, chlamydia, herpes**, and **human papilloma virus**. **AIDS**, which is caused by **HIV**, is transmitted through bodily fluids and poses a significant risk to adolescent populations, particularly in the inner city and among homeless youths.

F.   Sex Education
School-based sexual education programs rarely dissuade adolescents from having sex, but do help students choose to have "safer" sex.

G.   Teenage Pregnancy and Childbearing
1.   The United States has the highest teen pregnancy rate in the industrialized world. About one-third of these pregnancies end in abortion and one-sixth in miscarriage. Teens who give birth, though, predominantly keep their babies. Only one in ten teen pregnancies results in adoption.
2.   Teen pregnancy is more likely in economically disadvantaged communities, and occurs more frequently in nonwhite communities.

3.   Teen mothers are more likely to perceive their baby as difficult, and are less likely to interact with their baby in ways that promote cognitive and social development of the infant.

4.   Teen mothers experience a disruption in their educational and career development. Finishing high school and delaying subsequent childbearing helps teen mothers fare better over the long haul than teen mothers who do not complete high school and/or who have additional pregnancies.

III.   Eating Disorders
   A.   Obesity
   Obesity is an increasing problem among adolescents, largely because of lack of physical activity and over-consumption of high-calories/high-fat food.

   B.   Anorexia Nervosa and Bulimia
      1.   **Disordered eating** refers to patterns of eating attitudes and behavior that are unhealthy. It ranges from unnecessary preoccupation with weight and eating to actual eating disorders.
      2.   **Bulimia** is a pattern of overeating (binging) followed by induced vomiting (purging). **Anorexia nervosa** involves actual self-starvation. The incidence of these disorders is smaller than most people would expect, although they are much more likely to occur in females than males.
      3.   A variety of treatments have been successful in treating eating disorders.

IV.   The Adolescent Brain
   A.   Brain Maturation in Adolescence
      1.   Important changes occur in the brain during adolescence. First, the **prefrontal cortex** is pruned. The prefrontal cortex matures once a person reaches his or her twenties. Development in the **dorsolateral prefrontal cortex**, **ventromedial prefrontal cortex**, and **orbitofrontal cortex** is especially important.
      2.   Changes in **neurotransmitter** levels and the **limbic system** make adolescents more emotional, more responsive to stress, and more sensation-seeking. These changes explain why adolescents are more vulnerable to substance abuse and to over-concern for what peers think.
   B.   Implications for Adolescent Behavior
   The relatively late development of the prefrontal cortex, combined with limbic system changes may provoke a craving for novelty. This would correspond to adolescence as a period of experimentation with risk.

V.   Substance Use and Abuse in Adolescence
   A.   Prevalence of Substance Use and Abuse in Adolescence
      1.   Survey research indicates that alcohol and nicotine are the most used and abused drugs amongst adolescents, followed by marijuana. Use and abuse of other drugs is relatively rare in adolescence.
      2.   Among adolescents who report drug usage, nicotine is the only drug that those adolescents report using daily, although a noticeable percentage of teens also report some episodes (not daily) of **binge drinking** (having five or more drinks in a row).
      3.   Because illicit drug use beyond experimentation with marijuana is relatively rare in adolescence, it is unlikely that drugs explain many of the problems that adolescents in general experience. Education about cigarettes and alcohol are more urgently needed than targeting other drug usage.
      4.   The percentage of young adolescents (8th graders) who experiment with substances such as alcohol or marijuana has grown in recent years, though, which increases their risk for addiction as they mature.

5.   White adolescents are more likely to use drugs and alcohol than their minority counterparts.

B.   Drugs and the Adolescent Brain

1.   Changes in the brain at adolescence heighten the likelihood of addiction.

a)   Changes in the limbic system in adolescence affect the neurotransmitter **dopamine**, which is involved in the experience of pleasure.

b)   The main reason drugs feel good is because they affect the same receptors that are sensitive to naturally occurring dopamine.

c)   Frequent drug use signals the brain to reduce the amount of naturally occurring dopamine, which makes a person more dependent on the drug to stimulate those receptors.

d)   Because the limbic system is "remodeled" in adolescence, if this process occurs during that time period, it can permanently affect the way the dopamine system functions.

2.   The effects of nicotine and alcohol on brain function during adolescence are also significant. Alcohol can affect the **hippocampus**, which affects memory and the ability to stop impulsive behavior.

C.   Causes and Consequences of Adolescent Substance Use and Abuse

1.   **Substance abuse** is using drugs in a way that adversely impacts functioning at home, school, work, or other settings. **Substance dependence** refers to physical addiction.

2.   Moderate alcohol and marijuana use is somewhat normative for adolescents in the United States, and because these substances are typically used in social situations, adolescents who are more socially competent are more likely to have been part of social activities in which they are used.

3.   Substance *abuse*, however, is usually a sign of a prior psychological problem as a youngster, rather than a cause of the problem. Substance abuse in adolescence, however, is associated with physical and psychological problems, as well as social problems.

4.   Four sets of **risk factors** for substance abuse have been identified.

a)   Psychological risk factors include personality characteristics such as inattentiveness or impulsivity.

b)   Familial risk factors include having a distant, conflicted, or hostile family environment.

c)   Social risk factors include having friends who use and tolerate drug use.

d)   Contextual risk factors include living in an environment where drugs are easily available, law enforcement is weak, and drug usage is promoted in the media.

D.   Prevention and Treatment of Substance Use and Abuse

1.   Prevention can focus on limiting the availability of drugs, but may be more effective if it targets the motivation of adolescents to use them and the environment in which they are exposed to drugs.

2.   Programs focused on individual students (such as Project DARE) have largely been ineffective. The most promising interventions are not individually based, but community wide, targeting adolescents, their parents, and their teachers. They are most effective when they begin prior to adolescence and continue through high school.

KEY TERMS

1. **Puberty** refers to the biological changes of adolescence. (see Puberty and Its Consequences)

2. The **endocrine system** is the system of the body that produces, circulates, and regulates hormones. (see Puberty and Its Consequences)

3. **Hormones** are highly specialized substances secreted by one or more endocrine glands. (see Puberty and Its Consequences)

4. **Glands** are organs that stimulate particular parts of the body to respond in specific ways to particular hormones. (see Puberty and Its Consequences)

5. **Gonadotropin releasing hormone (GnRH) neurons** are specific neurons in the brain that are affected by hormones (gonadotropins) that stimulate sexual maturation and regulate reproductive activity. (see Puberty and Its Consequences)

6. A **set point** is a physiological level or setting that the body attempts to maintain through a self-regulating system. (see Puberty and Its Consequences)

7. The **pituitary gland** is one of the chief glands responsible for regulating levels of hormones in the body. (see Puberty and Its Consequences)

8. The **hypothalamus** is a part of the lower brain stem that controls the functioning of the pituitary gland. (see Puberty and Its Consequences)

9. **Gonads** are the glands that secrete sex hormones: in males, the testes; in females, the ovaries. (see Puberty and Its Consequences)

10. The **testes** are the male gonads. (see Puberty and Its Consequences)

11. The **ovaries** are the female gonads. (see Puberty and Its Consequences)

12. The **HPG (hypothalamic-pituitary-gonadal) axis** is the neuropsychological pathway that involves the hypothalamus, pituitary gland, and gonads. (see Puberty and Its Consequences)

13. **Androgens** are a class of sex hormones secreted by the gonads, found in both sexes, but in higher levels among males than among females following puberty. (see Puberty and Its Consequences)

14. **Estrogens** are a class of sex hormones secreted by the gonads, found in both sexes but in higher levels among females than among males following puberty. (see Puberty and Its Consequences)

15. **Adrenarche** refers to the maturation of the adrenal glands that takes place in preadolescence. (see Puberty and Its Consequences)

16. **Cortisol** is a hormone produced when we are exposed to stress. (see Puberty and Its Consequences)

17. **Leptin** is a protein produced by fat cells that may play a role in the onset of puberty. (see Puberty and Its Consequences)

18. The **adolescent growth spurt** is the dramatic increase in height and weight that occurs during puberty. (see Puberty and Its Consequences)

19. **Secondary sex characteristics** refer to the manifestations of sexual maturation at puberty, including the development of breasts, the growth of facial and body hair, and changes in the voice. (see Puberty and Its Consequences)

20. The **Tanner stages** are a widely used system to describe the five stages of pubertal development. (see Puberty and Its Consequences)

21. **Menarche** is the time of first menstruation, one of the important changes to occur among females during puberty. (see Puberty and Its Consequences)

22. A **rite of passage** is a ceremony or ritual marking an individual's transition from one social status to another, especially marking the young person's transition into adulthood. (see Puberty and Its Consequences)

23. **Delayed phase preference** is a pattern of sleep characterized by later sleep and wake times, which often emerges during puberty. (see Puberty and Its Consequences)

24. **Melatonin** is a hormone in the brain that affects the sense of sleepiness; when melatonin levels are higher, it causes one to feel sleepy. (see Puberty and Its Consequences)

25. A **secular trend** is the tendency, over the past two centuries, for individuals to be larger in stature and to reach puberty earlier, primarily because of improvements in health and nutrition. (see Puberty and Its Consequences)

26. **Sexual orientation** is an individual's orientation, or preference for, same- versus opposite-sex sexual partners. (see Sexual Activity During Adolescence)

27. **Sex-role behavior** is behavior that is consistent with prevailing expectations for how individuals of a given sex are to behave. (see Sexual Activity During Adolescence)

28. **Gender identity** refers to the aspects of one's sense of self that concern one's masculinity and femininity. (see Sexual Activity During Adolescence)

29. **Sexually transmitted disease (STD)** refers to any group of infections—including gonorrhea, herpes, chlamydia, and AIDS—passed on through sexual contact. (see Sexual Activity During Adolescence)

30. **Gonorrhea** is a sexually transmitted infection caused by a bacterium. (see Sexual Activity During Adolescence)

31. **Chlamydia** is a sexually transmitted infection caused by a bacterium. (see Sexual Activity During Adolescence)

32. **Herpes** is a sexually transmitted infection caused by a virus. (see Sexual Activity During Adolescence)

33. **Human papilloma virus** is one of several viruses that causes a sexually transmitted disease. (see Sexual Activity During Adolescence)

34. **AIDS (acquired immune deficiency syndrome)** is a disease, transmitted by means of bodily fluids, that devastates the immune system. (see Sexual Activity During Adolescence)

35. **Human immunodeficiency virus (HIV)** is the virus associated with AIDS.

36. **Disordered eating** is mild, moderate, or severe disturbance in eating habits and attitudes. (see Eating Disorders)

37. **Anorexia nervosa** is an eating disorder found chiefly among young women, characterized by dramatic and severe self-induced weight loss. (see Eating Disorders)

38. **Bulimia** is an eating disorder found chiefly among young women, characterized primarily by a pattern of binge eating and self-induced vomiting. (see Eating Disorders)

39. The **prefrontal cortex** is the part of the brain responsible for many higher-order cognitive skills, such as decision-making and planning. (see The Adolescent Brain)

40. The **dorsolateral prefrontal cortex** refers to the outer and upper areas of the front of the brain, important for skills such as planning ahead and controlling impulses. (see The Adolescent Brain)

41. The **ventromedial prefrontal cortex** refers to the lower and central area at the front of the brain, important for gut-level decision making. (see The Adolescent Brain)

42. The **orbitofrontal cortex** is the region of the brain located directly behind the eyes, important for the evaluation of risk and reward. (see The Adolescent Brain)

43. **Neurotransmitters** are chemical substances in the brain that carry electrical impulses across synapses. (see The Adolescent Brain)

44. The **limbic system** is an area of the brain that plays an important role in emotional experience. (see The Adolescent Brain)

45. **Binge drinking** involves consuming five or more drinks in a row on one occasion, and is an indicator of alcohol abuse. (see Substance Use and Abuse in Adolescence)

46. **Dopamine** refers to a neurotransmitter especially important in the brain circuits that regulate the experience of pleasure. (see Substance Use and Abuse in Adolescence)

47. The **hippocampus** is part of the brain that is important for memory, particularly forming new memories. (see Substance Use and Abuse in Adolescence)

48. **Substance abuse** is the misuse of alcohol or other drugs to a degree that it causes problems in the individual's life. (see Substance Use and Abuse in Adolescence)

49. **Substance dependence** is the misuse of alcohol or other drugs to a degree that it causes physical addiction. (see Substance Use and Abuse in Adolescence)

50. **Risk factors** are factors that increase individual vulnerability to harm. (see Substance Use and Abuse in Adolescence)

FILL-IN-THE-BLANKS KEY TERMS

This section will help you check your knowledge of the key terms introduced in this chapter. Fill in each blank with the appropriate term from the list of key terms in the previous section.

1. _____ is mild, moderate, or severe disturbance in eating habits and attitudes.

2. The region of the brain located directly behind the eyes that is important for evaluation of risk and reward is known as the _____.

3. _____ are the glands that secrete sex hormones.

4. _____ refers to the biological changes of adolescence.

5. The misuse of alcohol or other drugs to a degree that it causes problem in the individual's life is called _____.

6. _____ refers to the aspects of one's sense of self that concern one's masculinity and femininity.

7. The tendency over the past two centuries for individuals to be larger in stature and to reach puberty earlier is known as a _____.

8. _____ is the virus associated with AIDS.

9.   The _____ describe the five stages of pubertal development.

10. The _____ is the neuropsychological pathway that involves the hypothalamus, pituitary gland, and gonads.

APPLIED LEARNING AND CRITICAL THINKING

The content covered in this chapter provides a great many opportunities for service that will enhance your ability to think critically about the physical changes of adolescence. Working with community and local government agencies can give you an "up close" look at some of the issues discussed here, and allow you the opportunity to form your own opinions based on both the evidence in the chapter and the kinds of experiences you acquire as you serve your community.

1.   For an applied research project, survey a group of school districts in your region to identify what time schools start for different age groups. In general, do the junior high and high schools start later or earlier than elementary and middle schools? Research reported in this chapter suggests that adolescent attention will be greater later in the day. Do school start times work with that finding, or against it? Write a brief report that summarizes your findings, and then work with your instructor to find a way to disseminate the information to school districts for their consideration.

2.   If your psychology department offers a practicum or internship experience, you might try to land an opportunity with a hospital, pediatric clinic, or other health care or mental health provider that serves adolescents. In particular, you could develop a program for promoting greater levels of activity and lower levels of consumption for high-calorie or high-fat foods. Talk to the providers about what it would take to implement such a program. If you are able to obtain IRB approval and parental permission, you might pilot test your program with a small sample of adolescents to determine its effectiveness. Afterwards, present your results at a professional conference with your internship or practicum supervisor to gain feedback on your program and its effectiveness in the eyes of your colleagues.

3.   If you are at all interested in a career as a substance abuse counselor, find an organization in your area that works toward preventing substance abuse in adolescents and do some volunteer work for them. As you volunteer, observe the level of their interventions. Do they target the individual adolescent decisions? Do they attempt to address the parents and teachers as well? Do they try to affect the community as a whole? How do they assess the effectiveness of their interventions, and is their research strategy to do so appropriate? What might you change?

4.   Most communities have mentorship programs for adults who want to work with school-aged children. Consider enrolling in one of those programs and mentoring a student who is in adolescence. As you mentor that student in terms of their school programs and other matters, you can also get a sense of how well that student seems to "match" the research described in this chapter. Is the student "typical" or "atypical"? Does the student seem at risk to you for substance abuse or for engaging in unsafe sex or for developing an eating disorder? What risk factors can you identify in their life? Be sure to consider all four categories of risk factors: psychological, familial, social, and contextual. Having thought through those factors, consider what you as a mentor might do to reduce their risk.

MULTIPLE-CHOICE QUESTIONS

Quiz 1

1. The hormones that stimulate sexual maturation and regulate reproductive activity are called

    a. gonadotropin releasing hormone neurons.
    b. gonadotropins.
    c. cortisol.
    d. testes.

2. The HPG axis is a

    a. brain structure.
    b. hormone.
    c. feedback loop.
    d. delayed phase preference.

3. Cristina can't believe how fast her 13-year-old daughter is growing. It seems like she has grown four inches taller in the past year—it's like she is a toddler again, she is growing so fast! Cristina's daughter is probably

    a. in her adolescent growth spurt.
    b. entering menarche.
    c. entering adrenarche.
    d. Both B and C

4. A ceremony that certifies adolescents as entering the adult community, and confers new privileges and responsibilities on them, is known as

    a. a rite of passage.
    b. adrenarche.
    c. delayed phase preference.
    d. a Tanner stage.

5. Blake's parents are so irritated with him. He constantly tries to stay up late and wants to sleep in. His parents have explained to him that his high school starts at 8 a.m. and he has to go to bed earlier to be up at that time, but Blake just doesn't feel sleepy at 10 p.m. at night! Blake is experiencing

    a. the secular trend.
    b. a delayed phase preference.
    c. adrenarche.
    d. the Tanner stages.

6. Which of the following countries would be most likely to see a secular trend?

    a. Country X, where there is a famine
    b. Country Y, where there is a war
    c. Country Z, where there is prosperity
    d. All of these

7. Which of the following STDs are caused by bacteria?

    a. HPV
    b. AIDS
    c. Herpes
    d. Gonorrhea

8. Which method of *effective* birth control do most teens who use contraception select?

    a. "Pulling out"
    b. Rhythm method
    c. Birth control pill
    d. Condoms

9. Jenna is a senior in high school, and has been dating the same boy for four years. She has been contemplating having sex with her boyfriend, and took a sex education class. Based on the research reported in your text about the effectiveness of sex education in schools, what do you think is most likely to occur?

    a. Jenna will probably opt to wait for marriage before having sex.
    b. Jenna will probably opt to have sex with her boyfriend and not worry about birth control.
    c. Jenna will probably opt to have sex with her boyfriend and will likely use some form of contraception.
    d. Jenna will probably try to get pregnant on purpose.

10. Kessa eats next to nothing—just a couple of tablespoons of yogurt in the morning, water at lunch, and then a piece of turkey for dinner. She is skin-and-bones and looks completely emaciated. Kessa probably has

    a. obesity.
    b. bulimia.
    c. anorexia nervosa.
    d. chlamydia.

11. The outer and upper areas of the front of the brain, which are important for skills such as planning ahead and controlling impulses, are called the

    a. prefrontal cortex.
    b. dorsolateral prefrontal cortex.
    c. ventromedial prefrontal cortex.
    d. orbitofrontal cortex.

12. What percentage of high school *seniors* report binge drinking at least once in the past two weeks?

    a. 30%
    b. 20%
    c. 10%
    d. 5%

13. Mack feels like he has to have alcohol to function. Without it, he sweats and shakes and thinks about it constantly. Mack is

    a. a binge drinker.
    b. dependent on alcohol.
    c. abusing alcohol
    d. both abusing and dependent upon alcohol.

14. Zachary is at risk for substance abuse because he is angry and impulsive. This risk factor is _____ in nature.

    a. psychological
    b. familial
    c. social
    d. contextual

15. The most promising drug abuse prevention programs

    a. focus on trying to get the adolescent to "just say no."
    b. explain the risks of trying drugs.
    c. train the adolescent to resist peer pressure and also have a community wide intervention.
    d. None of these

Quiz 2

Use this quiz to reassess your learning after taking Quiz 1 and reviewing the chapter.

1. Highly specialized substances secreted by glands are called

    a. hormones.
    b. cortisol
    c. gonadotropins.
    d. melatonin.

2. When the body attempts to maintain the level of a hormone through a self-regulating system, the level it maintains is known as the

    a. feedback loop.
    b. delayed phase preference.
    c. GnRH.
    d. set point.

3. Which of the following is a relatively late development in puberty for females?

    a. Adrenarche
    b. Menarche
    c. Elevation of the breasts
    d. Development of pubic hair

4. As melatonin levels rise, one feels

    a. more alert.
    b. sleepier.
    c. sexually aroused.
    d. stressed.

5. Joni believes she should have been born a boy, even though physically she is a girl. Joni is struggling with

    a. sexual orientation.
    b. sex-role behavior.
    c. gender identity.
    d. All of these

6. Which one of the following STDs is caused by a virus?

    a. Herpes
    b. Chlamydia
    c. Gonorrhea
    d. All of these

7. The percent of adolescents at risk for obesity in the United States has _____ since 1980.

    a. been cut in half
    b. remained flat
    c. doubled
    d. tripled

8. Erica can eat more than anyone in her dorm suite. She goes on major binges where she eats enormous amounts of food, and then she secretly goes and throws up so she won't get fat. Erica has

    a. obesity.
    b. bulimia.
    c. anorexia nervosa.
    d. disordered eating.

9. The lower and central area of the front of the brain that is responsible for intuitive decision making is the
    a. dorsolateral prefrontal cortex.
    b. ventromedial prefrontal cortex.
    c. orbitofrontal cortex.
    d. hippocampus.
10. Drugs feel pleasurable because they affect the same receptors sensitive to
    a. dopamine.
    b. leptin.
    c. melatonin.
    d. estrogen.
11. Jared uses drugs to the point that it influences his performance at work and at school. Jared has
    a. substance abuse.
    b. substance dependence.
    c. Both A and B
    d. None of these
12. All of Shiloh's friends do drugs. Which type of risk factor is this for Shiloh?
    a. Psychological
    b. Familial
    c. Social
    d. Contextual
13. Drug education
    a. works well if it involves scare tactics.
    b. is helpful if it has lots of information.
    c. that targets resisting peer pressure is very effective.
    d. is helpful if it targets resisting peer pressure as well as has a community-wide intervention.
14. Based on the statistics reported in your text on ethnicity and rates of teen pregnancy, who is most likely to become an adolescent parent?
    a. Janae, who is white
    b. Jetta, who is Mexican
    c. Chantal, who is African American
    d. They are all equally likely to become adolescent parents.
15. The signs of sexual maturation, such as breast development and pubic hair, are called
    a. the Tanner Stages.
    b. secondary sex characteristics.
    c. puberty.
    d. risk factors.

ANSWERS TO FILL-IN-THE-BLANKS KEY TERMS

1. Disordered eating (see Eating Disorders)
2. orbitofrontal cortex (see The Adolescent Brain)
3. Gonads (see Puberty and Its Consequences)
4. Puberty (see Puberty and Its Consequences)
5. substance abuse (see Substance Use and Abuse in Adolescence)

6.   Gender identity (see Sexual Activity during Adolescence)

7.   secular trend (see Puberty and Its Consequences)

8.   HIV (see Sexual Activity during Adolescence)

9.   Tanner stages (see Puberty and Its Consequences)

10. HPG axis (see Puberty and Its Consequences)

ANSWERS TO MULTIPLE-CHOICE QUESTIONS

Circle the question numbers you answered incorrectly.

Quiz 1

1.   *b is the answer.*   Gonadotropins are the hormones that stimulate sexual maturation and regulate reproductive activity. They affect gonadotropin releasing hormone neurons in the brain. (see Puberty and Its Consequences)

2.   *c is the answer.*   The HPG axis stands for *hypothalamus-pituitary-gonad* axis. The pituitary controls hormone levels in general, while the hypothalamus controls the pituitary and has a concentration of GnRH neurons, which respond to the release of the hormone gonadotropin. As the gonads release sex hormones, this information "loops" back to the hypothalamus, which is sensitive to those hormones. The hypothalamus then factors that information that was looped back to it into whether or not it needs to stimulate, via the pituitary, the release of more sex hormones.   (see Puberty and Its Consequences)

3.   *a is the answer.*   Cristina's daughter is probably in her adolescent growth spurt, which involves a rate of growth similar to that seen in toddlers. Girls in this period of development usually see an annual rate of growth of 3.5 inches, on average. Menarche (the beginning of menstruation) and adrenarche (the maturation of the adrenal glands) may occur with this growth spurt, but this question does not describe either of those processes. (see Puberty and Its Consequences)

4.   *a is the answer.*   A rite of passage is a ceremony that confers privileges and responsibilities of adulthood on a person, formally recognizing their membership in the adult community. Adrenarche is maturation of the adrenal glands, and delayed phase preference is the tendency to want to stay up late and then sleep in. The Tanner stages describe the changes of developing secondary sex characteristics. (see Puberty and Its Consequences)

5.   *b is the answer.*   The delayed phase preference is the tendency for teens to want to stay up late and sleep in, and it is driven by biological changes of puberty. Blake's desire to stay up late and sleep in is entirely consistent with the delayed phase preference. (see Puberty and Its Consequences)

6.   *c is the answer.*   The secular trend is the tendency for puberty to occur at an earlier age in situations with high-quality nutrition and conditions that promote good health. Country Z, which is prosperous, is more likely to have good nutrition available to its inhabitants and be able to have structures making health care available than countries torn by war or famine. (see Puberty and Its Consequences)

7.   *d is the answer.*   Gonorrhea is the only one of these four caused by a bacteria. The other three are all caused by viruses. (see Sexual Activity During Adolescence)

8.   *d is the answer.*   Sixty percent of teens who do use contraception select condoms. Twenty percent use the birth control pill. The rhythm method is an ineffective method of birth control during adolescence, and pulling out is ineffective at any time. (see Sexual Activity During Adolescence)

9.   *c is the answer.*   School-based sex education programs generally have little impact on whether or not teens have sex, but do have an impact on teens' willingness to use contraception. (see Sexual Activity During Adolescence)

10.   *c is the answer.*   Anorexia nervosa involves self-starvation to keep one's weight down, which is what Kessa is doing. (see Eating Disorders)

11.   *b is the answer.*   The dorsolateral prefrontal cortex is the upper and outer areas of the front of the brain responsible for controlling impulses and planning. The ventromedial prefrontal cortex is in the lower and central areas of the front of the brain and is responsible for intuitive decision making. The orbitofrontal cortex is directly behind the eyes, and is useful in evaluating risks versus rewards. (see The Adolescent Brain)

12.   *a is the answer.*   Thirty percent of all seniors in high school report binge drinking at least once in the past two weeks. Twenty percent of sophomore report doing so, and 10% of 8th graders. (see Substance Use and Abuse in Adolescence)

13.   *d is the answer.*   Substance abuse involves usage of drugs or alcohol that interferes with functioning at home, school, work, and so on. Substance dependence is physical addiction. Mack's sweating and shaking suggests physical dependence, and all persons who are dependent by definition have substance abuse, as well. There is no information in this question about the number of drinks Mack has at a time, so the question cannot speak to if he is a binge drinker or not. (see Substance Use and Abuse in Adolescence)

14.   *a is the answer.*   Psychological risk factors refer to personal characteristics like being angry and inattentive. Familial ones refer to the nature of the family relationships, social ones the influence of peers, and contextual ones the broader community. (see Substance Use and Abuse in Adolescence)

15.   *c is the answer.*   The most promising drug abuse prevention programs do not focus solely on teaching teens to resist peer pressure ("just say no"), but combine that with a community-wide intervention targeting parents and teachers, as well. (see Substance Use and Abuse in Adolescence)

Now turn to the quiz analysis table at the end of this chapter to find which areas you know well and which areas you need to work on. Circle the numbers in the table for items on Quiz 1 that you answered correctly.

Quiz 2

1.   *a is the answer.*   Hormones are highly specialized substances secreted by glands. Cortisol, gonadotropins, and melatonin are all examples of specific types of these specialized substances, but the question asks about hormones in general, not specific exemplars. (see Puberty and Its Consequences)

2.   *d is the answer.*   The *level* maintained is the set point. The process by which it is maintained is known as a feedback loop. (see Puberty and Its Consequences)

3.   *b is the answer.*   Menarche, the beginning of menstruation, is relatively late development in puberty. Elevation of the breasts and development of pubic hair are early, and adrenarche usually begins around the age of ten. (see Puberty and Its Consequences)

4.   *b is the answer.*   As melatonin levels rise, one feels sleepier, not more alert. Arousal and stress are not related directly to melatonin levels. (see Puberty and Its Consequences)

5.   *c is the answer.*   Gender identity is which gender a person believes he or she is psychologically. Sexual orientation refers to one's attraction to the same or opposite sex, and sex-role behavior refers to what degree one's behavior corresponds to traditional masculine and feminine behavior. This question only describes a struggle with gender identity, not orientation or sex-role behavior. (see Sexual Activity During Adolescence)

6.   *a is the answer.*   Only herpes in this list is caused by a virus. Chlamydia and gonorrhea are caused by bacteria. (see Sexual Activity During Adolescence)

7.   *d is the answer.*   The percent of teens at risk for obesity has tripled since 1980 in the United States. (see Eating Disorders)

8.   *b is the answer.*   Bulimia is an eating disorder characterized by binging and then purging, usually by inducing vomiting. Although this is an example of "disordered eating" in general, the question provides sufficient information to discern which type of eating disorder Erica has, so bulimia is the best answer. (see Eating Disorders)

9.   *b is the answer.*   The ventromedial prefrontal cortex is located in the lower center portion of the front of the brain and is responsible for intuitive decision making. (see The Adolescent Brain)

10. *a is the answer.*   Dopamine is the neurotransmitter that plays a special role in the experience of pleasure. Drugs that feel good stimulate dopamine receptors, mimicking those effects. (see Substance Use and Abuse in Adolescence)

11. *a is the answer.*   Substance abuse occurs when drugs are used in a way that they cause significant problems at work, school, or home. Jared has trouble at work and school because of his drug use. Substance dependence involves physical addiction. This question does not describe any signs of physical addiction to drugs in Jared. (see Substance Use and Abuse in Adolescence)

12. *c is the answer.*   Peers who use drugs are a social risk factor. Familial risk factors focus on behavior within the family unit, contextual risk factors focus on the larger community, and psychological risk factors on individual characteristics. (see Substance Use and Abuse in Adolescence)

13. *d is the answer.*   Drug education alone—whether it be informational or a scare tactic—is ineffective unless it targets the community as a whole as well. (see Substance Use and Abuse in Adolescence)

14. *c is the answer.*   Chantal is most likely to become pregnant. Teen pregnancy rates are double amongst African Americans what they are for white youths; and Mexican American teen pregnancy rates are in the middle of those two groups. (see Sexual Activity During Adolescence)

15. *b is the answer.*   Secondary sex characteristics are the signs of sexual maturation, such as breast elevation and pubic hair. The Tanner stages describe the process and order in which these characteristics appear, and puberty refers to all of the biological changes associated with becoming an adult. None of these is considered a risk factor. (Puberty and Its Consequences)

Now turn to the quiz analysis table at the end of this chapter to find which areas you know well and which areas you need to work on. Circle the numbers in the table for items on Quiz 2 that you answered correctly.

For each question you answered correctly, circle its number. (Quiz 1 numbers are not shaded; Quiz 2 numbers are shaded.) Are there patterns in the types of questions or the topics you got wrong that could direct your further study? Did you improve from Quiz 1 to Quiz 2?

QUIZ REVIEW

Topic	Type of Question		
	Definition	Comprehension	Application
Puberty and Its Consequences	1, 4	2, 6	3, 5
	1, 2, 15	3, 4	
Sexual Activity During Adolescence		7, 8	9
		6	5, 14
Eating Disorders			10
		7	8
The Adolescent Brain	11		
	9		
Substance Use and Abuse in Adolescence		12, 15	13, 14
		10, 13	11, 12

Total correct by quiz:

Quiz 1:
Quiz 2:

CHAPTER 14

Cognitive Development in Adolescence

LEARNING OBJECTIVES

1. List the five ways in which thinking changes during adolescence.

2. Describe one way in which metacognition (the ability to evaluate your thinking processes) makes teens more effective thinkers.

3. Explain how the newly acquired ability to think in multiple dimensions contributes to adolescents' abilities to reason, make decisions, and understand sarcasm.

4. Give one example of relativistic thinking causing an adolescent to question a previously accepted truth.

5. Describe Piaget's stage of formal operational thinking.

6. Explain the information-processing view of adolescent cognitive development.

7. Define social cognition.

8. Explain how social perspective-taking (the ability to assess the thoughts and feelings of others) makes it possible for adolescents to make better social decisions.

9. Describe the changes in adolescents' views about, and practice of, religion. List three ways in which religious participation affects adolescents.

10. List four reasons why adolescents engage in risky behavior.

11. Describe how the transition to middle/jr. high or high school affects adolescents academically and socially.

12. Describe the kind of academic experience most likely to maximize an adolescent's cognitive development.

13. Explain how an adolescent's success is affected by: parenting style, her or his beliefs about her or his abilities and likelihood to succeed, the source (internal or external) of the adolescent's motivation, school environments, and peers.

14. Explain the ways in which ethnicity affects the academic achievement of adolescents.

15. List some of the reasons why adolescents drop out of school.

16. Describe the opportunities and problems facing adolescents who do not to go to college.

17. Explain the possible rewards and costs for an adolescent who works during the school year.

18. List the seven basic factors that influence adolescents' career choices.

OUTLINE

I. How Thinking Changes in Adolescence
    A. Thinking about Possibilities
        During adolescence, teens acquire the ability to think about what is possible, not just what actually is the case.

227

1.   Deductive and Inductive Reasoning
   a)   **Deductive reasoning** is a type of reasoning that involves drawing logically
         necessary conclusions from a set of premises. Adolescents acquire the
         ability to engage in this sort of reasoning, both drawing conclusions when
         appropriate and understanding when insufficient information is given for a
         particular conclusion.
   b)   **Inductive reasoning** is a type of reasoning that involves drawing, or
         inferring, a conclusion from a body of evidence. Inductive reasoning is
         present well before adolescence.
2.   Hypothetical Thinking
   a)   With the emergence of deductive reasoning, adolescents are able to engage
         in hypothetical, "if-then," thinking. This allows them to plan ahead and
         foresee consequences.
   b)   Hypothetical thinking affects adolescents' ability to argue in the abstract, as
         well as to take the perspective of another person, which makes them more
         effective arguers than they previously were.

B.   Thinking about Abstract Concepts
     During adolescence, teens are capable of thinking about abstract concepts more
     systematically. This newfound ability is reflected in their increased interest in
     thinking about things like relationships, politics, religion, and morality.

C.   Thinking about Thinking
1.   Adolescents gain the ability to think about thinking, a process known as
       metacognition.
2.   Adolescent egocentrism
       As adolescents adjust to their new thinking skills, they pass through a period of
       self-absorption, or adolescent egocentrism, which results in two major problems

   a)   The **imaginary audience** involves having an increased sense that other
         people are paying attention to you more than they actually are.
   b)   Adolescents often adhere to a **personal fable**, the usually false belief that
         one's experiences are completely unique and no one else can understand
         them. While this might enhance an adolescent's sense of self-esteem, it
         can also allow an adolescent to engage in risky behavior, falsely believing
         that a dangerous outcome can't happen to him or her.
D.   Thinking in Multiple Dimensions
1.   Adolescents are able to think about things from different vantage points
       simultaneously. This promotes more sophisticated self-conceptions and
       relationships, as teens become able to see that different people have competing
       perspectives, or that they themselves possess multiple traits at once.
2.   As adolescents gain in their ability to think about multiple things at once, they
       come to appreciate sarcasm. Understanding sarcasm requires one to pay
       attention to what was said as well as *how* it was said. As adolescents learn to
       distinguish sarcasm from sincerity, their appreciation for the *double-entendres*
       that pepper the dialogue in shows like *South Park* increases.
E.   Adolescent Relativism
     Adolescents tend to see the world as "gray" rather than "black and white." This
     increase in relativism makes them more likely to question things, and may lead to
     parents perceiving them as increasingly argumentative.

F.   Theoretical Perspectives on Adolescent Thinking
1.   Piaget's View of Adolescent Thinking

a)   Piaget felt that all development occurred in stages, and that adolescence was characterized by the stage of formal operations, or abstract logical thinking.

b)   Piaget felt this process unfolded in two steps. First, an "emergent" period in which the adolescent sometimes was capable of formal operations and at other times wasn't, occurs. Secondly, in middle or late adolescence, this skill is consolidated into a general approach to reasoning.

c)   A great deal of evidence, however, suggests that there is a distinction between *competence* (being able to reason formally) and *performance* (actually using formal reasoning on a consistent basis). People, including adolescents, often reason in less sophisticated ways than they are capable.

d)   Although Piaget's perspective helps to explain the major changes in the ways adolescents think (see A-E above), his notion that this occurs in stages is less than accurate. Cognitive development of abstract formal reasoning is more continuous than he proposed.

2.   The Information-Processing View of Adolescent Thinking

a)   Although Piaget's viewpoint speaks to general changes in adolescent cognition, the information-processing view addresses specific changes in adolescent cognition, such as attention, memory, and processing speed.

b)   Attention, memory, and reasoning ability tend to increase throughout childhood and level off at about age 15. Beyond 15, sophisticated skills such as making judgments about the costs and benefits of a risky decision or regulating the impact of emotion on decision making improve, probably through the mid-20s.

II.   Social Cognition
Social cognition involves thinking about people, relationships, and social institutions.

A.   Social Perspective Taking

1.   **Social perspective taking** refers to how, and how accurately, one makes assessments about the thoughts and feelings of others. This ability improves dramatically during adolescence.

2.   A young adolescent can engage in **mutual role taking**—acting as an objective third party to see how the thoughts and actions of one person influence those of another.

3.   Later in adolescence, a teen can move this perspective taking to a societal orientation, including in his or her analysis of a situation the impact of social roles and institutions on the perspectives people bring to the table.

B.   Social Conventions

1.   **Social conventions** are the norms that guide day-to-day behavior.

2.   Early adolescents see these norms as arbitrary and changeable—mere social expectations. Some adolescents do not view this expectancy as a good enough reason to comply with such norms.

3.   Older adolescents come to appreciate that social norms regulate behavior, with shared expectancies creating order and predictability.

C.   Religious Beliefs during Adolescence

1.   During adolescence, religious beliefs become more abstract and principled. They are increasingly oriented towards internal spiritual matters but not external social rituals, such as going to church.

2.   The decline in interest in organized religion during adolescence is steeper during college than the pre-college years, suggesting that college attendance may play some part in influencing religious belief.

3. There is some variability in religiosity, with adolescents from Latino and African-American backgrounds being more religious than youth from other ethnic backgrounds. Youth from the South and Midwest are also more religious than their West or East coast counterparts.

4. Religious involvement does appear to buffer adolescents from problem behavior and sexual involvement, and this is partly due to the fact that adolescents who are highly religious often have other positive influences in their life (e.g., supportive parents and pro-social peers).

III. Adolescent Risk Taking
Risk taking is frequent during adolescence. Two proposed reasons why this may be the case are that adolescents are less logical than adults and adolescents are more likely to develop personal fables. Research does not lend much support to either of these explanations.

A. One reason that may explain the difference in risk-taking behavior between adults and adolescents, however, is that adolescents may value the various potential consequences of risky decisions differently than adults do.

B. Additionally, the gap between the activation of brain regions responsible for **sensation seeking** and the maturation of the regions responsible for judgment, decision making, and impulse control may explain adolescent willingness to take unnecessary risks.

C. Peer pressure may also account for adolescent risk-taking behavior.

IV. Achievement in School
A. The Transition from Elementary to Secondary School
1. During the early years of compulsory secondary education, **junior high schools** were established to house 7th and 8th (and sometimes 9th) graders to adequately address their special intellectual and emotional needs. More recently, **middle schools** housing 7th and 8th grades, along with one or more younger or older grades, have often replaced junior high schools in some districts.

2. Junior high and middle schools increase the number of school transitions an adolescent has to make. In general, these transitions are disruptive, but only temporarily in most cases. Students who had academic or psychosocial problems before the transition tend to cope less well than their counterparts.

3. Some experts feel that junior high and middle schools fail to meet adolescent needs because there is a mismatch between the teachers' beliefs about adolescents and what adolescents of that age actually need.

B. The Best Classroom Climate for Adolescents
Some evidence suggests that educational programs for adolescents focus too much on rote memorization of concrete facts, which does not facilitate the adolescent's emerging cognitive abilities. Both adolescents and teachers are most satisfied with classes that have a moderate degree of structure with high student involvement and teacher support.

C. Achievement Motivation and Beliefs
1. The extent to which an individual strives for success is his or her **need for achievement**. Adolescents with parents who set high performance standards, reward academic success, and encourage autonomy in the context of a warm relationship tend to have higher need for achievement.

2. **Intrinsic motivation**, or mastery motivation, refers to the drive to achieve for the sheer pleasure of learning. **Extrinsic motivation**, or performance motivation, refers to the drive to achieve for an external reward associated with the achievement.

       a)   Adolescents who believe they are competent are more intrinsically motivated, and tend to maintain their efforts to do well in school.

       b)   Adolescents who doubt their ability tend to be extrinsically motivated and feel more anxiety about failing.

       c)   Adolescents with parents who attempt to directly reward school outcomes tend to promote extrinsic motivation. Parents who support school success without rewarding it concretely support intrinsic motivation.

    3.   **Achievement attributions** are how students explain their successes and failures.

       a)   When individuals succeed and attribute it to internal causes (e.g., ability or effort), they tend to approach future tasks with confidence. When individuals succeed and attribute it to external causes (e.g., luck or the assignment being easy), they remain uncertain about their abilities. High achievement motivation is associated with internal attributions.

       b)   When individuals attribute failure to lack of effort, they try harder on future tasks. When individuals attribute failure to bad luck, lack of ability, or task difficulty, they feel helpless and try less in future situations.

D.   Environmental Influences on Achievement

    1.   Students achieve more in schools which are more personal, less departmentalized, less rigidly tracked, and that use team-teaching.

    2.   Even more important than the school environment is the home environment in which adolescents live. Parents' values and expectations directly affect adolescents' school success.

       a)   Parents who set high standards support school success.

       b)   Parents who value school success are more likely to attend programs, help in course selection, and maintain interest in assignments.

    3.   Socioeconomic status is a powerful influence on school success. Middle-class adolescents tend to outperform their working-class counterparts.

    4.   Peers can influence the day-to-day behavior in school that inhibits or promotes school success. Peers can undermine academic success, but having friends who value high grades can also promote academic achievement. Unfortunately, the peer culture impact in the United States is more often negative than positive.

E.   Ethnic Differences in Educational Achievement

    1.   African American and Hispanic students' achievement tends to lag behind white students', which in turn perform more poorly than Asian students. This persists even after taking into account socioeconomic differences in these groups.

    2.   This difference is interesting because the aspirations among these groups are not significantly different, but their academic skills, study habits, and school-related behaviors are. It may be that fear of failure, which drives many Asian students to achieve, could explain this pattern of differences. Alternately, Asians tend to emphasize effort over ability in achievement, which promotes a mastery orientation. This mastery approach promotes school success.

    3.   Studies of foreign-born adolescents and children of immigrants in comparison to minorities who have been in the United States several generations tend to show the former groups outperforming the latter, perhaps because acculturation to American society results in devaluing academic success, or because of superior education prior to coming to the States.

F.   Dropping Out of High School

    1.   The number of years of school completed is a powerful predictor of adult occupational success. This makes dropping out of high school a great disadvantage in adulthood.

2.   The current dropout rate has declined over the years to a present average of 12%, although this varies widely amongst regions and ethnicities.

3.   Dropping out of high school is associated with low socioeconomic status, poor communities, single-parent or large families, permissive or disengaged families, and lack of reading material in the household. Additionally, adolescents who drop out tend to have a history of low performance, lack of involvement, many school transitions, and so forth.

4.   Dropping out is the culmination of a process of failure, not a discrete decision.

G.   Beyond High School

    1.   The Transition from High School to College

        a)   Today, 75% of high school graduates enroll in college, most upon graduation.

        b)   Only half of the students who enroll in a four-year college complete their degree within 6 years, and one-third of them leave after the first year.

    2.   The Non-College-Bound

        a)   College graduates earn substantially more than those who attend college but do not graduate, who in turn earn more than those who never attended college.

        b)   Although one-third of adolescents do not pursue college, most secondary schools are almost exclusively focused on the college-bound student.

        c)   Vocational tracks in high schools tend to emphasize higher-order thinking less than college-prep tracks, leading the students in vocational training under-prepared for employment.

        d)   As service jobs have replaced manufacturing jobs, students who do not pursue college have found it increasingly difficult to earn a livable wage.

        e)   Experts believe that it would be beneficial to strengthen the connection between the world of work and working during high school through apprenticeship models and the like.

V.   Work and Occupational Development

A.   Working During High School

    1.   Most high school students work part-time, with sophomores averaging 15 hours each week and seniors up to 20 hours a week.

    2.   Working during high school is equally likely for middle- and lower -class youth, as well as for males versus females. Employment is most likely for white youth and least for African American youth.

B.   Working and Adolescent Development

    1.   Research suggests that working does *not* teach adolescents responsibility and how to manage money, as they largely use their income to purchase designer clothes, to eat out and so forth. As a whole, they do not budget, save, or plan for their income's use.

    2.   Adolescent workers tend to have more cynical attitudes toward work, are more likely to endorse unethical business practices, and are less satisfied with their lives than their non-working counterparts. Working less than 20 hours a week seems to buffer one from these effects.

        a)   One reason for these effects may have to do with the nature of the work in which adolescents engage—often dull and stressful.

        b)   Another possibility is that working long hours jeopardizes school performance and engagement. Long hours in the summer do not seem to harm adolescents' school performance in the same way.

    3.   Employment in adolescence is associated with increased risk for problem behavior, including drug and alcohol use. It may be that the income from

working helps adolescents purchase these substances, or that working has disrupted relationships that would have buffered them from pursuing such activities.

C.   Influences on Occupational Choices

    1.   Theorists interested in predicting occupational choice have considered both personality variables (e.g., artistic, social, enterprising) and work values (e.g., *intrinsic rewards, extrinsic rewards, social rewards, altruistic rewards, security, influence,* or *leisure*).

    2.   The relative importance adolescents place on work rewards changes over adolescence. Early on, they tend to value all rewards equally, believing they can find a job that maximizes all of those values. As they come to realize this isn't the case, the relative importance of extrinsic, altruistic, and social rewards declines dramatically while intrinsic rewards and security remain strong values.

    3.   Although individual preferences and values are part of occupational choice, social influence and societal forces also constrain these decisions.

        a)   Socioeconomic status exerts the strongest influence on occupational choice. Middle-class youth tend to prefer middle-class jobs; lower-class youth are less likely to aspire to those. Additionally, socioeconomic status affects work values, with individuals from higher classes being more likely to value intrinsic rewards and influence than those from lower classes.

        b)   The community also influences students perceptions of what occupations will have demand in the labor market or will be acceptable in the community.

KEY TERMS

1.   **Deductive reasoning** is a type of logical reasoning in which one draws logically necessary conclusions from a general set of premises, or givens. (see How Thinking Changes in Adolescence)

2.   **Inductive reasoning** is reasoning that involves drawing an inference from the evidence one has. (see How Thinking Changes in Adolescence)

3.   **Metacognition** is the process of thinking about thinking itself. (see How Thinking Changes in Adolescence)

4.   The **imaginary audience** is the belief, often brought on by the heightened self-consciousness of early adolescence, that everyone is watching and evaluating one's behavior. (see How Thinking Changes in Adolescence)

5.   An adolescent's belief that he or she is unique and therefore not subject to the rules that govern other people's behavior is known as a **personal fable**. (see How Thinking Changes in Adolescence)

6.   **Social cognition** is the aspect of cognition that concerns thinking about other people, about interpersonal relationships, and about social institutions. (see Social Cognition)

7.   **Social perspective taking** is the ability to view events from the perspective of others. (see Social Cognition)

8.   **Mutual role taking** is the ability to act as an objective third party to see how the thoughts or actions of one person can influence those of another. (see Social Cognition)

9.   **Social conventions** are the norms that govern everyday behavior in social situations. (see Social Cognition)

10. **Sensation-seeking** is the enjoyment of novel and intense experiences. (see Adolescent Risk Taking)

11. **Junior high school** is an educational institution designed during the early era of public secondary education, in which young adolescents are schooled separately from older adolescents. (see Achievement in School)

12. **Middle schools** are three- or four-year educational institutions housing seventh and eighth grades with one or more younger grades. (see Achievement in School)

13. **Need for achievement** is a need that influences the extent to which an individual strives for success in evaluative situations. (see Achievement in School)

14. **Intrinsic motivation** is motivation based on the pleasure one will experience from mastering a task. (see Achievement in School)

15. **Extrinsic motivation** is motivation based on the rewards one will receive for successful performance. (see Achievement in School)

16. **Achievement attributions** are the beliefs one holds about the causes of one's successes and failures. (see Achievement in School)

FILL-IN-THE-BLANKS KEY TERMS

This section will help you check your knowledge of the key terms introduced in this chapter. Fill in each blank with the appropriate term from the list of key terms in the previous section.

1. _____ is the ability to view events from the perspective of others.

2. The process of thinking about thinking itself is _____.

3. _____ are three- or four-year educational institutions housing seventh and eighth grades with one or more younger grades.

4. _____ is a type of logical reasoning in which one draws logically necessary conclusions from a general set of premises, or givens.

5. The enjoyment of novel and intense experiences is called _____.

6. _____ refers to motivation based on the pleasure one will experience from mastering a task.

7. An adolescent's belief that he or she is unique and therefore not subject to the rules that govern other people's behavior is known as a _____.

8. _____ is the aspect of cognition that concerns thinking about other people, about interpersonal relationships, and about social institutions.

9. _____ is the ability to act as an objective third party to see how the thought or actions of one person can influence those of another.

10. The beliefs one holds about the causes of one's successes and failures are called _____.

APPLIED LEARNING AND CRITICAL THINKING

Cognitive changes during adolescence are significant and exciting. Working with adolescents in a service-learning project, in an internship, or as participants in a research project can give you some insight into the nature of these changes.

1. For an applied research project, develop a qualitative research study that assesses the content of the sorts of personal fables adolescents have. You know from your reading of the text that a personal fable is the belief that the normal "rules" don't apply to you, but that is a

pretty broad definition. Do a literature review to get some idea on what specific personal fables adolescents adhere to, and then develop a set of interview questions to administer to adolescents about their beliefs related to those fables identified in the literature. Be sure to work with a professor, to get IRB approval, and parental permission before actually collecting any data. Once your interviews are complete, work with a partner to categorize the adolescents' responses and then start consolidating them. What percent of your sample adhered to each of the personal fables identified in the literature? Was their variability? If so, can you identify any possible explanations for why some personal fables were more likely than others to occur?

2.   See if your local school district allows college students to sign up to mentor adolescents. In particular, see if you can do volunteer work at a junior high or middle school. As you mentor students there, see if you can see any evidence for the pros versus cons of having a junior high versus a middle school. Which do you think would be best for the kids you have mentored? Why? And why do you think the district chose the format (junior high or middle school) that they did?

3.   If you engage in a mentoring program that involves tutoring adolescents, you will have a great opportunity to actually apply what you've learned in this chapter about achievement motivation. One of the most persistent findings regarding adolescent achievement in school is that a mastery orientation (or intrinsic motivation) is associated with greater achievement in school than a performance orientation (or extrinsic motivation). What can you do to help instill a mastery motivation in the students you tutor? What does the research say will be helpful? How can you implement that in a tutoring session?

4.   This chapter talks about the development of social cognition as, in part, related to the acquisition of the ability to engage is social perspective taking and mutual role taking. These skills are often limited amongst adolescents who become involved in delinquent behavior. Consider seeking an internship with a community or government agency that works with juvenile delinquents and learn what they do to develop these skills in the delinquent population. Does it seem to work? Could you imagine a better training strategy? Talk to you instructor in the course about how you might approach your internship supervisor with ideas that you have to foster the emergence of these important cognitive skills in the population the agency serves.

MULTIPLE-CHOICE QUESTIONS

Quiz 1

1.   Which of the following statements about deductive and inductive reasoning in adolescence is true?
     a.   Deductive reasoning appears well before adolescence.
     b.   Inductive reasoning rarely appears before adolescence.
     c.   Deductive reasoning seldom appears before adolescence but inductive reasoning does.
     d.   Neither deductive nor inductive reasoning is seen until adolescence.

2.   Charlotte is fourteen. Her mom is worried about her. Charlotte seems to spend a lot of time thinking about "weighty issues" like the meaning of life. What would you tell Charlotte's mom, based on the research in this chapter, about this particular concern?
     a.   Charlotte is probably at abnormally high risk for depression.
     b.   Charlotte has recently developed hypothetical and abstract thinking skills and is adjusting to using them.
     c.   Thinking about such things is a normal part of developing one's personal fable.
     d.   Charlotte needs to quit thinking about such things and relax.

3. Thinking about the process of thinking itself is known as

    a.   deductive reasoning.
    b.   inductive reasoning.
    c.   sarcasm.
    d.   metacognition.

4. Carrie is so mortified! She thinks everyone noticed that she has a spot on her dress, and is probably making fun of her. In fact, the spot is barely noticeable and no one even is watching Carrie or her dress. Carrie is experiencing

    a.   the imaginary audience.
    b.   a personal fable.
    c.   mutual role-taking.
    d.   adolescent relativism.

5. Upon which cognitive ability that emerges during adolescence does being able to look at problems from multiple perspectives rest?

    a.   Deductive reasoning.
    b.   Inductive reasoning.
    c.   Metacognition.
    d.   Multidimensional thinking.

6. Thinking about people, relationships, and social institutions is

    a.   social cognition.
    b.   metacognition.
    c.   sarcasm.
    d.   adolescent relativism.

7. Adolescents are likely to

    a.   lose all interest in religion and spirituality.
    b.   be more interested in external aspects of religion, like going to church.
    c.   be more interested in internal aspects of religion, like what one believes.
    d.   None of these

8. Max is interested in bungee jumping, loves riding scary rides, and driving too fast. Max is

    a.   developing his personal fable.
    b.   engaged in social perspective taking.
    c.   sensation seeking.
    d.   has a high need for achievement.

9. Brad teaches at a school that has 6th, 7th, and 8th graders at it. It is most likely called a

    a.   junior high school.
    b.   middle school.
    c.   high school.
    d.   elementary school.

10. Who is most likely to have high need for achievement?

    a.   Kara, who has parents who monitor her schoolwork closely and always stay on her to get it done
    b.   Darrah, who has parents who hope she does well but let Darrah set her own standards and goals for school
    c.   Chloe, who has parents who reward her achievements in school and expect her to do well
    d.   None of these

11. Motivation that stems from the pleasure one anticipates once a task is mastered is called

    a. extrinsic motivation.
    b. intrinsic motivation.
    c. performance motivation.
    d. social convention motivation.

12. Dropping out of high school

    a. isn't a big deal because a person can land a good factory job.
    b. is a big deal because you earn more money more quickly if you do drop out and start working.
    c. is a big deal because you are more likely to live at poverty and be involved in delinquency if you do quit high school.
    d. is almost unheard of in most of the United States.

13. What percent of high school graduates enroll in college?

    a. 75%
    b. 66%
    c. 50%
    d. 40%

14. Garrison is working 20 hours each week during his senior year of high school. Which of the following statements is probably true about Garrison, based on the research you read in this chapter?

    a. Garrison is learning the value of a dollar.
    b. Garrison may well be less satisfied with his life because the number of hours he works.
    c. Garrison is probably developing a really positive set of work values.
    d. All of these

15. Krista highly values income in determining what career she will pursue. "Income" is an example of which one of the following individual work values?

    a. Extrinsic
    b. Security
    c. Social rewards
    d. Altruistic rewards

Quiz 2

Use this quiz to reassess your learning after taking Quiz 1 and reviewing the chapter.

1. When you draw logically necessary conclusions from a general set of premises, you are engaged in

    a. deductive reasoning.
    b. inductive reasoning.
    c. sensation seeking.
    d. multidimensional thinking.

2. Jarrett is reading his textbook. At the end of each paragraph, he asks himself, "Did I understand that?" When Jarrett assesses his own comprehension, he is engaged in

    a. egocentrism.
    b. social perspective taking.
    c. achievement attributions.
    d. metacognition.

3.   The imaginary audience and personal fable are both problems of adolescence that result from

    a.   multidimensional thinking.
    b.   adolescent egocentrism.
    c.   mutual role taking.
    d.   inductive reasoning.

4.   Ricki constantly argues with his parents' every assertion. If they say, "It is good to do your homework before watching T.V.," then Ricki counters that procrastinating could actually teach him how to perform well under pressure. It seems like Ricki thinks there are no solid "truths" and that every claim his parents make could have an alternate side to it. Ricki's unwillingness to accept facts as black and white statements illustrates

    a.   adolescent egocentrism.
    b.   adolescent relativism.
    c.   sensation seeking.
    d.   metacognition..

5.   Which theoretical perspective best explains specific gains in cognition during adolescence?

    a.   Piaget
    b.   Information-processing
    c.   Social cognition
    d.   Need for Achievement theory

6.   Edna told a fib to her dad, and she believes that her dad believed it. When Edna assesses what her dad's viewpoint is she is engaged in

    a.   social perspective taking.
    b.   mutual role taking.
    c.   social conventions.
    d.   adolescent relativism.

7.   Riding the elevator facing forward and not sitting too close to someone on a public bus unless that is the only seat open are both examples of

    a.   social perspective taking.
    b.   mutual role taking.
    c.   social conventions.
    d.   need for achievement.

8.   Which of the following explanations *best* addresses why adolescents are more likely to engage in risky behavior than adults?

    a.   Adolescents are less logical than adults.
    b.   Adolescents are more likely to develop personal fables than adults.
    c.   The differing rates of maturation in parts of the brain responsible for judgment versus sensation seeking during adolescence.
    d.   All of these explain this phenomenon equally well.

9.   In general, most adolescents would prefer a classroom climate that

    a.   is very tightly controlled by the teacher so that it is predictable and calm.
    b.   has moderate structure provided by the teacher, but with lots of student input.
    c.   has little structure so student interests drive the lessons each day.
    d.   has a classroom structure that doesn't really affect adolescent preference for classes.

10.   The extent to which an individual strives for success is called

    a.   sensation seeking.
    b.   work values.
    c.   egocentrism.
    d.   need for achievement.

11. Mastery motivation is to _____ as performance motivation is to_____.
    a. intrinsic motivation; extrinsic motivation
    b. extrinsic motivation; intrinsic motivation
    c. extrinsic motivation; extrinsic motivation
    d. intrinsic motivation; intrinsic motivation

12. _____ is/are how students interpret their successes and failures.
    a. Achievement attributions
    b. Mutual role taking
    c. Deductive reasoning
    d. Inductive reasoning

13. Asian cultures tend to explain school success as based on
    a. how difficult or easy the coursework is.
    b. how intelligent the student is.
    c. how hard the student tries.
    d. how lucky the student is.

14. What percentage of students enrolled in college complete their degree in less than six years?
    a. 80%
    b. 70%
    c. 50%
    d. 10%

15. Charlene wants a job that will have her working with people she really enjoys. Which of the following work values does Charlene's desire reflect?
    a. Influence
    b. Altruistic rewards
    c. Social rewards
    d. Leisure

ANSWERS TO FILL-IN-THE-BLANKS KEY TERMS

1. Social perspective taking (see Social Cognition)

2. metacognition (see How Thinking Changes in Adolescence)

3. Middle schools (see Achievement in School)

4. Deductive reasoning (see How Thinking Changes in Adolescence)

5. sensation seeking (see Adolescent Risk Taking)

6. Intrinsic motivation (see Achievement in School)

7. personal fable (see How Thinking Changes in Adolescence)

8. Social cognition (see Social Cognition)

9. Mutual role taking (see Social Cognition)

10. achievement attributions (see Achievement in School)

ANSWERS TO MULTIPLE-CHOICE QUESTIONS

Circle the question numbers you answered incorrectly.

Quiz 1

1. *c is the answer.*   Inductive reasoning is seen prior to adolescence, but deductive reasoning rarely occurs until adolescence. (see How Thinking Changes in Adolescence)

2. *b is the answer.*   Research on how thinking changes in adolescence reveals that hypothetical and abstract thinking skills emerge during this period. Thinking about the meaning of life deals with abstract concepts. Because abstract thinking skills emerge in adolescence, it is normal for one to spend more time thinking about such issues.   (see How Thinking Changes in Adolescence)

3. *d is the answer.*   Metacognition is thinking about the process of thinking itself. Deductive reasoning involves reaching conclusions based on premises, while inductive reasoning focuses on inferring a conclusion based on evidence. They are forms of thinking, but not thinking about thinking. Sarcasm involves using different meanings in different dimensions of speech.   (see How Thinking Changes in Adolescence)

4. *a is the answer.*   An imaginary audience is the heightened sense of self-consciousness characteristic of adolescence. It involves feeling as if everyone is watching you, which is exactly what Carrie is embarrassed about. (see How Thinking Changes in Adolescence)

5. *d is the answer.*   Multidimensional thinking is the ability to think about multiple aspects of something at the same time. Being able to understand a problem from multiple viewpoints is one way multidimensional thinking is used. This skill emerges during adolescence. So does deductive reasoning, but that is reasoning to a conclusion from a set of premises. This question does not describe a set of premises leading to a conclusion. Inductive reasoning emerges before adolescence so that cannot be the answer, and metacognition is thinking about the process of thinking itself, which is also not described here. (see How Thinking Changes in Adolescence)

6. *a is the answer.*   Social cognition is thinking about people, relationships, and social institutions. Metacognition is thinking about the process of thinking. Sarcasm is the use of two different meanings in different dimensions of speech, and adolescent relativism is the tendency for adolescents to see things as "gray" rather than black and white. (see Social Cognition)

7. *c is the answer.*   Adolescents tend to place more emphasis on internal aspects of religion than external ones. They do not necessarily see a decline in spirituality although they are less interested in religious rituals and customs. (see Social Cognition)

8. *c is the answer.*   Sensation seeking is the enjoyment of novel and intense experiences. The activities Max enjoys are novel and intense; therefore, he is engaged in sensation seeking. (see Adolescent Risk Taking)

9. *b is the answer.*   Middle schools contain 7th and 8th grades, and usually one grade either below or above those grades. A junior high is usually 7th through 8th or 9th grade, but would not include 6th grade. (see Achievement in School)

10. *c is the answer.*   Chloe's parents reward success and set high performance standards, both of which tend to lead to high need for achievement. Kara's parents do not encourage autonomy, which is important for high need for achievement. Darrah's parents allow her to set her own standards rather than setting their own high expectations, which also reduces the chances of high need for achievement. (see Achievement in School)

11. *b is the answer.*   Intrinsic motivation is motivation related to the anticipated pleasure of mastering a task. Extrinsic, or performance, motivation on the other hand stems from an anticipated reward for achieving a goal, not the pleasure of mastering the task. There is no such term as social convention motivation. (see Achievement in School)

12. *c is the answer.*   High school drop-outs are significantly more likely to live at poverty level or become involved in delinquent behavior. Factory jobs are harder and harder to find, and any benefit one might see by immediately earning wages upon quitting high school is erased by the difference in income over a lifetime for high school graduates versus those who did not graduate from high school. Unfortunately, high school drop-outs are not rare—on average 12% of high school students quit school. (see Achievement in School)

13. *a is the answer.*   Three-fourths (75%) of all high school students enroll in college. Two-thirds (66%) of them do so immediately upon graduation (see Achievement in School)

14. *b is the answer.*   High school students who work 20 or more hours each week tend to be less satisfied with their lives. Evidence indicates they do not use work experience to learn to manage money or value the dollar. Students who work this much, instead, learn to spend more frequently on "luxury" designer items, and are more likely to develop cynical attitudes towards work.   (see Work and Occupational Development)

15. *a is the answer.*   Income is an example of an extrinsic reward. (see Work and Occupational Development)

Now turn to the quiz analysis table at the end of this chapter to find which areas you know well and which areas you need to work on. Circle the numbers in the table for items on Quiz 1 that you answered correctly.

Quiz 2

1. *a is the answer.*   Deductive reasoning involves drawing logically necessary conclusions from a set of general premises. (see How Thinking Changes in Adolescence)

2. *d is the answer.*   Metacognition is thinking about the process of thinking itself. As Jarrett asks himself if he understands the reading, he is thinking about reading comprehension, which is itself thinking. (see How Thinking Changes in Adolescence)

3. *b is the answer.*   Adolescent egocentrism is the extreme self-absorption that often accompanies adolescence. Both the imaginary audience and the personal fable relate to self-absorption. The imaginary audience involves believing everyone is watching you, and the personal fable involves believing you are so special that the typical "rules" and consequences do not apply to your own behavior and outcomes. (see How Thinking Changes in Adolescence)

4.   *b is the answer.*   Adolescent relativism involves seeing the world as "gray" rather than "black and white." Ricki seems to believe that there aren't any absolute statements that could serve as general guidelines, if he is rejecting notions like "it is good not to procrastinate." Rejection of general guidelines—which are black and white—suggests that Ricki sees the world in relative terms. (see How Thinking Changes in Adolescence)

5.   *b is the answer.*   The information-processing perspective focuses on specific gains in cognition. Adolescents see improvements in five specific areas identified by these scientists: attention, working memory, processing speed, organization, and metacognition. In contrast, Piaget's perspective focuses on global qualitative changes in "formal reasoning" rather than specific areas of improvement. (see How Thinking Changes in Adolescence)

6.   *a is the answer.*   Social perspective taking is the ability to see another person's viewpoint. Edna is trying to see her dad's viewpoint to assess if he believed her fib. She is not engaged in mutual role taking because that would involve Edna acting as an objective third party, and in this example Edna is one of the two parties; there is no third party described. (see Social Cognition)

7.   *c is the answer.*   Social conventions are the social norms that guide day-to-day behavior. Riding elevators or public buses for many people are daily activities, and the rules of how to behave in those situations (face forward, don't sit too close) guide people to make the situation more predictable.   (see Social Cognition)

8.   *c is the answer.*   Scientists have suggested adolescent risk taking is rooted in the fact that during adolescence, the maturation of the parts of the brain responsible for sensation seeking occur more rapidly than the parts of the brain responsible for judgment and decision making that might modulate the risk taking driven by sensation seeking motives. Adolescents are just as logical as adults by around age 15 or so, and adults are at risk for developing personal fables just like adolescents, so neither of these explanations is as effective as the third one focused on brain maturation. (see Adolescent Risk Taking)

9.   *b is the answer.*   In general, both teachers and students prefer moderate classroom structure with high student involvement and high teacher support. (see Achievement in School)

10.   *d is the answer.*   Need for achievement is the degree to which one strives for success. (see Achievement in School)

11.   *a is the answer.*   Mastery motivation relates to intrinsic motivation—it's based on the pleasure one anticipates after mastering a task. Performance motivation relates to extrinsic motivation—it's based on how one's task performance will relate to obtaining a reward or avoiding a punishment. (see Achievement in School)

12.   *a is the answer.*   Achievement attributions are how people explain successes or failures. They generally involve some attribution to ability, effort, task difficulty, or luck. (see Achievement in School)

13.   *c is the answer.*   Asian culture tends to emphasize the role of effort in school success more so than other cultures do. How hard a student tries refers to the amount of effort they put forth. (see Achievement in School)

14.   *c is the answer.*   Only about half of the students enrolled in a four-year college complete their degree in six years or less. (see Achievement in School)

15. *c is the answer.*   Social rewards refer to being able to work with people you like.   This is Charlene's main concern. (Work and Occupational Development)

Now turn to the quiz analysis table at the end of this chapter to find which areas you know well and which areas you need to work on. Circle the numbers in the table for items on Quiz 2 that you answered correctly.

For each question you answered correctly, circle its number. (Quiz 1 numbers are not shaded; Quiz 2 numbers are shaded.) Are there patterns in the types of questions or the topics you got wrong that could direct your further study? Did you improve from Quiz 1 to Quiz 2?

QUIZ REVIEW

Topic	Type of Question		
	Definition	Comprehension	Application
How Thinking Changes in Adolescence	3	1, 5	2, 4
	1	3, 5	2, 4
Social Cognition	6	7	
			6, 7
Adolescent Risk Taking			8
		8	
Achievement in School	11	12, 13	9, 10
	10, 12	9, 11, 13, 14	
Work and Occupational Development		15	14
			15

Total correct by quiz:

Quiz 1:
Quiz 2:

CHAPTER 15

Socioemotional Development in Adolescence

LEARNING OBJECTIVES

1. List the social factors that caused psychologists to distinguish adolescence as a distinct life stage.

2. Describe Erik Erikson's idea of the identity crisis, and explain how his proposed moratorium would help adolescents resolve this crisis.

3. Define the four categories James Marcia used to categorize the identity status of adolescents.

4. Describe the four ways in which adolescents deal with their ethnic identities.

5. Explain why self-esteem fluctuates more during the transition into adolescence than it does over the course of adolescence.

6. List some of the variables that affect the transformation of family relationships during adolescence.

7. Show how the evolving relationships between adolescents and their siblings affect the adolescents' social adjustment.

8. Describe the ways in which peer relationships change during adolescence.

9. Explain how cliques and crowds fulfill particular needs in adolescent development.

10. Evaluate the differences between peer and parental influences on adolescents' behavior.

11. Explain why some adolescents are more popular than others.

12. Describe the differences in the friendships of male and female adolescents.

13. Show how the type and quality of dating may affect the course of an adolescent's development.

14. Distinguish between normal adolescent experimentation and long-term socio-emotional problems.

15. List what's known about the psychological and personal factors that contribute to adolescent delinquent behavior.

16. Describe the symptoms and causes of depression in adolescents.

17. Discuss the causes and prevalence of suicidal behavior in adolescents.

OUTLINE

I. The Invention of Adolescence
    A. Adolescence as we know it today began in the middle of the 19th century. With industrialization at the end of that century, the connection between what one learned in

245

childhood and what one needed to know for adulthood became weaker. Consequently, parents encouraged their children to stay in school longer, which increased the significance of the peer group in adolescent's lives.

B.   Additionally, because industrialization replaced numerous jobs with machines, adolescents were competing with adults for a limited number of jobs. To deal with this competition, society rationalized that teens were too immature to work and required additional schooling.

C.   Finally, because of industrialization, more people moved to cities and fewer remained in small farming communities with stronger relationships. **Child protectionists** argued young people needed to be protected from the workforce for their own good.

II.   Developing an Independent Identity
Adolescence is one of the most important periods for developing an independent identity.

A.   Erikson's Theoretical Framework
1.   Erikson viewed **identity versus identity diffusion** as the chief psychosocial task of adolescence. If this crisis is resolved effectively, previously disparate parts of one's identity become woven into a coherent whole. This is partly determined by other's responses to the adolescent and partly determined by sociocultural norms.
2.   To allow time for self-discovery to resolve this crisis, most cultures have a **psychosocial moratorium**—a time-out from responsibilities during adolescence. This allows adolescents to try on different roles, although this is largely a luxury for the affluent. Those who live in poverty tend to press forward towards survival rather than trying on roles.

B.   Determining an Adolescent's Identity Status
Identity status is determined by two dimensions: the degree to which the adolescent is engaged in a sustained search process for identity and the degree to which the adolescent has made commitments to an identity. High versus low scores on these two dimensions create four possible categories:

1.   *Identity achievement* indicates a sustained search has culminated in a coherent identity to which the adolescent is committed. Individuals in these categories tend to score high on achievement motivation, intimacy with peers, moral reasoning, reflectiveness, and career maturity.
2.   *Moratorium* indicates a search is in progress, but no commitments have yet been made to any particular identity. Individuals in this category score high on anxiety, have difficulty with authority, and lack a firm set of beliefs or values.
3.   *Identity foreclosure* indicates the adolescent had made commitments to an identity without a period of searching. Individuals in this category are the most authoritarian and prejudiced, have a strong need for social approval, lack autonomy, and are especially close to their parents.
4.   *Identity diffusion* indicates no search for identity has occurred, and no commitments to an identity have been made. Individuals in this category have the most psychological and interpersonal problems, are the most socially withdrawn, and have low intimacy with peers.

C.   The Development of Ethnic Identity
1.   For adolescents who are not part of the majority, developing a sense of **ethnic identity** is an important task. This development follows the same pattern as more general identity development. During adolescence the individual comes to realize he or she is "different" which initiates a period of exploration which may involve rejecting majority culture and immersion in one's own ethnic group.

This crisis is resolved as one develops a coherent ethnic identity and turns to helping other young people deal with similar issues.

2. Having a strong ethnic identity is associated with positive outcomes (higher self-esteem, better mental health, etc.) for minority youth, but the link is weaker for white youth.

3. Because minority youth must establish an ethnic identity that is separate from the general culture, their task is more complicated. Four possibilities are open to minority youth in dealing with this:

    a) *Assimilation* involves adopting the majority culture's norms and rejecting one's own ethnic group's norms.

    b) *Marginality* involves adoption of neither the majority nor ethnic group norms.

    c) *Separation* involves adoption of one's own ethnic group's norms and rejection of the majority culture's norms.

    d) *Biculturalism* involves acceptance of both the majority culture and one's own ethnic group's norms.

4. In the past, minority youth were encouraged to assimilate, but this often resulted in continued exclusion from majority society, leading to an end result of marginalization. Attempts to assimilate are also often scorned by the ethnic group, which leads many youth to seek separation or biculturalism as strategies.

5. In general, a strong and positive ethnic identity coupled with awareness of the potential for discrimination—but not outright rejection of the majority culture—yields the best outcomes for minority youth.

D. Changes in Self-Esteem

1. Evidence as to whether self-esteem increases or decreases during adolescence is mixed. What is clear is that self-perceptions do change during this time period.

2. The changes in self-perceptions are most significant during early adolescence (the transition into adolescence) rather than later adolescence.

III. Family Relationships in Adolescence

Adolescence is a period of disequilibrium for families. For families with boys, the disequilibrium peaks at around age 13 or 14. For families with girls, the peak is closer to age 11 or 12. These gender differences suggest that the disequilibrium may be driven by puberty.

A. Adolescents' Relationships with Parents

1. As adolescents try to play a more forceful role in the family, their attempts may be initially ignored by parents, leading to interrupting and other immature behavior. As parents come to allow them to have more influence, they no longer resort to such behavior as interrupting.

2. Parents and adolescents often perceive their day-to-day shared experiences quite differently. Young adolescents are especially sensitive (even oversensitive) to emotional signals from others, leading them to misinterpret emotional cues (e.g., "serious" is interpreted as "angry").

3. As adolescents age, they become more aware of their families' shortcomings.

4. Most families do weather the storm of adolescence successfully. Families with psychologically competent teens are characterized by interaction patterns that permit members to express their individuality and autonomy while remaining attached to other family members.

B. Adolescents' Relationships with Siblings

1. Adolescents rate their sibling relationships as similar to parental relationships in terms of companionship and importance, but more like friendships with respect to power, assistance, and satisfaction with the relationship.

2. Conflict amongst siblings tends to increase during adolescence, but improve as they move into young adulthood and have less competition for resources or attention.

3. Parent-child interactions influence sibling relations. Adolescents with positive relationships with parents also report more positive sibling relationships, and vice versa.

4. Sibling interaction also influences, and is influenced by, peer relationships outside of the family. Positive sibling interactions are associated with more positive peer interactions, although the direction of causality between this association is unclear.

5. Positive sibling interaction is also associated with adolescent adjustment. Good sibling relationships are associated with school success, sociability, self-esteem, and autonomy, and may provide a buffer even if an adolescent has few friends at school.

IV. Peer Relationships in Adolescence

Peer relationships during adolescence change in four major ways. First, adolescents spend far more time with peers than younger children. Secondly, that time is largely unsupervised in contrast to peer play in childhood. Third, adolescents spend more time with opposite-sex peers than their younger counterparts. Fourth, rather than socializing only in small peer groups, larger collectives tend to emerge (e.g., the "popular" crowd, "nerds," etc.).

A. Cliques and Crowds

1. **Cliques** are small groups ranging in size from 2 to 12 (usually around 5 or 6) that may be defined by common activities (e.g., drama club) or just friendship (e.g., we like to go to lunch together). It is the setting in which close friendships are formed.

2. Adolescents in the same clique tend to be from the same social background, and tend to have the same orientation towards school, towards the broader teen culture, and towards antisocial activity as each other.

3. **Crowds** are based on reputation and stereotypes (e.g., "brains" or "jocks" rather than actual social interaction. Crowds help to locate individuals in the broader school social structure, to channel adolescents into associations with some peers and away from others, and to provide contexts that reward certain lifestyles and discourage others.

4. Because crowd membership is based upon reputation, one need not actually be like the members of the crowd to be considered part of it. For example, someone who isn't that smart can be part of the "brain" group.

5. Adolescents learn how to be friends and end friendships within the context of cliques. Crowds, however, contribute to adolescent sense of identity and self-esteem. The crowd determines in large part the nature of the peer pressure the adolescent experiences.

B. Responding to Peer Pressure

1. Adolescents are mainly influenced by peers in short-term, day-to-day, social matters, but their values and long-term career plans are more influenced by parents.

2. Adolescents are most susceptible to peer pressure during early and middle adolescence, not later. At the same time, adolescent susceptibility to parental influence declines. This suggests that adolescents have a growing sense of

independence, and when the void is created by reduced parental influence they turn to peers to fill that void.

C. Popularity and Rejection in Adolescent Peer Groups
1. Social competence is the main determinant of popularity in adolescence. Social competence involves the ability to act appropriately in the eyes of one's peers, to perceive and meet the needs of others, and confidence without conceit.
2. Rejection in adolescence typically occurs for being overly aggressive, being withdrawn, or being both aggressive and withdrawn.

D. Sex Differences in Adolescents' Friendships
1. Girls tend to have more intimate friendships than boys during adolescence and tend to list more people as friends than boys do. Just because girls overtly emphasize intimacy, however, does not indicate boys have no intimacy in their relationships. Instead, intimacy in boys' friendships is based on shared activity rather than meeting emotional needs.
2. During adolescence, conflict in boys' relationships have to do with issues of power and control, while girls' conflict deal with betrayal and trust. This difference makes girls' emphasis on intimacy both an asset and a liability. While girls may have more confidantes and social support, their friendships are also more fragile as betrayal is more difficult to resolve than issues of power and control.

E. Dating and Romantic Relationships
1. During earlier eras, dating was a path to mate selection. That is no longer the case in present-day dating.
2. Half of all adolescents have had a date before they turn 12, and 90% of all adolescents have had a date by the time they are 16. The dating relationships adolescents have are not generally short-lived, contrary to stereotypes. Girls tend to date older boys, and Asian Americans are somewhat less likely to date than other ethnic groups.
3. The transition to romantic relationships is somewhat challenging for adolescents, even if they have had successful friendships in the past. Many adolescents mention communicating with the opposite sex as a challenge.
4. The impact of dating on adolescents depends largely on the age of the adolescent. Early and intensive dating can stunt psychosocial development. Adolescents who do not date at all show delayed social development. A moderate degree of dating, delaying serious involvement until the age of 15, seems to be somewhat beneficial.
5. Romance has a strong impact on adolescent emotional state. Forty percent of adolescent feelings about their romantic relationships are negative, and adolescents who have entered a romantic relationship are at higher risk for depression (in part because break-ups often trigger depression).

V. Socioemotional Problems in Adolescence
A. Some General Observations about Problems in Adolescence
1. Troublesome behavior in adolescence may be experimentation, or may be enduring.
2. Some problems have their origin and onset in adolescence, and other problems are rooted in earlier childhood.
3. Many problems of adolescence are transitory and resolved by adulthood.
4. Problem behavior in adolescence is not a direct consequence of going through the normative changes of adolescence.
5. Three major types of problems tend to occur during adolescence: substance abuse, **externalizing problems** (problems are turned outward and manifested in

antisocial behavior), and **internalizing problems** (problems are turned inward and manifested in emotional and cognitive distress).

B.   Externalizing Problems
1.   **Delinquency** is the most common externalizing problem of adolescence. The earlier it begins, the more likely the adolescent will become a chronic offender.
2.   For individuals who antisocial behavior begins before adolescence and continues through it, they are at great risk for continued criminal behavior in adulthood. This group is considered **life-course-persistent**.
3.   For individuals whose offending is **adolescent-limited**, delinquency appears first in adolescence and only in adolescence.
4.   Adolescents who engaged in externalizing behavior prior to adolescence are often psychologically troubled. Risk factors include being male, coming from a poorer background, coming from a family with a divorce, having a history of aggressive behavior, having problems with self-regulation as seen in **attention deficit/hyperactivity disorder (ADHD)**, and performing more poorly on intelligence and neuropsychological functioning tests as well as in school.
5.   Adolescent-limited offenders do not show this same sort of pathology; however, they do have more problems during adolescence than those who engage in no delinquent behavior. They tend to suffer more mental health, financial, and substance abuse problems than their non-delinquent counterparts. Risk factors for adolescent-limited offending include poor parenting and affiliation with antisocial peers.

C.   Internalizing Problems
1.   **Depression** is the most common internalizing problem of adolescence. It includes cognitive and physical symptoms as well as emotional ones. Depressed mood (feeling sad) is worth distinguishing from depressive syndromes (having multiple symptoms of depression) and a depressive disorder (having enough symptoms to merit a clinical diagnosis). Three percent of teens meet the diagnostic criteria for depression at any given time.
2.   Depression is half as common in childhood as it is in adolescence, with late adolescence being the time at which the risk for depression is highest. Mexican-American teens are at greater risk for depression than other ethnic backgrounds.
3.   The **diathesis-stress model** suggests that predispositions for depression interact with chronic or acute stressors to trigger depressive episodes.
     a)   Because depression is believed to have a strong genetic component, psychologists believe it is related to **neuroendocrine** functioning— hormonal activity in the brain and nervous system. Cognitive sets may also be related to depression.
     b)   Research focused on the environmental piece of the diathesis-stress model emphasizes three types of stressors: coming from a high-conflict/low-cohesion family, having poor peer relations, and having more acute or chronic stress than others.
     c)   Research on the increase in depression during adolescence suggests that the diathesis-stress model can explain this spike. The biological changes of puberty heighten one's sensitivity to stress, and the new cognitive skill of hypothetical thinking adds to this. These changes, coupled with new environmental demands, increase the likelihood of depression.
4.   Before puberty, boys are at greater risk for depression, but after puberty girls are. This may be related to the girls' concerns over boy-girl relationships coupled with heightened self-consciousness over appearance. Girls also tend to experience adolescence as more stressful (more change at once), to react by

turning their feelings inward, and are more sensitive to interpersonal relationships and thus more distressed by conflicts in them.

5. About 10% of females and 6% of males in high school attempt suicide each year. Twenty percent think about killing themselves, which is known as **suicidal ideation**. This peaks at age 15 and then declines. Most suicide attempts are preceded by attempts to seek help in which no support was found.

6. Risk factors for attempting suicide include having a *psychiatric problem*, having a *history of suicide in the family*, being under *stress*, and experiencing *parental rejection, family disruption, or extensive family conflict*.

7. Adolescent suicide attempts increased from 1950 to 1990, at which point antidepressants became more widely available. These treatments, though often accused of increasing one's risk for suicide, are effective and have helped to reduce the number of suicide attempts that adolescents make.

KEY TERMS

1. **Child protectionists** are individuals who argued, early in the twentieth century, that adolescents needed to be kept out of the labor force in order to protect them from the hazards of the workplace. (see The Invention of Adolescence)

2. **Identity versus identity diffusion**, according to Erikson, is the normative crisis characteristic of the fifth stage of psychosocial development, predominant during adolescence. (see Developing an Independent Identity)

3. The **psychosocial moratorium** is a period of time during which individuals are free from excessive obligations and responsibilities and can therefore experiment with different roles and personalities. (see Developing an Independent Identity)

4. **Ethnic identity** is the aspect of one's sense of identity concerning ancestry or racial group membership. (see Developing an Independent Identity)

5. **Cliques** are small, tightly knit groups of between two and twelve friends, generally of the same sex and age. (see Peer Relationships in Adolescence)

6. **Crowds** are large, loosely organized groups of young people, composed of several cliques and typically organized around a common, shared activity. (see Peer Relationships in Adolescence)

7. **Externalizing problems** are psychosocial problems that are manifested in a turning of the symptoms outward, as in aggression or delinquency. (see Socioemotional Problems in Adolescence)

8. **Internalizing problems** are psychosocial problems that are manifested in a turning of the symptoms inward, as in depression or anxiety. (see Socioemotional Problems in Adolescence)

9. **Delinquency** is juvenile offending that is processed within the juvenile justice system. (see Socioemotional Problems in Adolescence)

10. **Life-course-persistent offenders** are individuals who begin demonstrating antisocial or aggressive behavior during childhood and continue their antisocial behavior through adolescence and into adulthood (contrast with adolescence-limited offenders). (see Socioemotional Problems in Adolescence)

11. **Adolescence-limited offenders** are antisocial adolescents whose delinquent or violent behavior begins and ends during adolescence (contrast with life-course-persistent offenders). (see Socioemotional Problems in Adolescence)

12. **Attention deficit/hyperactivity disorder (ADHD)** is a biologically based psychological disorder characterized by impulsivity, inattentiveness, and restlessness, often in school situations. (see Socioemotional Problems in Adolescence)

13. **Depression** is a psychological disturbance characterized by low self-esteem, decreased motivation, sadness, and difficulty finding pleasure in formerly enjoyable activities. (see Socioemotional Problems in Adolescence)

14. The **diathesis-stress model** is a perspective on disorders that posits that problems are the result of an interaction between a pre-existing condition (the diathesis) and exposure to a stressful event or condition. (see Socioemotional Problems in Adolescence)

15. **Neuroendocrine** refers to hormonal activity in the brain and nervous system. (see Socioemotional Problems in Adolescence)

16. **Suicidal ideation** is thinking about ending one's life. (see Socioemotional Problems in Adolescence)

FILL-IN-THE-BLANKS KEY TERMS

This section will help you check your knowledge of the key terms introduced in this chapter. Fill in each blank with the appropriate term from the list of key terms in the previous section.

1. _____ are small, tightly knit groups of between two and twelve friends, generally of the same sex and age.

2. The aspect of one's sense of identity concerning ancestry or racial group membership is called _____.

3. _____ are individuals who begin demonstrating antisocial or aggressive behavior during childhood and continue their antisocial behavior through adolescence and into adulthood.

4. _____ are individuals who argued, early in the twentieth century, that adolescents needed to be kept out of the labor force in order to protect them from the hazards of the workplace.

5. Hormonal activity in the brain and nervous system are referred to as _____.

6. _____ are psychosocial problems that are manifested in a turning of the symptoms inward, as in depression or anxiety.

7. A period of time during which individuals are free from excessive obligations and responsibilities and can therefore experiment with different roles and personalities is called a _____.

8. _____ are antisocial adolescents whose delinquent or violent behavior begins and ends during adolescence.

9. _____ is the normative crisis characteristic of the fifth stage of psychosocial development, predominant during adolescence.

10. Thinking about ending one's life is called _____.

APPLIED LEARNING AND CRITICAL THINKING

Adolescence is a time of turbulence in a variety of ways, but particularly noticeable are the socioemotional "waves" that are part of this process. There are many real-world contexts that will allow you to begin to understand social developments of adolescence more deeply than simply completing a class. As you dig into these contexts, be sure to consider multiple perspectives of whatever aspect of socioemotional development that you are trying to learn about.

Consider the adolescent's view, as well as the others views in the context—parents, teachers, peers, and so forth. Part of critical thinking is explicitly taking into account varying points of view, and applied contexts are rife with opportunities to do so.

1. For many college students, university life is one of the more "diverse" communities of which they have ever been a part. Consequently, the university itself offers a wonderful vehicle in which to explore ethnic identity development. Because ethnic identity development tends to occur late in adolescence, many university students may still be addressing this important task. While the textbook describes research on African American, Asian American, Hispanic, Native American, and white adolescents, there are many ethnicities with which one could identify that do not fit into these five categories. Consider collaborating with a professor to extend research on ethnic identity development to address other ethnic backgrounds. Does ethnic identity development in those other backgrounds follow the same pattern? Or is it different? Why do you think that would be the case?

2. The psychosocial moratorium is an interesting social phenomenon. Consider the ways this is phenomenon occurs in different cultures. A really valuable way to apply what you are learning is to see if it occurs similarly in different parts of the world. If your university has such a program, consider studying abroad for a period of time. As you experience that culture, consider how the adolescent experience there is similar to, or different from, the experience of adolescents where you come from. Do they have a psychosocial moratorium? Is it formally recognized (as in an Amish rumspringa) or is it an informal structure? If there are differences, can you identify any possible reasons why based on the broader cultural situation? Does it seem connected to the structure of secondary education in that country? To the age at which adolescents begin full-time work? What factors can you identify to explain what you have observed?

3. Social workers take on many roles, but a common one is to work with juvenile delinquents. Consider completing a practicum experience under a social worker in your area who specializes in working with delinquents. As you observe in this capacity, see if you can get an understanding of his or her perspective on the distinction between life-course-persistent offenders versus adolescent-limited offenders. What are the ways that the social worker feels he or she can tell the difference between these two types of delinquents? Is it solely the age at which the offending begins, or are there other factors?

4. Consider doing a service-learning project with a middle or high school counselor. This chapter identifies social competence as one of the main determinants of popularity. Although social competence undoubtedly comes more naturally to some adolescents than others, it is an identifiable set of skills that can be taught with some success. For your project, work with the counselor to develop a social-skills training program that could be used to help adolescents who have not mastered social competency to improve their social skills. Then implement your project under their tutelage (after getting parental permission, of course) with a sample of students. How would you evaluate the success of your training program? Would sorts of measures would indicate to you that you'd helped these students improve their social skills?

MULTIPLE-CHOICE QUESTIONS

Quiz 1

1. People who argued early in the 20th century that young people needed to be protected from the labor force for their own good were called

    a.   social workers.
    b.   child protectionists.
    c.   psychologists.
    d.   liberals.

2. Samantha is fifteen years old. She is driving her mom nuts! Some days she acts like a prima donna, spending hours getting dressed and putting on make-up. Other days, she acts like a tomboy—running around with her hair shoved into a messy ponytail, playing sports. Still other days, she acts like an intellectual, wearing her glasses, reading poetry and drinking expensive coffee. Her mom is never sure who Samantha will be from one day to another. Samantha is experiencing which of Erikson's psychosocial crises?

    a.   Identity versus identity diffusion
    b.   Initiative versus guilt
    c.   Trust versus mistrust
    d.   Autonomy versus shame and doubt

3. Who is most likely going to enjoy the benefit of a psychosocial moratorium?

    a.   Jenna, who is from a family whose home is being foreclosed
    b.   Nduta, who lives in Kenya and subsists on very limited means
    c.   Miranda, who is from a middle-class family and is enrolled in college while working part-time
    d.   Edwina, who is from an affluent family and is studying abroad for the semester

4. According to psychologist Jean Phinney, which of the following strategies for dealing with a minority ethnic identity involves accepting the majority culture?

    a.   Biculturalism
    b.   Assimilation
    c.   Marginalization
    d.   Both A and B

5. When are changes in self-image most likely to occur during adolescence?

    a.   Early adolescence
    b.   Middle adolescence
    c.   Late adolescence
    d.   All throughout adolescence

6. Lindsey is a junior in high school. Her parents want to make sure she develops a really high self-esteem along with good coping skills for when things don't go her way. What would you advise her parents?

    a.   Make sure to control Lindsey's thinking and behavior so that she doesn't ruin her future with a big mistake.
    b.   Let Lindsey run wild and experience life; this is her time to grow!
    c.   Have lots of discussions where Lindsey can express her dissenting opinions while remaining connected to her family.
    d.   Any of the above would be fine.

7. Adolescents who have positive relationships with their parents tend to

    a. have negative relationships with their siblings.
    b. have negative relationships with their peers.
    c. have positive relationships with their siblings.
    d. Both A and B

8. Small groups of two to twelve individuals that are composed of members who are the same age and same sex are called

    a. crowds.
    b. cliques.
    c. moratoriums.
    d. adolescent-limited.

9. Which characteristic best predicts popularity during adolescence?

    a. Social competence
    b. Athleticism.
    c. Shyness
    d. Aggression

10. Which adolescent below is most likely to have his development stunted by dating?

    a. Kent, who started dating when he was 13, and got serious with his girlfriend right away
    b. Clarence, who didn't date until he was 16, and moved slowly from going out in groups to having a more serious girlfriend
    c. Ador, who started dating his girlfriend when he was 15
    d. Michael, who had his first date when he was 17

11. When a young person's problems are turned outward and manifested in antisocial behavior, it is considered a(n)

    a. internalizing problem.
    b. externalizing problem.
    c. sign of depression.
    d. diathesis.

12. Acts committed by juveniles violating the law are called

    a. internalizing problems.
    b. ADHD.
    c. delinquency.
    d. suicide ideation.

13. Monroe was always getting into trouble as a child. He set fires and hurt animals. During adolescence, he got in trouble for fighting, skipping school, and insubordination. He landed in prison shortly after graduating high school for peddling drugs. Monroe is a(n)

    a. adolescent-limited offender.
    b. life-course-persistent offender.
    c. internalized person.
    d. externalized person.

14. ADHD is to _____ as depression is to _____.

    a. externalizing problems; internalizing problems
    b. internalizing problems, diathesis
    c. diathesis; externalizing problems
    d. marginalization; separation

15. A predisposition is also known as a(n)

    a.   moratorium.

    b.   neuroendocrine.

    c.   ideation.

    d.   diathesis.

Quiz 2

Use this quiz to reassess your learning after taking Quiz 1 and reviewing the chapter.

1. Which factor is discussed in your textbook as one of the main reasons for the invention of adolescence as we know it today?

    a.   The prefrontal cortex began maturing at a faster rate.

    b.   The industrial revolution initiated social changes that affected adolescents.

    c.   Teenagers became more sexually active.

    d.   The development of the computer changed the way adolescents interact.

2. Erikson felt that the key to resolving the identity versus identity diffusion crisis was in

    a.   adolescents' interactions with others.

    b.   prefrontal cortex development.

    c.   having time alone to ponder who one wants to become.

    d.   employment.

3. Bradford was a really wild kid as a teenager. He tried everything—drugs, alcohol, lots of sex….his parents and teachers were sure he was a lost cause. But by the time he was 19 or so, he seemed to settle down and get comfortable with himself. Bradford's identity status is probably best characterized as

    a.   identity achievement.

    b.   moratorium.

    c.   identity diffusion.

    d.   identity foreclosure.

4. Ethnic minorities living within the majority culture but feeling estranged and outcast experience

    a.   biculturalism.

    b.   separation.

    c.   assimilation.

    d.   marginality.

5. Which pattern of findings suggests that adolescents become more aware of their families' shortcomings throughout adolescence?

    a.   The disparity between adolescents' actual and ideal family descriptions gets smaller over time.

    b.   The disparity between adolescents' actual and ideal family descriptions remains constant over time.

    c.   The disparity between adolescents' actual and ideal family descriptions widens over time.

    d.   None of these

6. Over the course of adolescence, sibling relationships become

    a.   more emotionally intense.

    b.   more conflicted.

    c.   less emotionally intense.

    d.   less distant.

7. Large, loosely knit groups of young people that are organized around shared activity are called

   a. cliques.
   b. crowds.
   c. siblings.
   d. delinquents.

8. On which sort of issue is Chris most likely to yield to peer pressure?

   a. Deciding what career to pursue
   b. Deciding whether or not to go to college
   c. Determining what church to join
   d. Deciding on what clothes to buy

9. Which characteristic is NOT associated with rejection amongst peers in adolescence?

   a. Social competence
   b. Aggression
   c. Being withdrawn
   d. Both B and C

10. Which of the following situations is most likely to foster the development of intimacy in a group of adolescent boys?

   a. Sharing disappointments and supporting each other through that
   b. Talking about their latest love interest and how they feel about him or her
   c. Doing a river rafting trip for two weeks during the summer
   d. All of these are equally likely to foster intimacy amongst boys.

11. The age at which one first gets married has

   a. remained constant over time.
   b. has increased over time.
   c. has decreased over time.
   d. has increased, and then decreased over time.

12. When one's problems are manifested in emotional and cognitive distress, the problem is characterized as

   a. internalizing.
   b. externalizing.
   c. delinquency.
   d. ADHD.

13. _____ engage in antisocial behavior during adolescence only.

   a. Life-course-persistent offenders
   b. Adolescent-limited offenders
   c. Delinquents
   d. Cliques

14. Kaizley is an extremely difficult-to-manage student. Her 9th grade social studies teacher has a hard time keeping her from blurting out comments when she does listen, and she seems to be paying attention to something other than the lecture more than half the time. She is constantly jiggling her leg or tapping her pencil, and generally distracting the rest of the class. Kaizley may have

   a. depression.
   b. an internalizing disorder.
   c. ADHD.
   d. suicidal ideation.

15.   _____ refers to hormonal activity in the brain and nervous system.
    a.   Neuroendocrine
    b.   Diathesis
    c.   Stress
    d.   Ideation

ANSWERS TO FILL-IN-THE-BLANKS KEY TERMS

1.   Cliques (see Peer Relationships in Adolescence)

2.   ethnic identity (see Developing an Independent Identity)

3.   Life-course-persistent offenders (see Socioemotional Problems in Adolescence)

4.   Child protectionists (see The Invention of Adolescence)

5.   neuroendocrine (see Socioemotional Problems in Adolescence)

6.   Internalizing problems (see Socioemotional Problems in Adolescence)

7.   psychosocial moratorium (see Developing an Independent Identity)

8.   Adolescence-limited offenders (see Socioemotional Problems in Adolescence)

9.   Identity versus identity diffusion (see Developing an Independent Identity)

10.   suicidal ideation (see Socioemotional Problems in Adolescence)

ANSWERS TO MULTIPLE-CHOICE QUESTIONS

Circle the question numbers you answered incorrectly.

Quiz 1

1.   *b is the answer.*   Child protectionists argued in the early part of the 20th century that adolescents should be sheltered from the labor force for their own good. Although some child protectionists might have been social workers, psychologists, or liberals, this was not necessarily the case. (see The Invention of Adolescence)

2.   *a is the answer.*   Identity versus Identity diffusion is the primary crisis during adolescence. It involves taking separate pieces of one's identity (in this case, feminine, athletic, and smart) and working to put them into a coherent whole. As Samantha tries on each identity, she can identify ways that they fit together to make her unique. Trust versus mistrust happens in infancy and autonomy versus shame and doubt and initiative versus guilt are more characteristic of early and middle childhood. (see Developing an Independent Identity)

3.   *d is the answer.*   Edwina is most likely to have the benefit of a psychosocial moratorium. Although ideally all adolescents are afforded this opportunity, *afford* is the key word. The psychosocial moratorium is largely a luxury of the affluent. Edwina is the only person described here who does not suffer some form of a financial strain.   (see Developing an Independent Identity)

4.   *d is the answer.*   Both biculturalism and assimilation involve acceptance of the majority culture. Biculturalism integrates majority culture with one's ethnic identity, while assimilation involves rejection of the ethnic identity in favor of the majority culture. Marginalization involves failure to successfully adopt the ethnic identity or the majority culture. (see Developing an Independent Identity)

5. *a is the answer.*   Changes in self-image are more dramatic early in adolescence than later. (see Developing an Independent Identity)

6. *c is the answer.*   Teens who are allowed to express disagreeing opinions within the context of a connected family develop the highest self-esteem and strongest coping skills. (see Family Relationships in Adolescence)

7. *c is the answer.*   Positive relations with one's parents tend to co-occur with positive sibling relationships, which in turn tend to co-occur with positive peer relationships. (see Family Relationships in Adolescence)

8. *b is the answer.*   Cliques are small groups of two to twelve members who tend to be the same age and same sex. Crowds, however, are larger social structures based more on reputation than actual interaction. (see Peer Relationships in Adolescence)

9. *a is the answer.*   Social competence is the best predictor of popularity in adolescence. This involves acting appropriately in the eyes of one's peers, perceiving and meeting the needs of others, and being confident without being conceited. Aggression tends to be associated with rejection, not with popularity. (see Peer Relationships in Adolescence)

10. *a is the answer.*   Kent is the most likely to suffer ill-effects from dating. Dating seriously and early in adolescence tends to stunt adolescent development. Clarence and Ador both waited until after they were 15, which is helpful. Michael may be somewhat delayed, given he didn't have his first date until he was 17, but that would be preferable to the early serious involvement that Kent experienced. (see Peer Relationships in Adolescence)

11. *b is the answer.*   Externalizing problems are those that are turned outward in the form of antisocial behavior. In contrast, internalization problems involve turning inward in the form of depression or anxiety. (see Socioemotional Problems in Adolescence)

12. *c is the answer.*   Delinquency refers to acts committed by juveniles that violate the law. It is a form of an externalizing problem, not an internalizing one. (see Socioemotional Problems in Adolescence)

13. *b is the answer.*   Life-course-persistent offenders tend to begin their antisocial behavior in childhood, and it continues through adolescence and into adulthood. In contrast, adolescent-limited offenders see antisocial behavior begin and end during adolescence. (see Socioemotional Problems in Adolescence)

14. *a is the answer.*   ADHD is associated with externalizing problems, while depression is an example of an internalizing problem. (see Socioemotional Problems in Adolescence)

15. *d is the answer.*   A diathesis is a predisposition. (see Socioemotional Problems in Adolescence)

Now turn to the quiz analysis table at the end of this chapter to find which areas you know well and which areas you need to work on. Circle the numbers in the table for items on Quiz 1 that you answered correctly.

Quiz 2

1. *b is the answer.*   The industrial revolution initiated changes in families, schooling, and work that significantly impacted adolescents. The move away from farming societies increased the amount of time in school, and the industrialization also created more competition between adults and adolescents for scarce jobs, so schooling was promoted as a way of decreasing that competition. (see The Invention of Adolescence)

2. *a is the answer.*   Erikson felt that the key to resolving the identity crisis was through interacting with others. Adolescents can respond to the reactions of others who matter to them, and in doing so learn about themselves. (see Developing an Independent Identity)

3. *a is the answer.*   Bradford is probably best described as having achieved his identity. Identity achievement involves establishment of a coherent identity after a period of experimentation. Bradford's wild years were the experimentation, and by the time he was 19 he has integrated these explorations into his self concept, or identity. (see Developing an Independent Identity)

4. *d is the answer.*   Marginality involves not really being part of the majority or the minority culture. Feeling estranged and outcast is part of experiencing marginality for minority youth. (see Developing an Independent Identity)

5. *c is the answer.*   If the actual family description is quite different from the ideal family description, the adolescent is aware of the shortcomings of his or her own family. If this difference gets larger over time, the adolescent has become more aware of those shortcomings. (see Family Relationships in Adolescence)

6. *c is the answer.*   Over the course of adolescence, sibling relationships become less emotionally intense and more distant. (see Family Relationships in Adolescence)

7. *b is the answer.*   Crowds are larger collectives of young people that are loosely connected and organized by shared activity, reputation, and stereotype. Cliques are smaller collectives knit together by friendship.   (see Peer Relationships in Adolescence)

8. *d is the answer.*   Conformity to peer pressure is greatest on day-to-day, short-term issues such as what clothes to wear, what music to listen to, and what leisure activities to engage in. Parental influence tends to hold sway over larger issues such as career or educational plans, religious and moral values and so forth. (see Peer Relationships in Adolescence)

9. *a is the answer.*   Both aggression and withdrawal ARE associated with rejection in adolescence. In contrast, social competence is associated with popularity. (see Peer Relationships in Adolescence)

10. *c is the answer.*   Adolescent boys are more likely to develop intimacy through shared activity than through explicit meeting of emotional needs. Sharing disappointments or talking about feelings explicitly addresses emotional needs, but a river rafting trip is a shared activity. (see Peer Relationships in Adolescence)

11. *b is the answer.*   Age at first marriage has increased since 1950. (see Peer Relationships in Adolescence)

12. *a is the answer.*   Internalizing problems involve turning the problem inward and manifesting the problem in emotional or cognitive distress (e.g., anxiety or depression). (see Socioemotional Problems in Adolescence)

13. *b is the answer.*   Adolescent-limited offenders begin and end their delinquency during adolescence. This is in contrast to life-course-persistent offenders who begin antisocial behavior during childhood and likely see it persist into adulthood. (see Socioemotional Problems in Adolescence)

14. *c is the answer.* ADHD is characterized by impulsivity (e.g., blurting things out), inattentiveness (e.g., not paying attention to the lecture), and restlessness (e.g., jiggling her leg, tapping her pencil), often in school situations. (see Socioemotional Problems in Adolescence)

15. *a is the answer.* Neuroendocrine refers to hormonal activity in the brain and nervous system. (see Socioemotional Problems in Adolescence)

Now turn to the quiz analysis table at the end of this chapter to find which areas you know well and which areas you need to work on. Circle the numbers in the table for items on Quiz 2 that you answered correctly.

For each question you answered correctly, circle its number. (Quiz 1 numbers are not shaded; Quiz 2 numbers are shaded.) Are there patterns in the types of questions or the topics you got wrong that could direct your further study? Did you improve from Quiz 1 to Quiz 2?

QUIZ REVIEW

Topic	Type of Question		
	Definition	Comprehension	Application
The Invention of Adolescence	1		
		1	
Developing an Independent Identity		4, 5	2, 3
	4	2	3
Family Relationships in Adolescence		7	6
		5, 6	
Peer Relationships in Adolescence	8	9	10
	7	9, 11	8, 10
Socioemotional Problems in Adolescence	11, 12, 15	14	13
	12, 13, 15		14

Total correct by quiz:

Quiz 1:
Quiz 2: